REEF CORALS OF THE WORLD
Biology and Field Guide

by Dr. Elizabeth M. Wood

All photos by the author unless otherwise credited.
Title Page: Photo by R. Scheer.

ISBN 0-87666-809-0

Distributed in the UNITED STATES by T.F.H. Publications, Inc., 211 West Sylvania Avenue, Neptune City, NJ 07753; in CANADA by H & L Pet Supplies Inc., 27 Kingston Crescent, Kitchener, Ontario N2B 2T6; Rolf C. Hagen Ltd., 3225 Sartelon Street, Montreal 382 Quebec; in ENGLAND by T.F.H. (Great Britain) Ltd., 11 Ormside Way, Holmethorpe Industrial Estate, Redhill, Surrey RH1 2PX; in AUSTRALIA AND THE SOUTH PACIFIC by T.F.H. (Australia) Pty. Ltd., Box 149, Brookvale 2100 N.S.W., Australia; in NEW ZEALAND by Ross Haines & Son, Ltd., 18 Monmouth Street, Grey Lynn, Auckland 2 New Zealand; in SINGAPORE AND MALAYSIA by MPH Distributors Pte., 71-77 Stamford Road, Singapore 0617; in the PHILIPPINES by Bio-Research, 5 Lippay Street, San Lorenzo Village, Makati, Rizal; in SOUTH AFRICA by Multipet Pty. Ltd., 30 Turners Avenue, Durban 4001. Published by T.F.H. Publications Inc., Ltd., the British Crown Colony of Hong Kong.

Preface

The invention of SCUBA (Self-Contained Underwater Breathing Apparatus) and advances in the development of more sophisticated and readily available gear are encouraging increasing numbers of people to learn about underwater life *in situ*. It is hardly surprising that coral reefs attract the attention of both amateurs and professionals alike. A visit to this most complex of marine ecosystems cannot fail to generate delight, excitement and interest.

Corals evolved and coral reefs flourished long before man appeared on earth. Coral types have appeared and disappeared, their structure and distribution modified by climatic and geological events. The evolutionary history of corals is relatively well known because the living animal produces such a well defined and characteristic skeleton. Paleontological studies have produced a solid foundation upon which the taxonomy of modern types is based. Conversely, there is much to be learned from the study of present-day corals, especially as regards their extraordinary plasticity in the face of different environmental conditions.

Work on this book began out of frustration at the lack of accurate yet comprehensible and informative texts on identification of corals in the field. It is not the purpose of this book to fulfill the needs of the specialist in coral taxonomy; there are other far more detailed papers and monographs to cater to these interests. It is instead intended primarily for professional marine scientists and reef workers, students of tropical marine biology, naturalists, amateur divers and underwater photographers.

It is a pleasure to acknowledge the various people and institutions that have helped me during my work on this book. My sincerest thanks go to Professor John Wells of Cornell University for all his assistance. Not only has he identified coral specimens and given freely of his long-standing knowledge of coral taxonomy, but he has also patiently read through the manuscript and made many useful comments. I am also indebted to Dr. John Veron of the Australian Institute of Marine Sciences for his invaluable and generous help. Dr. Paul Cornelius of the British Museum (Natural History) kindly assisted me by arranging access to the Museum's collection of corals and making working space available. I should also like to thank Gordon Paterson for his help. Bian Siew Tan collaborated in some of the work on Malaysian corals, and this led to useful discussions on taxonomic problems.

Christopher Wood has been a constant and patient diving companion and has given encouragement and help in many other ways. I am also grateful to the following for providing field assistance: David Jenkins, Frances Liew and other personnel of Sabah National Parks, Malaysia; Alan Robinson and the staff of Direktorat Perlindungan dan Pelastarian Alam (PPA), Bali, Indonesia; Professor A. Alcala and personnel of the Marine Station of Silliman University, Philippines; the staff of the Aquarium de Noumea, New Caledonia; and Dr. Jeremy Woodley and personnel of the Discovery Bay Marine Laboratory, University of the West Indies.

Photographs of the skeleton of *Goreaugyra* were kindly supplied by Dr. F. Bayer and those of *Clavarina, Catalaphyllia* and *Moseleya* by Dr. J. Veron. M. Melzak and Dr. C. Sheppard also generously responded to my requests for photographs for use in this book. These and other sources are acknowledged where appropriate.

3

Table of Contents

Introduction

CORAL AND CORAL REEFS

"Coral" is a general term used to describe a variety of related forms belonging to the phylum Coelenterata. It indicates the presence of skeletal material that is either embedded in the living tissues or encloses the animal altogether. This book deals only with those corals that build a solid calcareous skeleton around the polyps. These are known as hard corals and include scleractinians, hydrocorals and octocorals. Soft corals lay down skeletal fragments or horny material within the tissues, giving them a soft, fleshy texture.

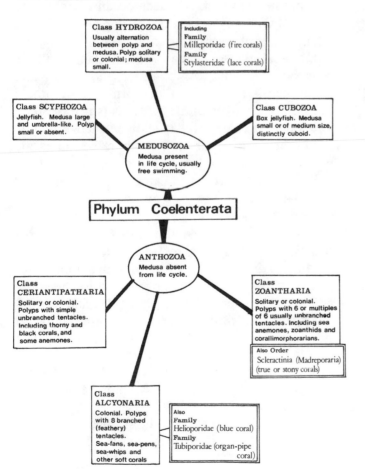

Hard corals do not invariably occur on coral reefs; neither do they always contribute to the building of reefs. To complicate matters still further, not all reefs are constructed entirely or predominantly of corals. There are many other organisms that help to build and strengthen coral reefs, of which red algae are of the greatest importance. *Lithothamnion, Porolithon, Hydrolithon* and several other genera of red algae grow as heavily calcified encrustations or nodules that bind the reef frame together. They are particularly successful and widespread on windward oceanic coral reefs, where they give added strength against the buffeting of waves. In both the tropical Atlantic and Indo-Pacific they may also form emergent algal ridges and non-coral reefs. Green algae such as *Halimeda* and *Udotea* have calcareous fronds that are not encrusted onto the reef but help to consolidate it by depositing coarse sediments. The death of molluscs, echinoderms, crustaceans, bryozoans, microscopic foraminiferans and other animals with limestone skeletons also adds calcareous matter to the basic framework.

GEOLOGICAL HISTORY

Since their appearance over 500 million years ago, corals have contributed to the formation of reefs in many parts of the world. The face of the earth has changed dramatically during that time, and the picture of reef distribution has altered many times. Early in the evolutionary history of corals a vast circumglobal sea known as the Tethys Sea connected the areas currently known as the

Corals and their relatives: the major taxonomic divisions (after George and George, 1979).

eastern Pacific, central Atlantic, Mediterranean, Indian Ocean and western Pacific. The warm-water fauna was continuous and there were no distinct biogeographical zones as there are today. The Mediterranean region was richest in coral species and remained so for many millions of years. Significant changes began to appear in the coral faunas at the beginning of the Miocene period, about 25 million years ago. This was the result of geological events that closed the Tethys Sea by a land barrier between Eurasia and Africa. The Indo-Malayan region took over as the center of coral development, while the tropical Atlantic became impoverished. This western Atlantic area was isolated from the central Indo-Pacific by a deep, extensive water barrier to the west and a land barrier to the east. The loss of genera was probably brought about by enormous changes in the physical environment (Newell, 1959), including changes in the pattern of surface ocean currents (Fell, 1967).

This situation persisted for about 10 to 15 million years, until disrupted by the closure of the link between the eastern Pacific and western Atlantic. The coral faunas on either side of the newly formed Isthmus of Panama were now completely isolated from each other and continued to develop separately until the present day. The subsequent history of the tropical West Atlantic is reasonably well understood, but that of the East Pacific is less certain. Dana (1975) believes that the entire coral fauna may have been obliterated during the ice ages by cooler temperatures and by fluctuations in sea level. He suggests that the area was then invaded from the Indo-West Pacific during the Pleistocene, less than a million years ago. Certainly the present day East Pacific coral fauna shows affinities with that of the Indo-West Pacific and not with the Caribbean. Porter (1972) explains the phenomenon in another way. He thinks that the similarity between the modern Indo-West Pacific and East Pacific faunas is due to their common Tethyan origin rather than to recent migration.

Despite the long evolutionary history of corals, the reefs as we know them today have only been in existence for a fraction of geological time. This is a result of sea level changes due to the melting and re-forming of ice during the ice ages. 15,000 years ago the seas were about 120 meters lower than they are now, and 7,000 years ago they were about 20 meters below the present level. Estimates show that modern reef growth related to present sea level

must have begun about 5,000 years ago (Stoddart, 1973). It also appears that modern reefs are only patchy in comparison with the flourishing reefs of the Pleistocene and pre-ice age eras. Throughout the world there are many drowned and raised reefs, but it is those related to present day sea levels with which this book is concerned.

FORMATION AND FORM OF REEFS

Present day reefs fall into two basic categories—shelf reefs and oceanic reefs.

Shelf reefs are close to continental land masses where the sea is mostly shallow, the bottom shelving gradually from the shore to a depth of about 200 meters. This coastal ledge of shallow sea bottom is known as the continental shelf, and in the tropics it provides a suitable base for the growth of coral reefs. In general the reefs grow upward from the sea bed and then spread outward upon reaching the surface waters, but they are capable of further upward growth should the sea level rise. If the sea level falls, then the reefs become stranded as dead, raised reefs.

Oceanic Reefs develop in deeper waters beyond the continental shelf. The deep ocean floor may be a virtually flat abyssal plain, but in places it rises to form ranges of submarine mountains. The highest peaks break the surface as oceanic islands and are often of volcanic origin (such as Tahiti and Raratonga). The reefs that form around these islands are younger than the atolls (such as Bikini and Enewetak) described below, which probably began their growth around comparable submarine mountains many millions of years ago.

Within these two basic categories are a number of different reef types, of which the major ones are outlined below.

Fringing Reefs: The majority of shelf reefs are of this type, but fringing reefs also develop around oceanic islands, provided the offshore slope is not too steep. Fringing reefs grow close to the shore and are characterized by a shallow, relatively impoverished back reef (reef flat) on the landward side that may be raised out of the water to give a reef crest. To the seaward side is a strongly growing fore reef that is usually divided into the shallow fore reef (reef rim, reef front) and the deep fore reef (reef slope).

Platform (Patch) Reefs: The sea bed of the continental shelf is often irregular and in places is raised up close to the surface. If this underwater

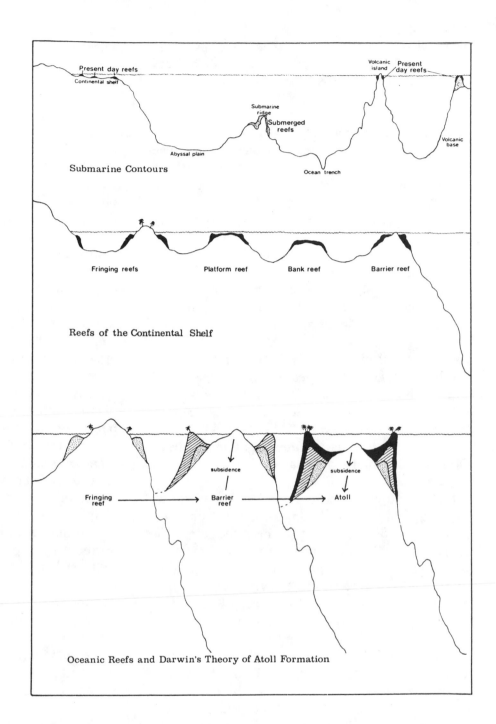

Submarine Contours

Reefs of the Continental Shelf

Reef types and their formation.

Oceanic Reefs and Darwin's Theory of Atoll Formation

hillock is suitably solid, then corals will settle on it and grow to form a platform reef. The top of the reef is usually exposed in places, and a sand cay or limestone bank may develop. In general the most prolific coral growth is around the reef front and the upper reef slope.

Bank Reefs: Bank reefs occur on bottom irregularities that lie deeper than the hillocks on which platform reefs are formed. Their tops are never exposed and may be as much as 40 meters below the surface. The most prolific growths of

coral are usually on the reef top, where light penetration is greatest. Bank reefs may occur both on the continental shelf and in oceanic waters.

Barrier Reefs: The width of the continental shelf varies, but at some point the gradient of the sea bottom becomes considerably steeper as it descends to the floor of the ocean basin. The edge of the shelf is known as the continental edge and the slope as the continental slope. Barrier reefs may develop along the continental edge, between the waters of the continental shelf and the open ocean. There are also oceanic barrier reefs that have probably developed from fringing reefs as a result of land subsidence. This process is described under the section concerned with atolls, which are thought to be the next stage on from the barrier reef.

Barrier reefs are separated from the mainland or island by a relatively deep, wide lagoon. The lagoon side and seaward side of the barrier reef are generally quite different in shape, structure and species composition. The lagoon fore reef tends to have an irregular outline and to be colonized by fragile corals. The seaward fore reef is more consolidated and regular, with prolific growths of calcareous algae and sturdy corals.

Atolls: An atoll is a roughly circular reef that encircles a central lagoon. The reef top is often exposed, and small islands of accumulated coral sand and fragments may form. Atolls are typically found in oceanic waters, rising abruptly from depths of thousands of meters. They range in size from Kwajalein in the Pacific, with a lagoon over 100 kilometers long and about 55 meters deep, to Astore in the Indian Ocean, only three kilometers across and with a lagoon about one meter deep. Occasionally small atolls may develop on the continental shelf.

Only the upper crust of an atoll is alive and growing, and the formation of the basal structure on which these reefs stand has been the subject of some interest. Darwin's theory is still the one most widely accepted. It proposes that the bases of present day reefs correspond to fringing reefs that were formed around islands millions of years ago. These islands then gradually became submerged below the surface of the water as a result of subsidence of their underlying mountainous bases. The only way contact was maintained with the surface was through the living corals. These were able to grow upward, compensating for the drop in level of the land. A similar sequence of events can also be applied to the evolution of barrier reefs from fringing reefs. Darwin's theory has been substantiated in a number of instances by test borings. For example, at Enewetak Atoll in the West Pacific the foundations of the atoll have been found at a depth of 1,219 meters, corresponding to the level at which corals were growing 50 million years ago (Kohn, 1961). In addition to Darwin's theory is the idea, proposed by Daly, that the land remained stationary while the water level rose. There were undoubtedly changes in sea level during the ice ages,

and these must have had an important influence on the more recent growth of reefs.

DISTRIBUTION OF PRESENT DAY REEFS

It is well known that coral reefs are restricted to the tropics, and it is clear that the capacity of corals to build reefs is controlled primarily by water temperature. Consistently high temperatures encourage growth through their effects on metabolic, physiological and reproductive processes. Additionally, precipitation of calcium from the water to form skeletons occurs readily when the temperature and salinity are high and the carbon dioxide concentration low, conditions typical of shallow tropical waters.

Reef-building corals generally occur within the latitudes 30°N and 30°S, which roughly coincide with the 20°C isotherms. The distribution and growth of reefs within this zone are influenced by a variety of factors. The flow of ocean currents is extremely important because not only do currents distribute coral larvae, nutrients, oxygen and food, but they also bring cold or warm streams of water to certain areas. Ocean currents result from a combination of factors, including temperature and density differences between adjacent bodies of water and the direction and velocity of the wind. In addition, the "Coriolis effect," caused by the rotation of the Earth, deflects currents clockwise in the northern hemisphere and counterclockwise in the southern hemisphere. These giant eddies swing into or away from the equatorial zone and in doing so become warmer or cooler. The final result is that warm water flows along the eastern shores of the major land masses while relatively cool water flows along the western shores. Thus the East Indies and the Caribbean are rich in corals while the Gulf of Guinea and western Central America are relatively poor.

This basic pattern of reef distribution and growth is influenced by temperature, but regional factors also play their part. Certain areas are exposed to strong wind-driven waves and swell and others to intermittent tropical storms and hurricanes. The degree of water movement and disturbance has profound effects on coral growth, reef morphology and sediment accumulation. Tidal range varies within the tropical zone, and this has additional effects on the development of reefs, as also do coastal geomorphology, water depth and type of substrate.

WESTERN ATLANTIC

Bahama Archipelago

This string of islands stretches from Florida toward Hispaniola and supports innumerable reefs, despite relatively low water temperatures. Around the Bahamas themselves there are estimated to be nearly 3,000 islands, cays and rocks, many with associated reefs (Colin, 1978). On the Atlantic side of Andros Island is the second largest barrier reef in the western Atlantic region. In general there is a great variety of reef types, even between one side of an island and the other. This is because southerly shores are relatively protected while northerly ones are subjected to the full force of the Atlantic swell.

The Antilles

The Antilles are formed by a long arc of islands that swing from Cuba in the north to Aruba in the south. Reefs have developed around many of these islands, but the degree of development and type of reef are influenced to a great extent by their aspect, the presence of a suitable substrate and the effect of hurricanes. In general the Caribbean shorelines are relatively sheltered and support extensive fringing reefs, while Atlantic shorelines are steeper and less luxuriant. Cuba, Hispaniola and Puerto Rico of the Greater Antilles have more extensive reefs than the islands of the Lesser Antilles, with the exception of the Dutch islands of Bonaire, Curacao and Aruba at the southeastern end of the Antilles chain.

Central Caribbean

Jamaica and the Cayman Islands lie in relatively deep water but are protected from the Atlantic by the Greater Antilles. Fringing reefs are well developed, and there are some spectacular slopes and caves with good growths of coral, especially off the northern coastlines of these islands.

Central and South American Coastlines

South American coastal waters receive a large influx of fresh water from the extensive mainland river systems, and in general reef development is poor. Little is known about Central American reefs, except for those off Panama, which are reasonably lush. North of the Gulf of Honduras is the Belize Barrier Reef, the longest such reef in the Atlantic. Outside this reef are several atolls, and inside within the lagoon are numerous patch and platform reefs.

Florida and the Gulf of Mexico

The southern Gulf of Mexico off Yucatan has the best developed reefs, but there are also coral communities around the western side of the Gulf and off the coast of Texas. The Florida reefs extend from Dry Tortugas to Key Largo, including the Marquesas Keys, all of which support reasonably good coral faunas.

Bermuda

The reefs around Bermuda occur further north than any others in the world and owe their existence to the warming influence of the Gulf Stream. The range of species is limited, but the reefs themselves are relatively varied and well formed.

INDO-PACIFIC

Red Sea and Persian Gulf

Fringing reefs grow along the shorelines of both these seas. The Red Sea is particularly rich, and many of the reefs here are steep and luxuriant. Conditions in the Gulf of Eilat, at the northern end of the Red Sea, also encourage prolific reef development, and the reefs here are popular and much-visited. Despite their relative isolation, the reef faunas of these two seas are closely allied to that of the Indo-Pacific in general.

Western Indian Ocean

Fringing reefs flourish along the continental coastlines of Kenya and Tanzania in East Africa but are less well developed off Somalia to the north. The large island of Madagascar supports good fringing reefs, especially on its northern and southern coastlines. To the northwest of this island, off Mayotte in the Comores Archipelago, is a fine barrier reef, and there are fringing reefs around other islands in the group. To the north of Madagascar are the Seychelles and to the east are the Mascarene Islands (Reunion and Mauritius), all of which have well developed fringing reefs. Between the Seychelles and the Mascarene Islands are Coetivy, Agalega, Tromelin and Carajos, with their linear or table reefs.

Central and Eastern Indian Ocean

Conditions along the coastlines of Saudi Arabia and the Indian subcontinent do not in general encourage the growth of fringing reefs, but there are some fine oceanic reefs in the central Indian Ocean. Here atolls are the dominant reef type; they are found throughout the Maldives and the Chagos Archipelago. Far to the south is Cocos Atoll. To the east are the Andaman and Nicobar Islands with their fringing reefs. The western and southern shorelines of Sumatra and Java support a variety of reef types, including small barrier reefs.

Australia

Only northern Australia lies within the reef-building zone, but within this area is the largest barrier reef in the world. The Great Barrier Reef of Australia is about 2,000 km in length and is separated from the mainland by a wide lagoon. Inside the lagoon are many smaller reefs. The barrier itself is marked by a string of islands, with Heron Island the most well-known landmark. Further north the reef is less easily visited because of its isolation and the effect of strong winds and oceanic swell.

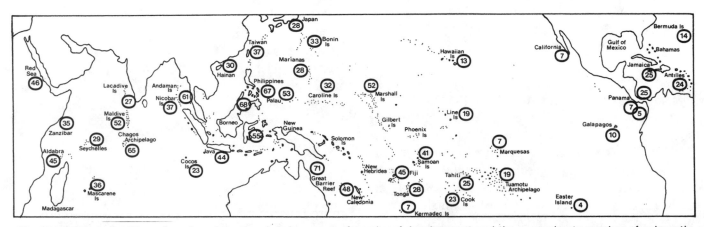

The tropical Indo-Pacific and western Atlantic, showing areas of coral reef development and the approximate number of scleractinian coral genera. (Sources of information: Bak, 1975; Barnes, et al., 1971; Burchard, 1980; Ditlev, 1976, 1980; Durham, 1962; Goreau, 1959; Goreau and Wells, 1967; Laborel, 1970; Loya and Slobodkin, 1971; Maragos, 1973; Pichon, 1977; Pillai, 1969, 1971; Porter, 1972; Rosen, 1971 a & b; Scheer, 1971; Scheer and Pillai, 1974; Smith, 1971; Stehli and Wells, 1971; Stoddart and Pillai, 1973; Veron and Pichon, 1976, 1980; Veron, Pichon and Wijsman-Best, 1977; Wells, 1950, 1954, 1972; Wells and Lang, 1973; Woodhead and Weber, 1969; Zou, 1975).

Southeast Asia and New Guinea

Southeast Asia includes the Malay Archipelago, Borneo and the Philippines and stretches southward through Sumatra and Java and eastward to the Moluccas. The water is shallow over extensive areas, and there are innumerable islands both large and small. In places such as the Straits of Malacca, the Gulf of Thailand and the Gulf of Papua the water is turbid from the inflow of large rivers and coral growth is restricted. Parts of the northern Philippines and New Guinea are affected by hurricanes or strong oceanic swells, but elsewhere in Southeast Asia the seas abound with reefs. There are innumerable fringing, platform and bank reefs, some small barrier reefs and a few atoll-like formations. The reef life is extremely rich and diverse, and the area is generally considered as the faunistic center of the entire Indo-Pacific region.

Western Pacific (Melanesia)

The western Pacific can be described as the region stretching outward from the Solomon Islands and New Hebrides to the Fiji and Tonga groups. The sea bottom in this area is traversed by a series of troughs and ridges that are considered continental remnants of Australia, New Guinea and New Caledonia (Whitehouse, 1973). The geological past is reflected in the reef formations seen in the western Pacific today. Typically, atolls are rare while fringing and barrier reefs are widespread. Reefs are scattered throughout the region and are associated with most of the islands, but the most extensive development is in the region of New Caledonia. There is a barrier reef running along both western and eastern coasts, each about 1,600 km long and enclosing around the island a large lagoon containing patch reefs, bank reefs, fringing reefs and other formations.

14

Central Pacific (Micronesia and Polynesia)

The central Pacific covers a huge area of sea dotted with clusters of islands of volcanic origin. These islands serve as foundations for the growth of fringing and barrier reefs and, when subsidence occurs, encourage the development of atolls. In comparison with those of the western Pacific, the central Pacific atolls are widespread, numerous and of a large size. The size of an atoll is a function of its age, rate of subsidence and extent of its foundations. Enewetak Atoll in the Marshall Islands is the top of a limestone cap 1,200 m deep that sits on a volcano rising over 3,000 m above the sea floor. The largest atoll is nearby Kwajalein, with a lagoon over 100 km wide. The second largest is Rangiroa in the Tuamotus, an area that supports about 80 atolls altogether and many bank reefs. The Central Pacific atolls may be circular, but often their shape is influenced by the prevailing winds so they take on a pear-shaped outline. Typically the windward sides are consolidated by coralline algae, while more extensive and varied coral growths occur on the leeward sides.

Hawaiian Islands

The Hawaiian Islands occupy rather a special position because they are on the fringe of the tropical zone. Reef-building is curtailed and much less extensive than it is around the central Pacific islands. It appears that the growth of present day reefs is poor or declining, probably as a result of erosion (Maragos, 1973). Vigorous growth is restricted to shallow areas, with little development below about ten meters.

Eastern Pacific

There is a wide gap in terms of both distance and water depth between the central Pacific islands and the islands and continental shorelines of the eastern Pacific. Coral reefs in this region are scattered and in a relatively poor state of development. Environmental conditions are marginal for coral growth, with fluctuations in temperature, salinity and tidal movements being the main limiting factors (Dana, 1975). The best reefs are in the Gulf of Chirique off western Panama, but even these are small and reach only to a depth of about ten meters.

GEOGRAPHICAL ASPECTS OF CORAL DISTRIBUTION

The distribution of coral reefs does not necessarily reflect the limits of distribution of the corals themselves. Hermatypic corals often grow successfully without actually forming reefs, for example around Easter Island in the eastern Pacific. Neither are coral reefs uniform in their composition. In some areas they are built from several hundred species (Great Barrier Reef), in others from 40 (Hawaii) or less (eastern Pacific).

Studies on the diversity and distribution of corals on a world-wide basis are made difficult because of the poor taxonomic understanding of the species (Rosen, 1975). This is amply illustrated by looking at a genus such as *Acropora*, which contains the familiar staghorn and elkhorn corals. At least 300 species have been described over the years, but a recent study (Wallace, 1978) suggests that as few as 70 are actually valid. There are many other genera that need to be revised before a complete picture of species distribution can be obtained. Investigations at the generic level, although complicated by some taxonomic problems, are more reliable and reveal some interesting trends.

A study of the number of genera present in tropical reef localities reveals two definite high diversity centers. These are in the Caribbean and the Indonesian-West Pacific, and there is possibly another focus in the central Indian Ocean. The Indonesian-West Pacific is the richest area, with well over twice as many genera as the Caribbean. This is presumably due to a long evolutionary history, stable environmental conditions and a wide variety of suitable habitats. The number of coral genera decreases in a fairly regular pattern from the high diversity centers to the edges of the coral reef zones. The most important factors in the formation of these gradients are a drop in temperature and the problems of larval dispersal. There is general agreement that sea water temperatures control reproduction in corals and that different genera have different critical minima for breeding. Thus, when Wells (1954) plotted the lines of equal minimum surface water temperature (isocrynes) against the generic diversity contours in the South Pacific, he found that they broadly corresponded.

In addition to the gradual shift in environmental conditions from favorable to unfavorable, it is also necessary to take the geological history of the different regions into consideration. Nowhere is this better illustrated than in the differences between the Atlantic and Pacific faunas, which were separated millions of years ago and have remained so until the present day. There are approximately 100 hermatypic scleractinian coral genera on a world-wide basis, but only eight are common to both areas. *Acropora, Porites* and *Montastraea* are reasonably prominent, but *Siderastrea, Madracis, Leptoseris, Cladocora* and *Favia* play only a marginal role in one region or the other. Porter (1972) believes that among these genera there is probably only one common species (*Siderastrea radians*). Ahermatypic (non-reef-building) corals show a slightly greater proportion of common genera (20 out of approximately 150), with several species in common (*e.g., Tubastrea aurea*). The hydrozoan corals *Millepora* and *Stylaster* also have a cosmopolitan distribution.

Geological events also appear to play a role in the distribution of genera across the Pacific. Stoddart and Pillai (1973) consider that a major faunistic discontinuity, rather than a gradual gradient, may exist between the Tonga and Cook Islands, and they suggest that this may be due to the geological history of the two areas. They point out that Tonga, Samoa and Fiji are associated with the ancient continental remains of Australia, New Guinea and New Caledonia, while the Cook and Society Islands and the Tuamotu Archipelago are isolated volcanic structures rising from the deep ocean floor.

Thus the richness of different reef areas, the position of faunal centers, the distribution of coral genera and species and the similarities between different reef areas are not attributable to any single factor. Instead they result from the combination of past and present geological and environmental events.

CONSERVATION

Coral reefs may be damaged by natural events such as hurricanes, temperature and salinity changes, sedimentation and a host of biological factors, but many of the most serious threats come from man himself. Coral reefs are exploited for food, trophies and building materials. They are abused by dynamite and other destructive fishing methods. They are choked by silt washed into the sea from erosion on land or are disturbed during dredging operations or sand extraction in shallow waters. They are polluted by sewage, oil, pesticides and industrial wastes and are damaged by warm-water outflows.

Healthy coral reefs are one of the most exotic and varied habitats known to man, but they also pose problems for conservationists. This is partly because man tends to consider the sea both as a convenient dustbin and a useful provider and partly because the sea has few barriers to prevent the spread of harmful substances. The creation of marine parks provides suitable legislation for the prevention of direct assaults on the reefs and their fauna, but it is not so easy to prevent detrimental environmental changes such as sedimentation and pollution. Often the sources of such trouble lie outside park boundaries and are elusive to trace and difficult to control. Ultimately, protection of the underwater world must come from a greater public awareness and from integrated and wide-ranging conservation policies, a difficult but not impossible task.

Biology of Corals

BASIC DESIGN

The living part of a coral is relatively simple and resembles an anemone. It is referred to as a polyp and is generally cylindrical in shape, varying from less than a millimeter to several centimeters in diameter. It may be tall or flattened and produces a skeleton to match. The polyp mouth is at the top of the cylinder and is surrounded by one or more rings of tentacles. Apart from a few rare cases these are unbranched, but size and shape vary tremendously. In most species the tentacles can be retracted and sometimes introverted. This may be a regular day/night activity or a rapid response to food, touch or some other stimulus. Internally the mouth leads to a short stomodaeum or pharynx, and this opens out into the gastrovascular cavity. Here digestion and absorption of food take place. The cavity is divided longitudinally by a series of radial partitions called mesenteries that bear the gonads and also play an important role in digestive processes. Adjacent polyps in a colony are frequently, but not invariably, connected by living tissue containing extensions of the gastrovascular cavity. The connection may be made by a sheet called the coenosarc that stretches over the surface of the skeleton. This can be regarded as a horizontal extension of the column wall and is responsible for depositing the parts of the skeleton that lie between the polyps. Some corals have perforated skeletons that allow adjacent polyps to be connected through as well as over the corallite wall.

The skeleton of either a solitary or a colonial coral is called the corallum, and the skeletal parts deposited by a single polyp form a corallite. Each corallite is usually enclosed by a wall (theca) and the upper open end is the calice. As a colonial coral grows, corallites leave beneath them horizontal layers of skeletal material known as endothecal dissepiments. Outside the corallite wall are porous or solid exothecal dissepiments, which have been deposited by the polyps and their interconnecting tissues. This skeletal material between the corallites forms what is known as coenosteum or peritheca. The surface of the coenosteum is visible in intact corals, but details of the dissepiments can only be seen when the coral skeleton is sectioned.

Within the corallite are a series of vertical radiating septa that alternate with the mesenteries. The septa are formed in cycles, with six in the first or primary cycle, six in the second, 12 in the third, 24 in the fourth and so on. Septa may be equal, subequal or unequal in size, thus forming distinct orders. Orders do not necessarily correspond to cycles.

When the septa pass over the top of the corallite wall and continue over perithecal areas they are referred to as costae. In some cases the distinction between septa and costae is indistinct and they are termed septocostae. Septa are exsert if they protrude above the top of the corallite wall, insert if they lie below. The upper free margins of septa, costae and septocostae may be smooth, granular or toothed, and a structure known as a paliform lobe may be formed at the inner end of some septa. Septal sides are smooth or ornamented, and in some cases adjacent septa are linked by bars called synapticulae. An axial structure called the columella is usually developed at the center of each corallite. This sometimes stands alone but more typically is connected to the inner edges of the septa. It can be rod-like (styliform), spongy (papillose or trabecular) or consist of a series of interconnecting vertical plates (lamellar).

STRUCTURAL DIVERSITY

A glance at some corals quickly reveals the basic corallite, but in others fusion or modification has led to a structure more difficult to interpret. It is a

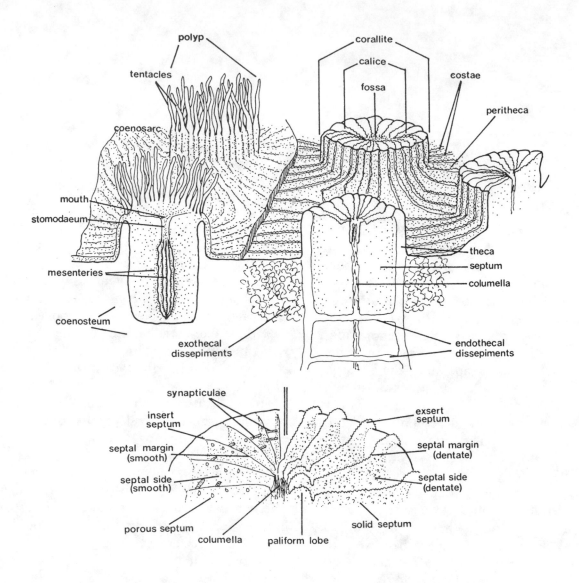

Diagrammatic representation of the basic features of coral polyps and skeletons.

fascinating study in itself to trace the way in which corals have advanced from simple to complex, and it also helps to explain some of the principles of classification.

The simplest type of coral is small and cup-like (solitary). It is rarely seen on shallow reefs but prefers deeper and often cooler waters. There is, however, an important group of solitary corals that have become discoid, much larger, and are a common sight on many reefs. These are the mushroom corals, which are attached as juveniles but become detached as adults (solitary, free-living).

Progressing from the simple corallum in another direction leads to the colonial corals with separate, well defined corallites (plocoid). Here an enormous range of species exhibit an equally daunting range of growth forms. Often the corallites are round, but they may be irregular and when packed together are often polygonal. They may protrude, be level with the general surface or even be slightly below it. Size varies from several centimeters down to less than a millimeter.

A further stage is reached when the corallites are packed closely together with adjacent calice walls fused (cerioid). Sometimes a line indicates where fusion has occurred, but in many cases only a single wall is apparent. The next step is loss of the wall so that septa run uninterrupted from one calice center to the next (thamnasterioid). Often the corallites are closely packed and easily

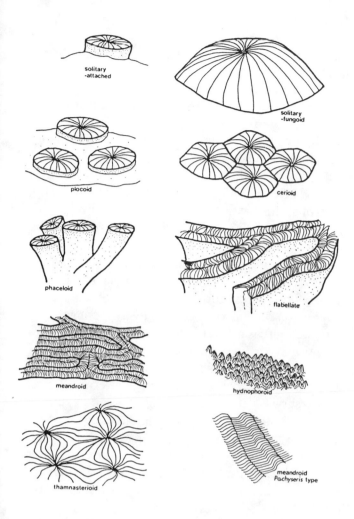

Structural diversity in corals: the basic types.

recognizable, but they are also sometimes small, irregular and difficult to distinguish. The situation is confused still further in several species by the presence of small hillocks called collines situated between corallites or groups of corallites. A special case is the peculiar condition reached in the highly modified genus *Pachyseris*, where the septa do not converge to separate centers but run parallel and at right angles to a series of ridges.

Finally there is an assemblage of corals whose corallites and polyps no longer have their own recognizable identity. They have joined in longitudinal series to produce a pattern of valleys and ridges (meandroid). The polyps lie in the valleys, and the ridges represent fused walls. The width, shape and length of the meanders vary from one species to another, and the patterns they form are most clearly seen in the familiar brain corals. In several species of meandrine corals the meanders arise from a common base but then become independent with unfused walls (flabellate). A peculiar condition occurs in the genus *Hydnophora*, where the ridges are split into a series of pointed cones (hydnophoroid).

The basic skeletal patterns of the groups described above are in most cases clearly visible in living corals, but occasionally the corallites are not easily seen because of a covering of living tissue.

GROWTH FORMS

The simplest form is the solitary cylinder, but types such as this are rarely seen on the reef. In contrast, colonial corals show an astonishing variety of form. This is largely determined by the way in

Variations in growth form:
typical variation of a massive coral
with depth.

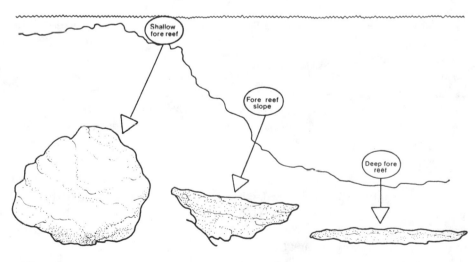

which new polyps are added and then modified by environmental factors, particularly light intensity and swell. There are four principal forms—branching, foliaceous, encrusting and massive—and many intermediates. Often a single species occurs in several of these forms, and this has created a certain amount of taxonomic confusion. However, with the advent of SCUBA diving it has become easier to identify series of coralla and to describe the full variation within a species.

Exposure to swell tends to favor the development of robust colonies, whereas a sheltered site allows the growth of more delicate skeletons. Calm conditions also allow establishment of stouter types, and as a result these areas generally support a more varied assemblage of growth forms than exposed reefs. Light intensity drops as depth increases and has an important effect on growth form. A coral that is massive and rounded in well lit shallow waters generally becomes conspicuously flattened or even foliaceous in deeper, dimmer conditions. A flat form is able to make better use of the available light than a spherical one and needs to add less skeletal matter for the addition of a new polyp (Dustan, 1975).

COLOR

Not only can a single species grow in a variety of forms (*i.e.*, polymorphic), but it may also occur in different colors. Conversely, the color is sometimes diagnostic for a particular species. Many corals are a shade of brown, but others are blue, green, yellow, pink, purple, red or even black. The color is contributed in part by microscopic plants that associate with living corals. Filamentous algae, usually red or green, bore their way into the polyps or skeleton. Additionally, the tissues of all reef-building (hermatypic) corals are packed with yellow, brown or green unicellular algae called zooxanthellae. When a coral is under stress or dies, these algae are ejected and their loss results in whitening of the colony. Apart from these "imported" colors, there are pigments within the tissues of the coral itself that produce a wide range of hues from opaque to black.

REPRODUCTION AND GROWTH RATES

Some mature adult corals are hermaphroditic, others are exclusively male or female. A few even change sex as they grow. It has been suggested that corals with small polyps (*e.g.*, *Stylophora*) produce

fewer eggs in each gonad than those with large polyps (*e.g.*, *Favia*) and that fertilization takes place internally in the former and externally in the latter (Rinkevich & Loya, 1979). Subsequent development produces a tiny larva, known as a planula, which in some species is brooded within the adult colony. Release of eggs or planula larvae usually occurs at night and is sometimes in phase with the lunar cycle. Studies on *Favia* (Lewis, 1974) and *Pocillopora* (Harrigan, 1972) reveal that recently released planulae are attracted toward the light but that prior to settlement they reverse this behavior and seek dark surfaces and crevices. The period from release to settlement usually lasts only a few days, but some planulae can survive afloat for several weeks. They are vulnerable at this time to heavy predation and adverse environmental conditions and may also be carried away from suitable settlement areas by water currents. For the relatively few that survive to implant themselves on the reef, there is evidence that at least some are gregarious in their settlement patterns. Lewis (1974) showed that *Favia fragum* planula larvae could recognize their own species either as the adult colony or as previously settled juveniles.

Further growth involves both the production of new polyps (asexual reproduction) and the deposition of skeletal material. There are two main ways in which new polyps are added:

a) Intratentacular (= intracalicular) reproduction. Referred to as "fission." The oral disc invaginates to produce a new mouth *within* the parental ring of tentacles.

b) Extratentacular (= intercalicular) reproduction. Referred to as "budding." The new mouth is produced from the edge zone or coenosarc and thus lies *outside* the parental ring of tentacles.

In addition to asexual reproduction, colonies can also spread by a phenomenon termed "vegetative" reproduction (Bak, 1975). This involves regrowth of whole colonies or fragments that have been overthrown but have subsequently cemented themselves to the substrate.

The rate of coral growth depends on many factors. It varies from one species to another according to the age of the corallum and the condition of the symbiotic algae. Growth rate may also be affected by factors such as light intensity, day length, water temperature, food supply, sedimentation, predation and competition. Testing the effect of a single variable in isolation from other factors is not

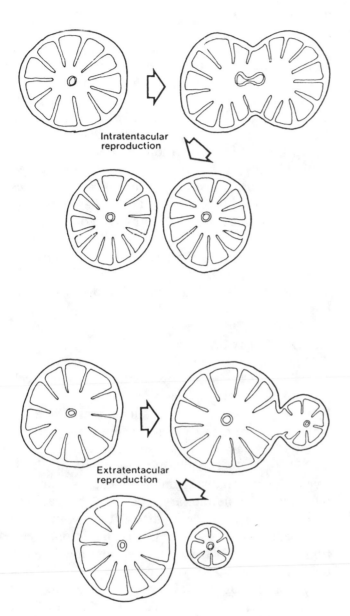

The two main types of asexual reproduction in corals: intratentacular (intracalicular) and extratentacular (intercalicular).

an easy task. How, also, can growth be best recorded? By weight gain, increase in the number or length of branches or increase in colony diameter or surface area? And over what period should growth be measured? It is highly probable that coral growth is a discontinuous process. As with many animals, it may slow down or stop during sexual activity or as a response to some short-term environmental change.

Despite all these problems and the lack of useful comparative data, various interesting facts have emerged from growth rate studies. Corals with porous skeletons increase in size more rapidly than those with solid ones, but although a solid skeleton may occupy less space, its weight may exceed that of a porous skeleton of comparable age. In relation to the overall dimensions of a coral and the area that it covers, branched forms grow more quickly than massive, rounded ones. Studies on the Great Barrier Reef have shown that the difference can be up to ten times as fast (Stephenson & Stephenson, 1933). *Acropora* species appear to be among the fastest growing corals, with upward growth between 10 and 20 cm per year. In contrast, a massive coral such as *Montastraea annularis* grows only about 0.5 to 1.0 cm per year (review in Buddemeier & Kinzie, 1976).

ZOOXANTHELLAE

The secret of success for reef-building corals lies in the presence of minute plants called zooxanthellae packed in large numbers in their tissues. These symbiotic plants require sunlight, using it during photosynthesis to build up organic matter. It has been shown experimentally that the number of hours of sunshine is probably the most important influence on coral growth (Connell, 1976). Sunshine is also essential for the survival of reef-building types. Colonies shaded under opaque domes on the Great Barrier Reef died within two to six months, while unshaded colonies lived for six years or more. This explains why the most luxuriant coral growths are found in well lit, relatively shallow waters (less than 30 meters), why there is a maximum depth at which corals can actively build reefs (46 meters), and why reef-builders will not live at all where the light intensity is too low (below 90 meters) (Vaughan & Wells, 1943). Non-reef-building corals are not affected in this way and can thrive many thousands of meters down in the ocean depths. This is because their tissues do not contain the light-dependent zooxanthellae.

The precise way in which corals benefit from the presence of zooxanthellae has been hotly debated for many years. It has been suggested that excess oxygen produced by the algae is used by the coral for its own respiration. Another possibility is that corals digest fragments of zooxanthellae, or even whole cells, as a supplement to their basic diet. Additionally, zooxanthellae may serve a useful role in conserving and recycling nutrients produced as "waste" products of coral metabolism. It appears, however, that the most important single factor is the role played by algal photosynthetic products in coral calcification (Muscatine, 1973). Corals may be able to induce the release of these organic products, or they may be released naturally, and they are then used either as specific substrates or as general energy sources (Pearse & Muscatine, 1971). In some cases there is a sophisticated transport system to carry the photosynthetic products to the required site. This was demonstrated by the use of radioactive tracers in *Acropora* to explain why calcification proceeds more rapidly in the branch tips than elsewhere, despite the smaller number of zooxanthellae (Pearse & Muscatine, 1971).

Whatever the precise relationship between zooxanthellae and coral calcification, the influence of the light-dependent algae on skeletal growth is clear. It explains why growth in reef-builders is severely curtailed with increasing depth and decreasing light and why skeletons formed in deeper waters are more fragile.

FOOD AND FEEDING

Corals utilize a number of different methods and tap a variety of sources in order to satisfy their nutritional requirements. It is known that they can absorb certain inorganic and organic materials from the surrounding sea water, but the relative importance of this activity is still under debate. The same applies to the utilization of fragmented or complete zooxanthellae. The most important food for corals is zooplankton, but they may also catch dead or moribund animal material and even bacteria. Many corals are active and efficient predators, catching small floating prey on their tentacles. These are armed with batteries of stinging cells called nematocysts, which both poison and capture. Some corals only extend their tentacles at night when the density of zooplankton in the water is at its highest. However, this does not explain why other species (*e.g., Euphyllia, Goniopora*) consistently expand their tentacles during the day.

The tentacles may pass captured food directly to the mouth, but in many cases it is carried on ciliated tracts. In *Pachyseris* there are no tentacles and the mucus-covered tracts are important in both capture and transport of food. In all corals the cilia also play an important role in ejecting unwanted sediments. In addition to tentacles and cilia, some corals catch food on digestive filaments derived from the internal mesenteries. These filaments are long and mobile and can be extruded through the mouth or through temporary openings in the body wall.

Coral polyps appear to have an acute sense of "smell" and can detect potential food substances by chemical means. For example, one part of homogenized plankton in ten million parts of water has been shown to stimulate *Cyphastrea*, causing the polyp mouth to open and the tentacles to search around in expectation of food (Mariscal & Lenhoff, 1968). The voracious *Montastraea cavernosa* responds to a variety of chemical substances from amino acids to sugars, and it has been suggested that punctured zooplankton could release such substances and elicit capture and ingestion behavior (Lehman & Porter, 1973). Such behavior may involve increased tentacular movements, opening of the mouth and muscular activity by the lips.

ASSOCIATED FAUNA

Corals and their skeletons provide a microhabitat for numerous organisms. Some seek shelter, food or living space on a temporary basis, but many others form permanent symbiotic associations. Symbiosis literally means "living together" of unlike organisms and does not indicate the feeding habits of the animals involved. Typically, the smaller symbiont benefits from the relationship while the larger host, in this case the coral, may or may not be affected by its presence and feeding activities. The precise nutritional relationships between the species is described by the terms parasitism and commensalism. A parasite is a symbiont that derives energy from living host tissues, whereas a commensal obtains energy from other sources. In addition to organisms that form symbiotic associations with living corals, there is a specialized flora and fauna that live in or around dead coral skeletons. These skeletons provide both hiding places for small animals and a convenient substrate for sessile and burrowing organisms.

a) Casual Associates

There are innumerable small organisms, including protozoans, flatworms and copepods, that creep about on the surface of corals. Other, larger animals such as molluscs, feather stars and crabs hide in nooks and crannies, emerging periodically to feed. Countless fishes also seek shelter, especially among branched coral colonies and beneath coral heads. Juveniles rarely venture out, but adults often spend the day feeding in open water and only

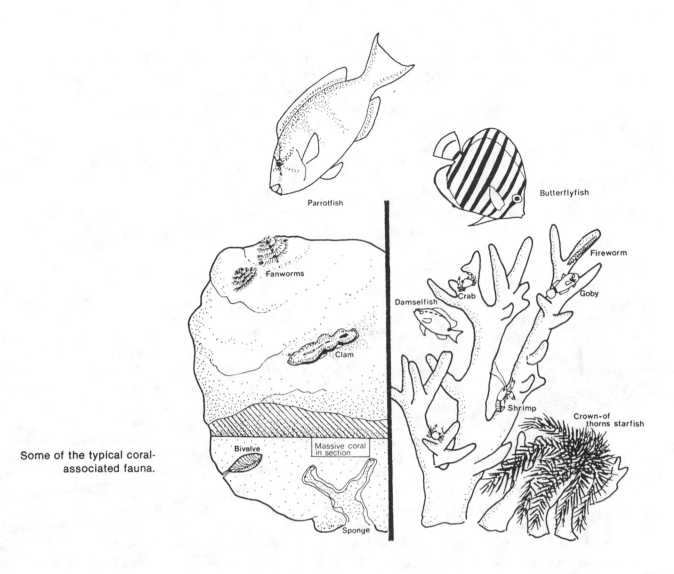

Some of the typical coral-
associated fauna.

retire among the branches at night. Some fishes use parts of the coral skeleton as spawning sites, the eggs being attached to a suitable dead surface.

b) Symbionts

Numerous small crabs and shrimps have permanent associations with corals, and it is common to find a high degree of species specificity. Thus, one particular species of crustacean may always be symbiotic with a certain species of coral. Most of the crabs and shrimps are small, cryptically colored and difficult to locate in the living coral. Some feed on mucus secreted by the corals, but many are of more help to their host because they remove and feed on settled sediments. Most of the crabs are fairly active. Others are less so, and because of their almost static habit they induce the coral skeleton to grow around them to varying degrees. The most curious of all is the gall crab *Hapalocar-*

cinus marsupialis, which lives in branches of corals of the family Pocilloporidae. Its presence induces abnormal growth and the development of a tiny gall or cage. The crab is trapped forever inside, filtering out tiny particles of food that float through. Only females inhabit galls. The male is smaller, lives in an open hollow on the coral surface and probably fertilizes the female before her gall is closed (Patton, 1976). There are also shrimps that live in similarly enclosed surroundings, such as the bloated *Paratypton siebenrocki* that lives in a cyst in the corallum of the coral *Acropora.* Male and female may live together or may have interconnecting chambers, which themselves only open to the outside through a tiny pore (Bruce, 1976).

There are various other animals that live in coral skeletons, lodging when young inside a corallite and taking over the cavity for their own use. As the coral grows so the cavity grows, usually with the new inhabitant doing little harm except perhaps to compete with the coral for food. There are a variety of worms that fall into this category, best known of which are serpulids of the genus *Spirobranchus*. These are often associated with *Porites* or *Acropora* but may inhabit other species and are easily recognized by their brightly colored crown of spiralling tentacles. *Spirobranchus* and other serpulids have calcareous tubes, but there are other coral-associated worms with membranous tubes, such as the fanworm *Sabellastarte*. This worm may be 10 to 15 cm long, but only the circle of feathery tentacles protrudes—the rest is hidden.

Barnacles may also take up residence in coral skeletons. The majority are filter-feeders, but an extreme condition has been reached in *Hoekia*, which is parasitic on the coral *Hydnophora*, feeding exclusively on host tissues (Patton, 1976).

Relatively large holes, probably previously inhabited by crabs, are often taken over by blennies such as *Petroscirtes* or *Plagiotremus*. The fish use these holes as permanent shelters and vantage points from which they can dart out to catch small prey. The gobies *Paragobiodon* and *Gobiodon* are also associated with living corals but differ because they do not occupy holes. Instead, they seek shelter among the closely knit branches of *Pocillopora*, *Acropora* and some other corals. They feed on small invertebrates and probably spend their entire life in a single coral colony.

In addition to the passive, generally non-destructive coral associates mentioned above, there are others that actively bore their way through coral skeletons. A serious threat to the health of living coral is posed by boring sponges such as *Cliona*. They excavate their way into the older basal parts of the colony, working their way up, and sometimes even penetrating, branches. They methodically remove tiny chips of calcium carbonate by chemical and mechanical means (Pomponi, 1979). This does not appear to damage the living polyps, but the skeleton is seriously weakened and may collapse. A variety of molluscs also burrow into the skeleton, weakening it in the same way. The date mussel, *Lithophaga*, is foremost in abundance and number of species and is common in *Porites*, *Favia*, *Favites* and *Goniastrea*. Individuals start life by settling on the coral surface then gradually penetrate the skeleton, forming long tunnels with slit-like or dumbbell-shaped openings. Date

mussels bore principally by chemical means, unlike the piddock *Petricola*, which uses its strong shell valves to mechanically wear away the skeleton.

The majority of organisms described above seek shelter in or on corals but are not dependent on their host for food. However, parasitism has developed among various crustaceans and prosobranch gastropods that consistently feed on the mucus and living tissues of their host. The family Coralliophilidae contains the most modified of all prosobranch coral associates, for these snails lack both jaws and radulae and apparently suck out their host's tissues (Robertson, 1970).

c) Predators

There are many predatory animals, including worms, crabs, starfishes, snails, nudibranchs and fishes, that feed on living coral tissues. Fishes are by far the largest and most diverse group of predators, with individuals from at least 12 families browsing on polyps, algae or skeletons. Parrotfishes are probably the most notorious in this respect, and their powdery excrement is thought to make a substantial contribution to the accumulation of coral sand. Butterflyfishes and angelfishes present a more attractive profile and a more delicate approach as they nibble at the coral polyps. The activities of these and other fishes are localized rather than extensive, and the coral will usually regenerate lost tissues and continue growing.

Sometimes white scars are seen on a coral surface where a mass of polyps has died. The culprit is frequently the large and voracious crown-of-thorns starfish, *Acanthaster planci*, which feeds by thrusting out its stomach and digesting living coral polyps. At the "normal" density of two or three individuals on a reef several hundred meters long, patches of dead coral occur but the reef as a whole remains healthy. For some reason as yet not fully understood, population explosions occur in this particular starfish with devastating results. A virtual plague sweeps across the reef, causing catastrophic destruction and encouraging growth of algae and other "fouling" organisms.

DISTRIBUTION, ECOLOGY AND COMPETITION

Distribution of corals is governed by a multitude of factors and is not a predictable subject. Larval settlement involves a certain amount of choice of substrate and location, and often the selected site lies close to an adult colony of the same species.

Environmental factors such as water depth, type of substrate and forces of swell and current also play a part both in successful establishment and subsequent growth. Newly settling planula larvae may be devoured by filter-feeding animals already established on the reef, and young corals are especially vulnerable to wandering predators.

Living space on reefs is at a premium, and corals have evolved methods of fighting for space and maintaining a living area (Lang, 1971, 1973). This is of vital importance to slower growing species otherwise in danger of being smothered by ones that may grow ten times faster. The corals use polyps to sting or internal mesenterial filaments to literally digest away the tissues of an encroaching coral. It has also been suggested that a toxic secretion may be involved (Sheppard, 1979). It appears that dominance of one coral over another is well established and that a definite "peck order" exists. Species can be described as aggressive, intermediate or subordinate, and the response of one species to another is consistent (Lang, 1973; Sheppard, 1979). Sheppard found that the most aggressive coral in the Chagos area was *Galaxea clavus*, which was capable of dominating certain reefs to the virtual exclusion of all other species. This contrasts with observations made by Lang (1973) in the Caribbean that showed that the most aggressive corals tended to be relatively minor components.

The final pattern of distribution of coral colonies and the way in which they and the reef grow produce a variety of habitats and microhabitats. These habitats each encourage growth of certain species or forms of coral and a particular type of associated or visiting fauna. The zone generally subjected to the most variable conditions is the reef crest or reef flat. Corals may be exposed to air and direct sunlight during low tides, to changes in salinity and to strong wave action. Species diversity is often limited because of these environmental constraints. Much the same applies to the back reef zone, which lies to the leeward and usually land-ward side of the reef crest. Here, corals have to withstand exposure to sun and air. In addition, there is relatively little water movement and sediments tend to accumulate. The fore reef lies to the seaward side of the reef crest, and the shallower regions are typically the most actively growing and diverse within the reef habitat as a whole. Water movement and food supply are good and environmental conditions are relatively stable, without the extremes encountered on the reef crest and back reef. Various microhabitats are found that support a specialized fauna and add to the diversity of this zone. For example, there may be a system of spurs (or buttresses) and grooves (or channels). The grooves are predominantly sandy and carry sediments down the fore reef slope away from the mounds of dense coral growth to either side. Sometimes the corals of adjacent buttresses grow together, forming a cavern over the top of the groove. Caves and underhangs may also be found on deep, steep fore reefs or in association with coral heads in shallower regions.

CORALS IN THE AQUARIUM

Aquarium owners around the world demand both dead bleached skeletons and living coral. As a result, innumerable coral colonies are taken from reef areas every day by private and commercial collectors. The damage and wastage involved in this largely uncontrolled trade is of concern both to conservationists and to those who simply wish to enjoy visiting and watching undisturbed reefs. A private collector may only seek a few skeletons to adorn his home or aquarium, but he must remember that he is not alone in his activities. As regards living coral, it is virtually impossible to recreate the coral reef environment within small man-made aquaria. Corals are demanding in their requirements and do not respond well to handling or sudden changes in their surroundings. A few large, well balanced and controlled aquaria do exist, but these need constant care and attention and are expensive to run.

Coral Taxonomy

HISTORICAL ASPECTS

Taxonomic studies on corals began early in the nineteenth century with Lamarck and his contemporaries. These early workers had a restricted amount of material at their disposal and often based their designation of species on single specimens or at most a small series. They did not appreciate that the majority of corals show a considerable range of variations in skeletal characters. Thus early taxonomic work led to an unnecessarily complicated situation that is still in the process of being disentangled today. The advent of major oceanographic expeditions toward the end of the nineteenth century enabled the first steps to be made in this direction. Veron & Pichon (1976) note, "It is the great merit of Quelch, in his report on the corals collected by the *Challenger* (1886), that he was the first to relate very clearly intraspecific variations with environmental factors."

GENUS AND SPECIES: EXPLANATION AND PROBLEMS

In his desire to classify living creatures, man has devised a hierarchical system in which related forms are linked together under the principal divisions of phylum, class, order, family, genus and species. Animals constituting a species can breed successfully among themselves and produce viable offspring. Closely related species do not interbreed successfully but have many characters in common and are grouped under the same generic name. A species is always referred to by both its generic and specific names and, to be strictly correct, the surname(s) of the author(s) who originally described it then follows. A species originally described in one genus then transferred to another has the name of the original author in parentheses. For example, *Maeandrina crispa* Lamarck, 1816 is now referred to as *Oulophyllia crispa* (Lamarck, 1816).

The concept of a species is relatively easy to appreciate in theory but not always easy to apply in practice. This is especially so in the case of corals, where physiology and reproductive biology are poorly known and matters are complicated by the extent to which polymorphism occurs. The different forms are generally referred to as ecomorphs because they are believed to be produced in response to ecological conditions. Thus it is essential to study a species throughout its ecological as well as geographical range in order to determine the full extent of its variability. It was difficult for early workers to do this, but the opportunity for detailed studies of different biotopes now exists, and work in progress is very revealing.

Definitions of coral genera must include both the range of variation among species and the common features that unite these species into a discrete group. In many cases this is clearly apparent, in some the differences between genera are less obvious and in a few they are minute and questionable. It is possible, for example, for a species to be so variable that some specimens have features of other genera. Certain groups are in particular need of revision, and it is hoped that some of these complex taxonomic problems will be cleared up as a result of future work.

IN SITU IDENTIFICATION

It is the aim of this book to encourage *in situ* identification of corals wherever possible. This would have been an impossible task before the advent of SCUBA diving and underwater photography, and even with these aids there are several problems. The major one is that corals are still classified principally on skeletal features. Some of these are obscured by living tissues and others are so small as to be difficult to distinguish underwater. This difficulty can either be overcome by carrying a magnifying lens or by removing a small portion of the colony for examination on land. This should be done with great care in order to minimize damage, and never in protected areas where collecting restrictions apply. Many genera are distinct and can be readily recognized from good photographs. Others are less easy, and thus it is advisable to combine photographs with detailed notes. It takes several minutes to complete this exercise, and if time underwater is limited then it is essential to be suitably prepared before entering the water.

USEFUL EQUIPMENT
1. Plastic ruler marked in centimeters and millimeters.
2. Laminated plastic board and pencil for making notes underwater.
3. Underwater camera and flash.
4. Hand lens.

WHAT TO RECORD
1. General features: solitary/colonial . . . attached/unattached . . . size . . . growth form . . . color
2. Corallites: arrangement . . . shape . . . size . . . pattern of asexual reproduction
3. Septa and costae: arrangement . . . exsert/insert . . . margins
4. Polyp: visible/retracted
   Tentacles: size . . . arrangement . . . shape
5. Peritheca/Coenosteum: general features

"MISLEADING" GROWTHS
1. Not all hard calcareous growths are corals—they may be algae or sponges. The surface should be examined carefully for corallites and polyps.
2. Juvenile corals are often strikingly different from mature specimens and may not have developed sufficient features to enable identification.
3. Growing edges and branch tips may show "strange" features when compared with the rest of the colony.
4. Some corals, notably the fungiids, are always detached as adults, but others become "accidentally" free-living. This can happen as a result of the juvenile becoming attached to a small rock fragment or a piece of seaweed. If the coral overgrows the rock fragment or the seaweed dies, then the colony may be deposited on a substrate to which it is unable to attach.

USING THE KEYS
It has already been emphasized that corals are extremely plastic organisms and that even a single species is capable of showing great morphological variation. Keys to genera must encompass an even wider range of form and are inevitably complex. The keys used here are based on the concept of the dichotomous key, a type of key used widely in the identification of plants and animals. Single or multiple characters are given in contrasting pairs (occasionally in groups) and a choice must be made between these alternatives. Thus each genus is eliminated in turn. The main reef-building forms are divided within the main key into "groups" according to the arrangement of calices on the corallum. There is then a subsidiary key for each group. A few genera fall into more than one group because the species that occur in that genus themselves show a range in calice morphology. For example, *Goniastrea* includes both cerioid and meandroid forms.

It is crucial that the keys be read carefully; all the features presented in the keys are essential for diagnosis and must be considered in turn. Many relate to the living coral and can be seen underwater. In cases where field diagnosis is difficult, skeletal characters that can be seen with a 10 X lens are given. Terminology relating to the keys is shown in the accompanying illustration and is also explained in the glossary.

NOTES ON THE DESCRIPTIONS
Atlantic and Indo-Pacific corals are considered separately since they are, for the most part, significantly distinct.

Many corals do not have common names; only where names are in regular and widespread usage have they been included. Scientific names are not always easily understood or remembered. For this reason their formation and meaning (etymology) are explained.

Where genera are monospecific or include only two or three species, then the species involved are described. For other genera the description of all known species is beyond the scope of this book. Instead, the ranges of species characters are merged to compile the generic description. References to more detailed texts are given in the bibliography.

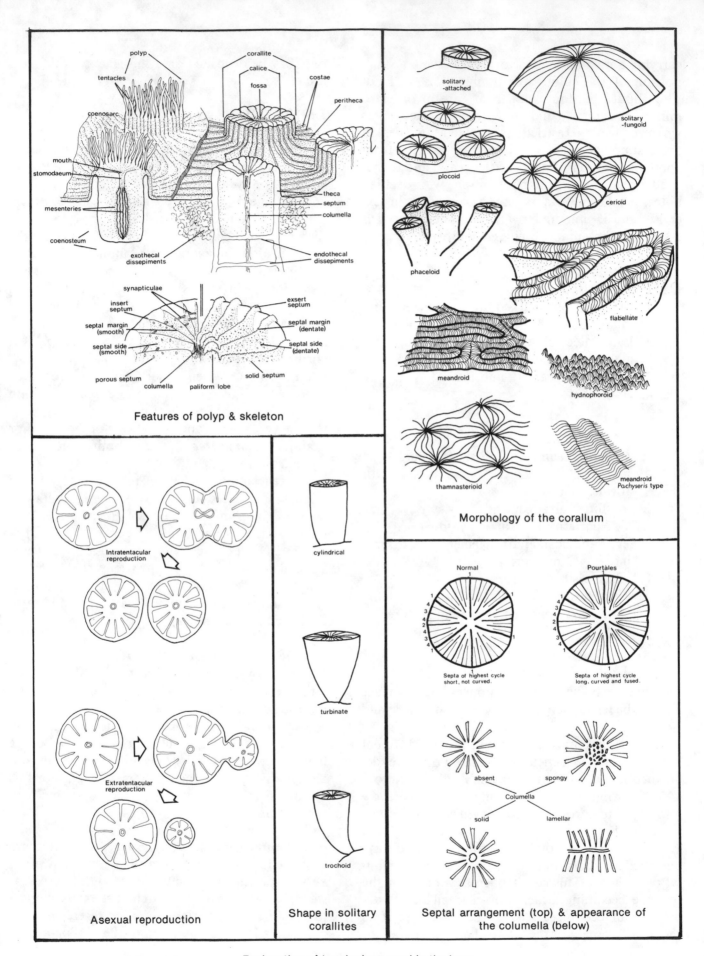

Features of polyp & skeleton

Morphology of the corallum

Asexual reproduction

Shape in solitary corallites

Septal arrangement (top) & appearance of the columella (below)

Explanation of terminology used in the keys.

Keys to Reef Coral Genera

KEYS TO ATLANTIC REEF CORALS

1. Corallum formed from a single corallite (solitary)..................................2
   Corallum formed from several or many corallites (colonial)...........................4
2. Corallite disc-like, about 5 cm in diameter; septal margins spiny..............*Scolymia*
   Corallite cylindrical or trochoid; septal margins smooth to dentate.....................3
3. Septa with smooth margins, costae absent; columella formed from small pillars; wall solid .... *Gardineria*
   Septa with smooth or minutely dentate margins, costal margins toothed; columella broad and spongy; wall porous.....................................*Balanophyllia*
   Septa with irregularly dentate margins, costal margins granulated; columella absent or feebly developed; wall solid.......................................*Astrangia*
   Septal and costal margins smooth; columella broad and spongy; wall solid....**Caryophylliidae**
4. Polyp-bearing chambers as tiny dots, 0.1 mm in diameter or less, with no visible walls; coral surface smooth, without costae...5
   Polyp-bearing corallites over 0.5 mm in diameter.....................................6
5. Corallum robust, either branched, plate-like, massive or encrusting; skeleton white or pale yellow ....*Millepora*
   Corallum delicate and branched, seldom over 10 cm high; usually pink or purple......*Stylaster*
6. Majority of corallites separate and rounded, each with its own wall; wall usually distinctly raised, but may be virtually superficial; narrow groove or wider trough present between corallites; coenosteum present or absent...**Group A**

A   B   C

Examples of Group A corals: a. *Dichocoenia*; b. *Mussismilia*; c. *Cladocora*.

Calices rounded or polygonal, superficial and often closely packed, each surrounded by a wall or coenosteum shared with adjacent corallites; no groove or trough between calices; occasionally 2 or 3 centers are enclosed...**Group B**

Examples of Group B corals: a. *Stephanocoenia*; b. *Isophyllastrea*; c. *Madracis*.

A   B   C

Most calices in colony elongate or indistinct in outline, some may be rounded; walls or collines present, either shared or distinct and separate; a few may encircle individual calices, but the majority form longitudinal ridges between groups or series of calices (meanders)........**Group C**

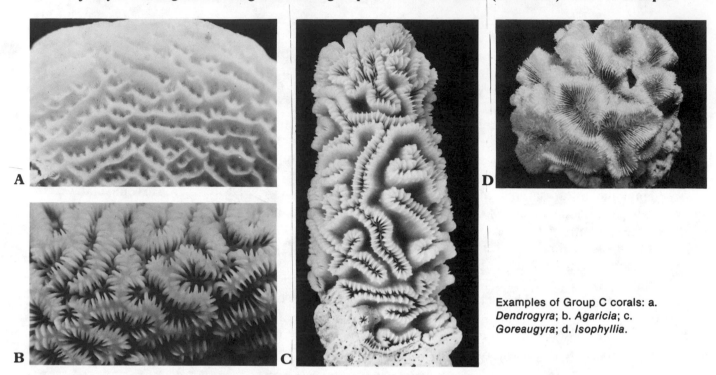

Examples of Group C corals: a. *Dendrogyra*; b. *Agaricia*; c. *Goreaugyra*; d. *Isophyllia*.

Calices lack distinct outline and are without walls, they may be closely packed or separated by coenosteum; septocostae cross the coenosteum between adjacent calice centers.......**Group D**

An example of a Group D coral: *Mycetophyllia*.

Group A

The majority of corallites separate and rounded, each with its own wall. The wall usually distinctly raised, but may be virtually superficial. A narrow groove or wider trough present between corallites; coenosteum present or absent.

KEY TO GROUP A

1. Corallite diameter 1 to 3 mm; septa small and not visible in living coral; costae absent; corallum porous . . . . ***Acropora***
   Corallite diameter usually over 5 mm (may be as little as 2 mm); septa visible in living coral; costae present or absent; corallum solid, rarely porous (only in *Tubastraea*) 2

2. Colony massive; corallites 2 to 10 mm in diameter...3
   Small colonies consisting of corallites joined laterally at their bases; septa numerous, margins finely dentate; costae short; corallum solid..............................**Family Rhizangiidae**
   Colony formed from thin branches or low clumps of corallites; branches or corallites less than 10 mm in diameter...5
   Colony formed from tall corallites arising from a common base (phaceloid growth form); corallites over 10 mm in diameter..7
3. Septal margins smooth; costae reduced or absent
   a. Corallite diameter 2 to 3 mm; paliform lobes present on first 2 cycles of septa...*Stephanocoenia*
   b. Corallite diameter 3 to 4 mm; paliform lobes absent.........................*Dichocoenia*
   Septal margins dentate; costae present...4
   Septal margins with sharp, often ragged spines; costae present.................*Mussismilia*
4. Costae short, those of adjacent corallites do not fuse; peritheca uneven or blistered...*Solenastrea*
   Some costae fuse on perithecal areas.
   a. Calices rounded and regular due to extratentacular budding.............*Montastraea*
   b. Some calices irregular in shape due to intratentacular fission.................*Favia*
5. Corallum porous; septal margins smooth to finely dentate.....................*Tubastraea*
   Corallum solid; septal margins minutely dentate...6
6. Colony bushy; costae reduced to ill-defined ridges............................*Oculina*
   Branches short, each representing single corallite; costae well developed, with dentate margins
   ....*Cladocora*
7. Septa exsert, their margins strongly dentate
   a. Septal teeth triangular; septa non-porous; restricted to the Caribbean............*Mussa*
   b. Septal teeth slender; septa porous; restricted to Brazil.......................*Mussismilia*
   Septa exsert and leafy, their margins smooth.................................*Eusmilia*

Group B

Calices rounded or polygonal, superficial and often closely packed, each surrounded by a wall or coenosteum shared with adjacent corallites. No groove or trough between calices. Occasionally 2 or 3 centers are enclosed.

KEY TO GROUP B

1. Calice diameter greater than 5 mm..2
   Calice diameter less than 5 mm..3
2. Septal margins with sharp spines, making the coral surface rough to touch......**Isophyllastrea**
   Septal margins finely serrated, making the coral surface smooth to touch........***Colpophyllia***
3. Walls or collines not distinct or raised; calices 1 to 2 mm in diameter; costae absent..........4
   Walls or collines usually distinct and raised; calices over 2 mm in diameter; costae present or absent..5
4. Corallum solid; usually 10 (rarely 8) septa.................................***Madracis***
   Corallum porous; 12 septa...***Porites***
5. Costae reduced, not continuous between centers; septal margins smooth; paliform lobes present..***Stephanocoenia***
   Costae run uninterrupted between centers; septal margins smooth or minutely dentate; collines tend not to form a regular polygonal pattern throughout the colony.................***Agaricia***
   Septocostae continuous or interrupted by narrow groove on top of wall; septal margins finely serrated; walls regular and polygonal.......................................***Siderastrea***

Group C

Most calices in the colony elongate or indistinct in outline; some may be rounded. Walls or collines may be present, either shared or distinct and separate. A few may encircle individual calices, but the majority form longitudinal ridges between groups or series of calices (meanders).

KEY TO GROUP C

1. Corallum detached; only a single sinuous valley system (meander)............................2
   Corallum attached; several or many meanders that are free laterally, *i.e.*, each ridge separated from its neighbor by deep and distinct groove..3
   Corallum attached; several or many meanders that are joined laterally, *i.e.*, each ridge shared with its neighbor; groove, if present, narrow and shallow................................5
2. Septal margins serrated; large paliform lobes present; columella broad and spongy...*Manicina*
   Septal margins smooth; no paliform lobes; columella with spongy lamellar centers and lamellar linkage...*Meandrina braziliensis*
3. Septal margins smooth; non-flabellate growth form...4
   Septal margins smooth; flabellate growth form...*Eusmilia*
   Septal margins dentate; meandrine growth form.................................*Diploria labyrinthiformis*
4. Width from mid-ridge to mid-ridge greater than 5 mm; meanders long; costae present.........
   ....*Goreaugyra*
   Width from mid-ridge to mid-ridge less than 5 mm; meanders short; costae absent..............
   ....*Dichocoenia*
5. Septa fine and numerous, continuous over collines; mid-ridge to mid-ridge less than 5 mm; septal margins smooth or minutely dentate..6
   Septa stout or leafy, with serrated margins; septa run over walls but may be interrupted by narrow groove or ridge along midline; mid-ridge to mid-ridge over 5 mm....................7
   Septa stout and their margins with long, sharp spines; mid-ridge to mid-ridge over 5 mm.....10
6. Growth form of corallum variable, from foliaceous to encrusting or semi-massive; corallites generally small (usually 2 to 3 mm), superficial and crowded.......................*Agaricia*
   Corallum delicate, foliaceous bowl-shaped or branched; corallites to 6 mm in diameter, usually protuberant and well spaced...*Leptoseris*
7. Septal margins dentate; 9 or more large septa per cm.......................................8
   Septal margins smooth; fewer than 9 large septa per cm......................................9
8. 13 to 45 septa per cm; width mid-ridge to mid-ridge 4 to 15 mm.....................*Diploria*
   11 to 14 large septa per cm, plus smaller ones between; width mid-ridge to mid-ridge 10 to 20 mm..*Manicina*
   9 to 12 septa per cm; width mid-ridge to mid-ridge 13 to 20 mm; teeth on septal margins minute..*Colpophyllia*
9. 6 to 8 large septa per cm (may be smaller ones between); width mid-ridge to mid-ridge 10 to 15 mm...*Meandrina*
   6 to 7 septa per cm (may be smaller ones between); width mid-ridge to mid-ridge 5 to 6 mm...*Dendrogyra*
10. Shared walls regular, forming continuous ridges...............................*Isophyllia*
    Shared walls discontinuous...*Mycetophyllia*

Group D

Calices lack a distinct outline and are without walls. They may be closely packed or separated by coenosteum. Septocostae cross the coenosteum between adjacent calice centers.

1. Calices closely packed; septa low and fine, their margins smooth or finely dentate . . . . . *Agaricia*
   Calices widely spaced; septa and costae with long sharp spines . . . . *Mycetophyllia*

KEYS TO INDO-PACIFIC REEF CORALS

1. Corallum unattached, either solitary or colonial (mushroom corals and small ahermatypic corals) 2
   Corallum attached, either solitary or a small low colony consisting of a few corallites joined at their bases (some adult mussids, large juvenile corals and small ahermatypic corals) 3
   Corallum attached and colonial (this category includes all the major hermatypic corals) 8
2. Corallum solitary or colonial, flattened or domed, disc-like or elongate, 2 cm to 50 cm or more in diameter or length; septa radiate from center of corallum to its outer edge . . . .
   . . . . **Family Fungiidae**
   Corallum solitary, rounded or oval, turbinate to tympanoid, generally less than 15 mm in diameter
     a. Solid skeleton . . . . *Heterocyathus*
     b. Perforated skeleton . . . . *Heteropsammia*
   Corallum colonial; growth form variable, branched to massive; septa do not radiate from center of colony to its outer edge 8
3. Corallum rounded and disc-like, seldom exceeding 4 cm in diameter, attached by a narrow stalk; septal margins smooth or with small spines . . . . **Juvenile fungiids**
   Corallum rounded and disc-like, 3 to 14 cm in diameter, attached by a broad base; septal margins with prominent sharp teeth; usually a single mouth, occasionally several . . . . . *Scolymia*
   Corallum cylindrical, turbinate or trochoid 4
4. Corallum porous; corallite diameter generally about 1 cm; septa fuse in calice (Pourtales plan); septal margins rarely smooth, usually granular to finely dentate; costae present, columella well developed and spongy . . . . **Family Dendrophylliidae**
   Corallum non-porous; corallite diameter usually 5 mm to several cm; a few septa may join in calice, but not according to Pourtales plan; septal margins smooth, dentate or lobate; costae and columella present or absent 5
5. Corallite diameter often about 5 mm (may be less or up to 15 mm); tentacles not usually extended during day 6
   Corallite diameter generally over 10 mm and may be several cm; polyp tentacles either extended and prominent, or retracted and corallum covered with fleshy or bubble-like expansions of polyp tissue 7
6. Usually solitary, may be small, creeping colonies; septal margins smooth; a few septa may join in calice; costae present (may be short); columella well developed and spongy . . . .
   . . . . **Family Caryophylliidae**
   Solitary; septal margins smooth; septa do not join; costae absent; columella absent to moderately developed . . . . **Family Flabellidae**
   Usually small, creeping colonies; septal margins smooth to dentate; septa do not join; costae short; columella usually feebly developed and spongy, rarely solid or absent . . . .
   . . . . **Family Rhizangiidae**
7. Septal margins smooth; septa leafy and often exsert; paliform lobes absent . . . .
   Juvenile (hermatypic) caryophyllids
   (see descriptions for *Plerogyra, Euphyllia, Catalaphyllia*)
   Septal margins with regular, small teeth; septa slightly exsert, not leafy; paliform lobes present .
   . . . . **Juvenile** *Trachyphyllia*

Septal margins with large, dentate lobes; major septa distinctly broad and exsert; paliform lobes present..*Cynarina*

8. Polyp-bearing chambers as tiny dots, 0.5 mm or less in diameter; no visible walls or septa; coral surface smooth, without costae; polyps minute.......................................9
Polyp-bearing corallites over 0.5 mm in diameter...11

9. Corallum large, branched to massive; skeleton blue; largest pores about 0.5 mm in diameter; polyp tentacles branched..*Heliopora*
Corallum variable in size and form; skeleton usually white, yellow or pink, never blue; largest pores about 0.1 mm in diameter; polyp tentacles simple.......................................10

10. Corallum large, branched to massive; skeleton pale yellow; pores scattered over coral surface..*Millepora*
Corallum branched, less than 20 cm high; skeleton white, pink or purple; pores scattered over coral surface...*Stylaster*
Corallum branched, less than 10 cm high; skeleton white, pink or purple; pores arranged in rows along sides of branches...*Distichopora*

11. Calices in series surrounding walls, which are reduced to cone-shaped processes...*Hydnophora*
Calices and walls not arranged as above..12

12. The majority of corallites separate and rounded, each with its own wall; wall usually distinctly raised, but may be virtually superficial; narrow groove or wider trough present between corallites; coenosteum present or absent..**Group A**

Examples of Group A corals: a. *Blastomussa;* b. *Diploastrea;* c. *Echinopora.*

Calices rounded or polygonal, superficial and often closely packed, each surrounded by a wall or coenosteum shared with adjacent corallites; no groove or trough between calices; occasionally 2 or 3 centers are enclosed...**Group B**

Examples of Group B corals: a. *Stylocoeniella;* b. *Moseleya;* c. *Gardinoseris.*

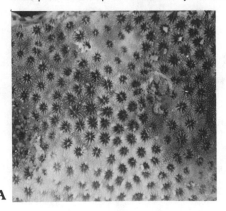

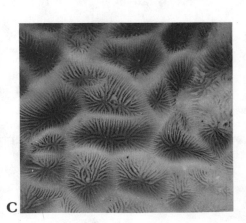

Most calices in colony elongate or indistinct in outline, some may be rounded; walls or collines present, either shared or distinct and separate; a few may encircle individual calices but the majority form longitudinal ridges between groups or series of calices (meanders)........**Group C**

Examples of Group C corals: a. *Trachyphyllia;* b. *Ctenella;* c. *Scapophyllia.*

Calices lack distinct outline and are without regular walls or collines; calices may be closely packed or separated by coenosteum; septocostae cross coenosteum between adjacent calice centers..**Group D**

Examples of Group D corals: a. *Leptoseris;* b. *Podabacia;* c. *Oxypora.*

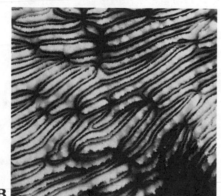
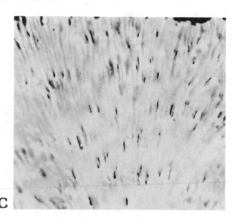

Group A

The majority of corallites separate and rounded, each with its own wall. The wall usually distinctly raised, but may be virtually superficial. A narrow groove or wider trough present between corallites; coenosteum present or absent.

KEY TO GROUP A

1. Corallum branched, with a dendroid form, in tufts or tree-like growths; skeleton porous; corallites well spaced and about 10 mm in diameter (5 to 15 mm); septa and costae visible in living coral 2
   Corallum may be branched, but not dendroid; if skeleton porous then corallites about 2 to 3 mm in diameter 3
2. Septa numerous, many united at their inner ends according to the Pourtales plan ....
   .... *Dendrophyllia*
   Septa fewer, seldom united at their inner ends .... *Tubastraea*

3. Corallites in "organ-pipe" arrangement, red in color and 5 mm or less in diameter; septa and costae absent; polyps normally extended during day, each with 8 tentacles that bear small side branches . . . . ***Tubipora***
   Corallites and polyps not as above 4
4. Corallum phaceloid, consisting of separate corallites arising from an encrusting base; corallites usually several cm tall and 15 to 20 mm in diameter (range 10 mm to several cm) 5
   Corallites may form clumps, but corallum not distinctly phaceloid, corallites less than 1 cm tall 7
5. Septa widely spaced, margins smooth or rarely minutely dentate; columella absent 6
   .Septa crowded and in cycles, margins with regular, small teeth; columella spongy and distinct . . . . ***Caulastrea***
   Septa stout and widely spaced; margins with long, either rounded or pointed spines; columella trabecular . . . . ***Lobophyllia***
6. Septa widely spaced and leafy; balloon-like vesicles cover corallum during day . . . . ***Plerogyra***
   Septa widely spaced, but not leafy; elongate, simple or compound tentacles cover corallum during day . . . . ***Euphyllia (Euphyllia)***
7. Corallum small; corallites 5 to 15 mm in diameter, either crowded or well separated and several mm tall; septa prominent, their margins with relatively few tall blunt lobes or sharp teeth; columella solid . . . . ***Blastomussa***
   Combination of characters not as above 8
8. Corallite diameter about 8 mm; costal ridges well developed; septal and costal margins with small compound teeth; septa perforate, often join in calice . . . . ***Horastrea***
   Combination of characters not as above 9
9. Corallites well spaced, generally tall and narrow, diameter usually 3 to 5 mm (range 1.5 to 8 mm); height about 5 mm (range 2 to 15 mm); septa prominent, typically leafy, delicate and exsert, margins smooth; costae short and low; columella absent or weak .10
   Combination of characters not as above 11
10. Corallum usually massive, occasionally branched; calices usually about 5 mm in diameter; coenosteum cellular . . . . ***Galaxea***
    Corallum branched and delicate; calices seldom exceed 3 mm in diameter; coenosteum solid . . . . ***Acrhelia***
11. Corallites usually well spaced and about 2 to 3 mm in diameter (range 1 to 5 mm), rarely superficial, and generally raised by 2 to 5 mm; septa obscured or just visible in living coral; septal margins smooth or granular, occasionally with irregular small teeth; skeleton porous 12
    Combination of characters not as above 14
12. Corallum foliaceous or plate-like; corallites cone-shaped, 1 to 5 mm in diameter; septa well developed, more than 12; columella spongy . . . . ***Turbinaria***
    Corallum branching, encrusting or massive; corallites 0.5 to 4 mm in diameter; septa 12 or less, often poorly developed; columella absent or minute 13
13. Corallum branching to semi-massive; corallites usually 1.5 to 2.5 mm in diameter; larger axial corallite present; septa 12 or less . . . . ***Acropora***
    Corallum branching, seldom over 10 cm high; corallites 0.5 to 1.0 mm in diameter, well spaced and often almost superficial; axial corallites lacking; septa 12 or less . . . . ***Anacropora***
    Corallum encrusting to massive; corallites cone-shaped, usually 3 to 4 mm at base; axial corallites lacking; septa poorly developed . . . . ***Astreopora***
14. Corallites well spaced or crowded, usually about 3 mm in diameter (range 2 to 5 mm); septa and septocostae prominent, fine, crowded and low, with smooth to coarsely serrated margins; columella pinnacle-like, may be poorly developed 15
    Combination of characters not as above 16
15. Calices closely set; septal margins smooth or finely serrated; calice diameter 2 to 3 mm . ***Pavona***
    Calices widely spaced and usually protruberant; septal margins granular to coarsely serrated;

calice diameter 2 to 5 mm occasionally more..................................*Leptoseris*

16. Corallum usually foliaceous or encrusting, occasionally semi-massive or partially branched; corallites usually well spaced; calice diameter generally 5 to 10 mm (range 3 to 20 mm); septa and costae widely spaced, their margins with irregular sharp teeth; columella consists of a few twisted trabeculae...17

Combination of characters not as above...18

17. Calices usually protrude and have vertical walls; corallum without pores or slits . *Echinophyllia*

Calices usually protrude, but are inclined at an angle; corallum without pores or slits.........
....*Mycedium*

Calices superficial (although may appear raised due to exsert septa); corallum penetrated by pores or slits...*Oxypora*

18. Corallites tall (about 10 mm), in clumps or low tufts.........................*Bikiniastrea*

Corallites less than 10 mm tall, neither in clumps or tufts..........................19

19. Corallum encrusting; corallites often 3 to 4 mm in diameter (range 2 to 10 mm); corallite walls fused basally and separated by a fine furrow above; coenosteum absent............*Leptastrea*

Growth form variable; corallites 2 to 20 mm in diameter; corallite walls seldom fused basally; coenosteum present or reduced..20

20. Corallites crowded, coenosteum reduced; corallite diameter about 15 mm (range 10 to 25 mm); costae usually present, may be discontinuous; septal margins with long, sharp, mussid teeth....
....*Acanthastrea*

Corallites crowded or well spaced; coenosteum present or reduced; corallite diameter 2 to 20 mm; costae present or absent; septal margins finely or coarsely serrated...................21

21. Corallites low and usually separated by a gap of several mm; calice diameter 3 to 5 mm; coenosteum black (even in cleaned specimens), calices white; corallum small and rounded.....
....*Oulastrea*

Corallum not colored as above..22

22. Corallum massive; calices regular, closely packed and in the shape of low cones, approximately 10 mm in diameter; septa conspicuous and thickened where they cross corallite wall; major septa meet between calices and alternate with shorter, narrow ones...........*Diploastrea*

Calices and septa not arranged as above..23

23. Corallum usually foliaceous, may be encrusting or branched; corallite diameter usually 3 mm (range 2 to 7 mm); calices separated by several mm; coenosteum usually with rows of small teeth, sometimes with smooth edged or dentate costae........................*Echinopora*

Corallum usually massive and rounded, may be encrusting, plate-like or branched; corallite diameter usually 1 mm (range 1 to 2.5 mm); calices separated by several mm; coenosteum non-costate, either blistered or with fine spines.................................*Cyphastrea*

Corallum usually massive, occasionally encrusting; corallite diameter 2 to 20 mm; calices crowded or well separated; coenosteum costate, costae either continuous or discontinuous, with dentate margins...24

24. Corallite diameter 2 to 3 mm; new corallites added primarily by extratentacular division (budding); paliform lobes well developed on larger septa........................*Plesiastrea*

Corallite diameter about 10 mm (range in mature corallites 7 to 15 mm); new corallites added primarily by extratentacular division (budding); paliform lobes usually present....*Montastraea*

Corallite diameter often about 10 mm (range 2 to 20 mm); new corallites added primarily by intratentacular division (fission); paliform lobes present or absent....................*Favia*

Group B

Calices rounded or polygonal, superficial and often closely packed, each surrounded by a wall or coenosteum shared with adjacent corallites. No groove or trough between calices. Occasionally 2 or 3 centers are enclosed.

KEY TO GROUP B

1. Calices 0.5 to 3 mm in diameter, crowded or well spaced; coenosteum and/or shared walls low, not ridge-like; up to 24 septa, their margins smooth or granular; septocostae absent; columella small, sometimes absent; skeleton porous...2

    Combination of characters not as above...3

2. Polyps long (usually over 10 mm), with both column and tentacles extended during day; calices crowded, 1 to 3 mm in diameter; usually 24 septa..................................*Goniopora*

    Small to medium sized polyps (usually less than 10 mm long), with both column and tentacles extended during day; calices crowded, about 1 mm in diameter, occasionally more; 12 to 24 septa, reduced to tiny spines; calice walls highly perforate.................................*Alveopora*

    Polyps small, not usually extended during day (if extended, only tentacles, not column, protrude); calices crowded, 1 to 1.5 mm in diameter; 12 septa, generally with paliform lobes ......

    ....*Porites*

    Polyps small, often extended during day; calices crowded or widely spaced; coenosteum often covered with papillae or tubercles; calices 0.5 to 1.0 mm in diameter; septa small or rudimentary

    ....*Montipora*

    Polyps small, occasionally extended during day; calices widely spaced, 0.5 to 1.0 mm in diameter; coenosteum smooth; septa 12 or less..................................*Anacropora*

3. Corallum often branched, may be sub-massive or encrusting; calices 0.5 to 1.5 mm in diameter, crowded or well spaced; coenosteum and/or shared walls low, not ridge-like; septa 6 to 20, their margins smooth or beaded; septocostae absent; columella styliform; skeleton imperforate....4

    Calices over 2 mm in diameter; shared walls prominent and ridge-like; costae present; skeleton imperforate...7

4. Small encrusting or knobby colonies; small intercorallite pillar protrudes between calices; 12 septa...*Stylocoeniella*

    Colony branched, sub-massive or encrusting; no intercorallite pillar; 6 to 20 septa...........5

5. Corallum branched, usually delicate, with branches anastomosing; calices well spaced and in rows up the branches; septa 6, often poorly developed, sometimes rudiments of a second cycle..

    ....*Seriatopora*

    Corallum usually branched, may be sub-massive or encrusting; calices often borne on ends of rudimentary branchlets (verrucae); calices crowded or well spaced, not in rows; septa 12, often poorly developed..*Pocillopora*

    Corallum branched, sub-massive or encrusting; calices not borne on verrucae and not in rows; septa well developed, at least 6 reach columella..6

6. A "hood" often arches over top of each calice; 6 septa reach columella...........*Stylophora*

    No "hood" over calices; 6 thick septa reach columella; columella often exsert.....*Palauastrea*

    No "hood" over calices; 10 narrow septa reach columella (rarely 8, 18 or 20)........*Madracis*

7. Calice diameter usually about 10 mm (range 4 to 60 mm); septa and costae prominent, their margins finely to coarsely serrated; columella present and spongy.............................8

    Calice diameter 2 to 5 mm; septa and costae prominent and crowded, their margins smooth to finely serrated, rarely coarsely serrated; columella absent, or present and styliform.........10

8. Mature colony small, less than 10 mouths; large central calice (to 60 mm in diameter), plus smaller peripheral ones present; paliform lobes present..........................*Moseleya*

    Mature colony large, more than 10 mouths; calices approximately equal in size, none reaching 60 mm in diameter; paliform lobes present or absent...9

9. Spines on septal margins small and closely set; calice diameter 4 to 10 mm; paliform lobes well developed...*Goniastrea*

    Spines on septal margins well developed, sometimes ragged; calice diameter 5 to 20 mm; paliform lobes absent in some species, well developed in others......................*Favites*

    Spines on septal margins well developed, coarse, large and sharp; calice diameter 10 to 25 mm;

paliform lobes absent . . . . *Acanthastrea*

10. Fossa narrower than walls, walls flat-topped; septa fine, margins smooth or extremely finely serrated 11
    Fossa deep, but wider than walls; walls steep and tall, meeting at a sharp angle; septa fine, margins smooth or granular . . . . *Gardineroseris*
    Fossa deep or shallow, wider than walls; walls rounded or meet at an angle; septa fine or stout, margins smooth or finely to coarsely serrated 12

11. Septa well spaced, 20 to 30 in 3 mm diameter calice; septal margins smooth or with a few fine spines; restricted to eastern Indian Ocean, western Pacific . . . . *Coeloseris*
    Septa crowded, 35 to 45 in 3 mm diameter calice; septal margins with small, either simple or dentate, spines; restricted to western Indian Ocean . . . . *Siderastrea*

12. Corallum often large, great variety in growth form; synapticulae absent or present; septal margins smooth or finely serrated . . . . *Pavona*
    Corallum small and inconspicuous, encrusting to massive; synapticulae present; small dentate spines on septal margins 13

13. New calices produced by intratentacular fission; septa may be partially perforated; septa often fuse in calice; synapticulae rare; western Indian Ocean . . . . *Anomastrea*
    New calices produced by extratentacular budding; septa nearly imperforate; septa often fuse in calice; synapticulae present; eastern Indian and western Pacific Oceans . . . . . *Pseudosiderastrea*
    New calices produced by intratentacular fission; septa perforate; septa occasionally fuse in calice; synapticulae present; Indo-Pacific . . . . *Coscinaraea*

Group C

Most calices in the colony elongate or indistinct in outline, some may be rounded. Walls or collines present, either shared or distinct and separate. A few may encircle individual calices, but the majority form longitudinal ridges between groups or series of calices.

KEY TO GROUP C

1. Meanders free laterally except at base of colony, *i.e.,* each ridge separated from its neighbor by deep and distinct groove 2
   Meanders joined laterally throughout the colony, *i.e.,* each ridge shared with its neighbor; if a groove is present it is narrow and shallow 5

2. Septal margins smooth, granular, or with minute or small teeth; surface of living coral smooth to touch 3
   Septal margins with long, sharp spines; surface of living coral rough and spiky to touch . . . . *Lobophyllia*

3. Polyp fleshy, but tentacles not extended during day; septa slightly exsert, their margins with small, regular teeth; columella well developed and spongy . . . . *Trachyphyllia*
   Tentacles or vesicles extended during day; septa slightly to highly exsert, their margins smooth, rarely minutely dentate; columella absent or weakly developed 4

4. Tentacles cover corallum, long and finger-like, usually with kidney-shaped tips, either simple or subdivided; septa slightly exsert; valley a deep V-shape . . . . *Euphyllia (Fimbriaphyllia)*
   Tentacles form fringe along top of walls, long and finger-like, with slightly bulbous tips; septa slightly exsert; valley a relatively shallow V-shape . . . . *Catalaphyllia*
   Expanded vesicles cover corallum; often rounded and balloon-like or may be bulbous only at base, then tapering upward; septa highly leafy and exsert . . . . *Plerogyra*

5. Width from mid-ridge to mid-ridge 10 mm or more 6
   Width from mid-ridge to mid-ridge less than 10 mm 9

6. Septal margins non-dentate and smooth 7

Septal margins with small teeth, but living coral feels almost smooth to touch 8

Septal margins with long sharp spines; living coral feels rough and spiky to touch . . . *Symphyllia*

7. About 20 septa per cm; width mid-ridge to mid-ridge about 15 mm; lamellar columella . . . .
. . . . *Ctenella*

Fewer than 10 septa per cm; width mid-ridge to mid-ridge 10-15 mm; no columella . . . .
. . . . *Physogyra*

About 10 septa per cm; width mid-ridge to mid-ridge 6-10 cm; no columella; distinct groove
along top of wall . . . . *Gyrosmilia*

8. Calices scattered along floor of valleys and on sides of collines; teeth on septal margins widely
spaced . . . . *Pectinia*

Calices in single row along floor of valleys, never on walls; teeth on septal margins crowded . . . .
. . . . *Oulophyllia*

9. Septa not converging to calice centers but arranged in parallel series crossing ridges at right
angles; septa in living coral distinct on walls and in valleys . . . . *Pachyseris*

Some or all septa converge to calice centers, not arranged as above; septa in living coral some-
times difficult to see in valleys 10

10. Septa numerous, closely packed and non-exsert, margins smooth or finely serrated; collines
tend to be irregular, not in typical "brain coral" arrangement; width mid-ridge to mid-ridge
usually less than 5 mm 11

Septa relatively well spaced, often slightly exsert, margins distinctly serrated; fused walls
regular, giving a typical "brain coral" appearance; width mid-ridge to mid-ridge generally be-
tween 3 to 10 mm 13

11. Septa usually arranged in petaloid pattern; calices seldom over 2 mm in diameter; septa may
bifurcate or trifurcate at periphery of calice . . . . *Psammocora*

Septa occasionally arranged in petaloid pattern; calices usually 3 to 5 mm in diameter, occasionally more; septa may fuse in calices . . . . *Coscinaraea*

Septa not in petaloid pattern; septal spines simple, not minutely serrated as in *Psammocora* and
Coscinaraea 12

12. Collines high and prominent; colony massive, often columnar, occasionally encrusting;
monocentric or short valleys . . . . *Gardineroseris*

Collines high or low; colony leafy, encrusting or massive; valleys short or long . . . . *Pavona*

13. Septa stout, with small teeth on margins and sides; centers distinct, marked by a ring of radiating septa; columella poorly developed (or absent), trabecular or solid 14

Septa narrow, with regularly dentate margins; calices distinct or indistinct; columella well
developed, trabecular or lamellar 15

14. Corallum massive . . . . *Scapophyllia*

Corallum foliaceous or partly encrusting, sometimes with irregular branched outgrowths . . . . . .
. . . . *Merulina*

Corallum branched . . . . *Clavarina*

15. Septal margins finely toothed; paliform lobes usually present; columella small and spongy . . . . .
. . . . *Goniastrea*

Septal margins coarsely toothed; paliform lobes generally absent; columella well developed and
spongy . . . . *Platygyra*

Septal margins finely toothed; paliform lobes absent; columella narrow and plate-like (lamellar)
. . . . *Leptoria*

Group D

Calices lack a distinct outline and are without regular walls or collines. Calices may be closely packed or separated by coenosteum. Septocostae cross the coenosteum between adjacent calice centers.

KEY TO GROUP D

1. Calice centers widely spaced, but seldom more than 10 in a colony (this coral is often solitary); calice diameter over 10 mm; corallum flat and encrusting; septal margins with long sharp teeth; costae prominent and spiny...*Scolymia*
   Never as few as 10 centers in mature corallum; calice diameter usually about 5 mm or less; septal and costal margins may be serrated, but spines are not of mussid type as *Scolymia*............2
2. Calices closely packed, sometimes difficult to distinguish; septa fine and low; septa and septo-costal margins smooth or finely dentate..3
   Calices closely packed; septa stout and often arch up between calices; septal and septocostal margins spinulose to spiny..6
   Calices usually widely spaced, may be closely packed in places; septal margins smooth or with fine or sharp teeth; costal margins similar, or costae may be reduced to rows of teeth........7
3. Septal and septocostal spines crowded and minutely dentate; synapticulae present...........4
   Septal and septocostal spines simple; synapticulae absent or few...........................5
4. Calices seldom exceed 2 mm in diameter; septa generally arranged in distinct petaloid pattern; septa usually imperforate, may bifurcate or trifurcate at periphery of calice......*Psammocora*
   Calices 2 to 7 mm in diameter; septa occasionally arranged in petaloid pattern; septa perforate and may fuse in calices..*Coscinaraea*
5. Calice diameter 2 to 3 mm; margins of septa and septocostae smooth or very finely serrated; calices superficial..*Pavona*
   Calice diameter 2 to 5 mm, occasionally more; margins of septa and septocostae finely or coarsely serrated; calices often slightly raised.................................*Leptoseris*
6. Corallum solid, not perforated by slits or pores; septal margins granular or minutely spinulose
   ....*Lithophyllon*
   Corallum perforated by slits or pores; septal margins with well developed, serrated spines......
   ....*Podabacia*
7. Corallum delicate, at least partly foliaceous, and perforated by pores or slits; calices super-ficial; septal margins with sharp teeth, septocostae may be reduced to rows of spines..........
   ....*Oxypora*
   Corallum delicate to robust, but not penetrated by pores or slits; calices superficial or raised; septal and septocostal margins smooth to spiny..8
8. Some corallites in the colony protrude; septal margins with sharp teeth; costae also spiny or reduced to rows of teeth...9
   Calices superficial; septal and septocostal margins either smooth or with small teeth........10
9. Alveoli (small pits formed at insertion of new septocostae) present; if corallites protrude they are inclined at an angle to surface of corallum.......................................*Mycedium*
   Alveoli absent; if corallites protrude they generally have vertical walls..........*Echinophyllia*
10. Septa and septocostae well spaced (2 to 5 mm apart); margins smooth or finely toothed; corallum partly foliaceous, partly encrusting.....................................*Physophyllia*
    Septa and septocostae 2 mm or less apart; margins with small teeth; corallum foliaceous or branched...*Pectinia*

Atlantic Reef Corals

LIST OF ATLANTIC CORALS
IN SEQUENCE COVERED

SCLERACTINIANS

FAMILY ASTROCOENIIDAE
- *Stephanocoenia*

FAMILY POCILLOPORIDAE
- *Madracis*

FAMILY ACROPORIDAE
- *Acropora*

FAMILY AGARICIIDAE
- *Agaricia*
- *Leptoseris*

FAMILY SIDERASTREIDAE
- *Siderastrea*

FAMILY PORITIDAE
- *Porites*

FAMILY FAVIIDAE
- *Cladocora*
- *Montastraea*
- *Solenastrea*
- *Favia*
- *Diploria*
- *Manicina*
- *Colpophyllia*

FAMILY FLABELLIDAE
  Gardineria

FAMILY RHIZANGIIDAE
  Astrangia
  Phyllangia

FAMILY OCULINIDAE
- *Oculina*

FAMILY MEANDRINIDAE
- *Dichocoenia*
- *Meandrina*
  Goreaugyra
- *Dendrogyra*

FAMILY MUSSIDAE
- *Scolymia*
  Mussismilia
- *Mussa*
- *Isophyllastrea*
- *Isophyllia*
- *Mycetophyllia*

FAMILY CARYOPHYLLIIDAE
  Solitary caryophylliids
- *Eusmilia*

FAMILY DENDROPHYLLIIDAE
  Balanophyllia
  Tubastraea

NON-SCLERACTINIANS

FAMILY MILLEPORIDAE
  Millepora

FAMILY STYLASTERIDAE
  Stylaster

CLASS ANTHOZOA

FAMILY ASTROCOENIIDAE

Stephanocoenia Milne-Edwards & Haime, 1848

(Gr: *stephos*, crown; Gr: *koinos*, shared. Presumably relating to the crown of paliform lobes and the shared calices.)

DESCRIPTION
Living coral   (Col. pl. p. 84)

Stephanocoenia forms encrusting or massive colonies, brownish in color. Tentacles are not usually extended during the day. Calices are either crowded with shared walls or more widely spaced and separated by coenosteum. Where walls are shared there is a faint line around the calices that corresponds to the narrow gap between septa of adjacent corallites. This becomes a definite groove in coralla with more widely spaced corallites.

Calices appear flat or slightly raised, and the fossa is shallow. They are rounded or polygonal with a diameter of 2 to 3 mm. Septa are visible as they radiate from calice centers on to the walls. The 12 septa of the primary cycle protrude slightly and can just be counted underwater.

Skeleton

Septa are arranged in three cycles, but only the

Stephanocoenia michelinii (X 4). Jamaica.

septa of the first two cycles reach the columella. These septa are also distinctly exsert and have well developed paliform lobes. Septal margins are smooth, but the sides bear tiny spines. Septa are discontinuous between adjacent calices, separated by either an extremely narrow groove or by coenosteum. In the latter case septa may join to a fine ridge that runs around the calices, otherwise the coenosteum is smooth.

SIMILARITIES

Colonies of *Stephanocoenia* that have corallites crowded and united by common walls can be mistaken for *Siderastrea*. However, the diameter of mature calices is about 2.5 mm in *Stephanocoenia* (4 mm in *Siderastrea*) and there are about half as many septa (no more than 24). An examination of the skeleton reveals that *Stephanocoenia* has smooth septal margins (serrated in *Siderastrea*) and well developed paliform lobes (absent in *Siderastrea*).

Other *Stephanocoenia* colonies have well spaced, slightly elevated calices and can resemble *Montastraea* or *Solenastrea*. There are several striking differences between these genera, but because of their small size diagnosis may be difficult underwater. Both *Montastraea* and *Solenastrea* have serrated septal margins and a spongy columella. *Stephanocoenia* has smooth septal margins, a solid columella and a distinctive ring of paliform lobes.

DISTRIBUTION AND ECOLOGY   (Map #1)

Stephanocoenia is a small or moderate sized coral that occurs on most reefs, especially along the fore reef. There is probably only a single species: *Stephanocoeniu michelinii* Milne-Edwards & Haime, 1848.

FAMILY POCILLOPORIDAE

Madracis Milne-Edwards and Haime, 1849

(Ital: *madre*, mother; Gr: *akis*, point. Possibly a reference to the small spines that surround the calices.)

DESCRIPTION
Living coral   (Col. pl. p. 89)

Madracis forms encrusting, nodular or branched colonies. The width of the branches varies from

Madracis mirabilis (X 5). Jamaica.

one species to another but seldom exceeds 1.5 cm. The corallum is cream, yellow, brown, green or reddish in color. Polyps are often partially or completely extended during the day, and rings of small simple tentacles can be seen.

Calices are small, superficial and may be well spaced or crowded. They are rounded or polygonal and about 1 to 2 mm in diameter. Corallite walls are indistinct, but the septa may be raised up at their outer ends to form a distinct ring that can be mistaken for a wall. The surface of the coral between calices is either smooth or slightly rough.

Skeleton

There are ten well developed septa (only eight in *Madracis formosa* Wells), all of which reach the columella. Paliform lobes are absent, but the septa are often raised up and exsert at their outer ends. Septal margins are smooth. The columella is solid and styliform. Septa do not cross perithecal areas. The coenosteum is smooth or granulated, and the granules may be united to form a low ridge just outside the calice margin.

SIMILARITIES

Madracis is unlikely to be confused with any other coral except perhaps *Porites*, which also has small, superficial corallites. *Madracis* is identified by its more widely spaced corallites and distinct septa. In addition, the skeleton in *Porites* is porous, while in *Madracis* it is imperforate.

DISTRIBUTION AND ECOLOGY (Map #2)

Madracis occurs on most reefs and is a fairly common coral. Some *Madracis* species (especially *Madracis mirabilis sensu* Wells, 1973) form large clumps in shallow areas; others occur in deeper water and beneath overhangs. There are probably six species; the genus *Axhelia* is synonymous.

FAMILY ACROPORIDAE

Acropora Oken, 1815
Elkhorn and staghorn coral
(Gr: *akron*, extremity; L: *porous*, pore.
Relating to the presence of a corallite at
the tip of each branch.)

DESCRIPTION

Living coral (Col. pl. p. 85)

Acropora is usually branched, except when young, but the size and shape of the branches vary according to the species concerned.

A. palmata: in exposed conditions this species may be totally encrusting, but it usually forms stout, thick branches. These are generally flattened horizontally and aligned to face the current or swell.

A. cervicornis: the branches in this species do not arise from a substantial base as they do in *A. palmata* and are much more slender. They may be 50 cm or more in height and seldom fuse together.

A. prolifera: this species is profusely branched and the branches are thin and delicate. They often fuse to form small, plate-like colonies.

Acropora colonies are brown or yellowish in color, often with the branch tips and the tips of the corallites paler. Small white tentacles can sometimes be seen but are often retracted during the day. The corallites are distinct and separate and are of two types. At the branch tip is a symmetrical and usually larger axial corallite; down the length of the branches are smaller, asymmetrical ones. Axial corallites are hardly distinguishable on the stout branches of *A. palmata*.

Corallites are round in cross section and protrude several millimeters from the surface. Radial corallites are often inclined at an angle, with the

44

lower wall longer than the upper. Corallite walls are usually thick, and the fossa is relatively small. Corallite diameter is around 1 to 3 mm. Septa are not visible in the living coral, and perithecal areas appear smooth.

Skeleton

The coenosteum is distinctly pitted and porous and is covered with tiny blunt spines. These may unite to form closely set parallel ridges that run up the outside of the corallite wall. There may be 12 septa, but they are usually reduced in number and poorly developed.

SIMILARITIES

Acropora is a distinctive coral and is unlikely to be confused with any other Atlantic genus.

DISTRIBUTION AND ECOLOGY (Map #3)

Acropora is an important reef-building coral and often dominates shallow areas. The three Atlantic species have different habitat preferences and characteristically occur in distinct zones.

A. palmata (elkhorn coral) is a robust species that is particularly common in water 6 m or less in depth and is seldom found below about 15 m. It adopts different growth forms according to the prevailing conditions and can thus thrive in many situations. It may be broken or overturned in tropical storms but is capable of re-cementing and continuing to grow.

A. cervicornis (staghorn coral) is less resistant to wave action than *A. palmata* and occurs in slightly deeper water or more sheltered sites. It may form dense tracts and be the dominant coral between about 6 to 12 m, but is also found in much deeper water. It has one of the most rapid growth rates of all western Atlantic corals.

A. prolifera is the least common of the three species and also forms the smallest colonies. It is usually found in similar habitats as *A. cervicornis* but does not occur in such dense thickets.

Acropora species provide shelter for a variety of small fishes and other animals. There are only three Atlantic species: *Acropora palmata* (Lamarck, 1816), *Acropora cervicornis* (Lamarck, 1816) and *Acropora prolifera* (Lamarck, 1816).

Agaricia sp. (X 2.1). Jamaica.

FAMILY AGARICIIDAE

Agaricia **Lamarck, 1801**
Leaf coral
(Gr: *agarikon*, mushroom. Etymology rather obscure, but possibly relating to the growth form, which can be flattened and rounded like a mushroom.)

DESCRIPTION
Living coral (Col. pl. pp. 88, 89)

Agaricia is usually foliaceous or encrusting, occasionally semi-massive. Colonies often consist of vertical crests or fronds with calices on both sides. Sometimes they are cup or plate-like with calices only on the upper surface. The corallum may be thin and fragile in some species, but in others it is stouter and stronger. Many colonies are shades of brown or green; others are pink, purple or yellow. Tiny dot-like mouths are visible and sometimes contrast in color with the rest of the colony. Tentacles are usually retracted during the day.

Corallites are crowded and the walls shared. Calices are round, polygonal or oval, and in the majority of specimens hillocks called collines are present between them. The collines sometimes enclose a single calice, but more often surround a short or long series, giving rise to a well defined system of ridges and grooves. The collines may be low and rounded or high and acute. Calice diameter, or distance between collines, is usually 2 to 3 mm but sometimes is as much as 5 mm.

Septa are visible as fine lines radiating from the calice centers. They run uninterrupted over collines

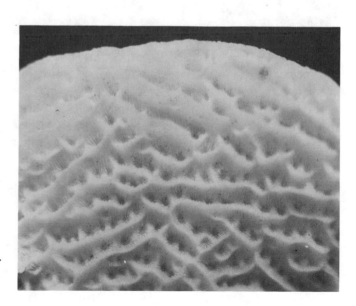

and are closely packed and smooth to the touch. Often they form characteristic star-shaped patterns over the surface of the corallum.

Skeleton

Septa are in cycles with thick and thin ones alternating in some species. Septal margins are smooth or minutely dentate. There is a pinnacle-like columella which usually lies deep in the calice.

SIMILARITIES

Agaricia could be confused with *Siderastrea,* but the latter is massive, lacks collines and has large (3 to 4 mm) regular calices with distinct shared walls. Some *Agaricia* colonies resemble the closely related *Leptoseris*; differences are explained under that genus.

DISTRIBUTION AND ECOLOGY   (Map #4)

Agaricia is a common coral that occurs in most reef habitats, including back reef areas. It is particularly important on deep reefs, where it can thrive under overhangs and in poor light conditions. Several species are known to occur at depths of around 80 m. Colonies often exceed 50 cm in diameter and may grow considerably larger. There are probably seven species.

Leptoseris Milne-Edwards & Haime, 1849

(Gr: *leptos,* slender; Gr: *seris,* lettuce. Referring to the leafy forms of this coral.)

DESCRIPTION

Living coral   (Col. pl. p. 92)

Leptoseris forms thin, fragile colonies that are usually either bowl-shaped or branching (see note on species below). They are brown or greenish in color, often with the polyp mouth contrasting in color with the rest of the corallum. Tentacles are tiny and are not generally extended during the day.

Corallites are rounded or elliptical and usually between 2 and 4 mm in diameter. Calices are usually protuberant and inclined toward the perimeter of the corallum. They are present only on the upper surface and may be arranged in approximately concentric rings following the outline of the coral perimeter. Collines are often present, usually in the form of conspicuous elongate ridges. Septa and septocostae are visible as fine lines running over the

collines and to calice centers. They are closely packed and feel smooth to the touch.

Skeleton

Septa are in cycles with thick and thin ones alternating. Margins of septa and septocostae are smooth, uneven or dentate. The columella is small or absent.

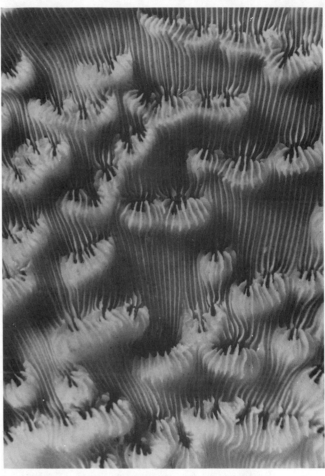

Leptoseris cucullata (X 3). Cayman Islands. BM(NH) 1976.4.14.5.

SIMILARITIES

Leptoseris is closely related to *Agaricia*, and in some respects the differences between the two genera hardly appear significant. In general, however, the calices in *Leptoseris* are larger and more protuberant than in *Agaricia*. Additionally, the corallum in western Atlantic *Leptoseris* is characteristically small and fragile.

TAXONOMIC NOTE

The presence of this genus in the western Atlantic has only recently been recognized (Dinesen, 1980). It includes two corals that were previously referred to as *Helioseris cucullata* (Ellis & Solander, 1786) and *Agaricia cailleti* (Duchassaing & Michelotti, 1864).

DISTRIBUTION AND ECOLOGY (Map #5)
Leptoseris usually occurs at depths between 8 and 50 m and has been found at depths of 90 m. Colony size does not generally exceed 20 cm, so this coral is less important than *Agaricia* in terms of reef building.

There are two species: *Leptoseris cucullata,* which forms thin bowl or plate-shaped colonies; and *Leptoseris cailleti,* a rare deep-water form with a corallum of delicate twisted branches.

FAMILY SIDERASTREIDAE
Siderastrea de Blainville, 1830
Starlet coral
(L: *sideris,* star; Gr: *aster,* star. Relating to the regular star-like arrangement of the calices and septa.)

DESCRIPTION
Living coral (Col. pl. p. 84)
Siderastrea is normally massive and rounded, occasionally encrusting, and is brown, green or red-

Siderastrea siderea (X 5.4). Bermuda. BM(NH) 1928.10.10.11.

dish in color. Tentacles are usually retracted during the day. If extended, they are in two rings, with those of the inner ring bifurcated. Calices are crowded, regular and have shared walls. They are rounded and deep in *Siderastrea siderea,* angular and shallower in *S. radians.* There is usually a faint line around the calices along the top of the corallite wall. Calice diameter is between 2 and 4 mm. Septa are clearly visible as fine lines radiating from the fossa to neighboring calices and feel smooth to the touch.

Skeleton
Septa are numerous and in cycles. There are less than 48 in a mature calice of *S. radians,* more than 48 in *S. siderea.* Only the large septa reach the columella. Septal margins are armed with tiny regular spines. The lateral walls of the septa are linked by synapticulae.

SIMILARITIES
Siderastrea bears a superficial resemblance to *Agaricia* but is readily distinguished by the regular shared walls that surround each calice, the larger calice diameter and the lack of collines.

DISTRIBUTION AND ECOLOGY (Map #6)
There are three Atlantic species of *Siderastrea,* two of which: *Siderastrea siderea* (Ellis and Solander, 1786) and *Siderastrea radians* (Pallas, 1766) occur in the Caribbean. *S. siderea* can exceed 2 m in diameter; it occurs from the shallow to deep fore reef but does not thrive in back reef areas or muddy bays. *S. radians* seldom reaches 30 cm in diameter and is found in these latter, turbid areas, but does not occur on deep reefs. *Siderastrea stellata* Verrill, 1868, is restricted to Brazilian waters.

FAMILY PORITIDAE
Porites Link, 1807
Finger or porous coral
(L: *porus,* pore; Gr:-*ites,* suffix denoting likeness. Relating to porous nature of the corallum.

DESCRIPTION
Living coral (Col. pl. pp. 89, 92, 93)
Porites forms massive, branched or encrusting colonies. Most are brownish or yellowish in color,

whereas some are blue, green or pinkish. Polyps are sometimes extended during the day but retract rapidly when the coral is touched. They are elongate and surmounted by a ring of simple tentacles.

The surface of the coral is smooth or slightly granular to the touch. Calices are about 1.0 to 1.5 mm in diameter, round or polygonal and closely united by their walls. This arrangement gives a characteristic honeycomb appearance. Septa may just be visible in the calices.

Skeleton

There are 12 septa, some of which have a paliform lobe at their inner end. Septa are perforate, and their margins are granular or armed with uneven tubercles. Tubercles are also present on the corallite wall, and the whole corallum is porous.

SIMILARITIES

Porites could possibly be confused with *Madracis*, but the latter does not have the long polyps characteristic of *Porites,* has more widely separated calices and has a non-porous skeleton.

DISTRIBUTION AND ECOLOGY (Map #7)

Porites is a common coral which is especially successful in shallow reef areas. Branched colonies often form large tracts along the reef front, while massive and encrusting species thrive at more exposed sites. There are probably five species of Atlantic *Porites*. This partly depends on the status of *Porites porites,* which is split by some authors into varieties and by others into separate species.

FAMILY FAVIIDAE

Cladocora Ehrenberg, 1834
(Gr: *klados,* branch; Gr: *keras,* horn. Relating to the appearance of this coral, with its branch-like protruding corallites.)

DESCRIPTION

Living coral (Col. pl. p. 93)

Cladocora forms small, low-growing colonies that are brown in color. Corallites arise from an encrusting base and may divide to give a branched colony. Each branch represents a single corallite; these are narrow (2 to 3 mm) but elongate (usually

Cladocora caespitosa (X 3.5). Italy. BM(NH) 1978.2.5.195.

5 to 8 mm). Some newly budded branches are shorter.

Calices are round in cross section, and septa are visible and slightly rough to touch. Costal striae can be seen running down the outside of the corallites.

Skeleton

Septa are in cycles and exsert by about a millimeter as they pass over the walls. They run down the outside of the corallites as well developed costae. Margins of septa and costae are finely dentate. The columella is deep, well developed and papillose.

SIMILARITIES

Cladocora is a distinctive coral that is unlikely to be confused with other genera, except possibly with *Oculina*, which has a superficially similar growth form. A basic difference, however, is that calices occur along the length of the branches in *Oculina*, whereas in *Cladocora* the branches themselves correspond to the calices; *i.e.,* each short branch ends in a calice.

DISTRIBUTION AND ECOLOGY (Map #8)

Cladocora normally occurs on soft substrates in shallow, turbid areas. There is a single shallow water species, *Cladocora arbuscula* (Lesueur, 1821), and one or two other species occurring in deeper water.

Montastraea de Blainville, 1830
Star coral
(L: *mont*, mountain; Gr: *aster,* star.
Relating to the protuberant calices and
the star-like arrangement of septa.)

DESCRIPTION
Living coral   (Col. pl. pp. 96, 97)

Montastraea forms massive colonies that are
usually rounded or lobed in shallow water and flattened or plate-like on deep reefs. The corallum is
brown or greenish, and sometimes the mouths contrast in color with the rest of the colony. Polyps are
normally retracted during the day, but a ring of
simple tentacles is sometimes extended from calices
that lie in shaded positions.

Corallites are distinct, with separate walls, and
may be crowded or separated by coenosteum. They
are raised several millimeters above the surface of
the coral, and in *Montastraea cavernosa* are raised
by as much as a centimeter. Corallites are rounded,
and there may be a distinct difference in average
calice size according to species. For example, in *M.
annularis* mature calices are about 3 mm in
diameter, but in *M. cavernosa* they are about 10
mm. In all *Montastraea* species small calices produced by intercalicular (extratentacular) division
can be seen between the mature ones.

Septa are numerous and clearly visible. They

Montastraea cavernosa (× 1.4). Jamaica.

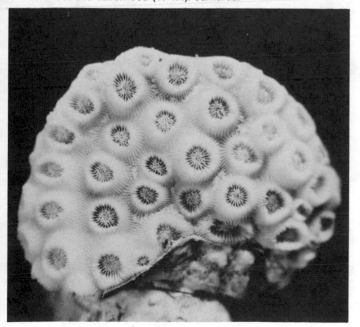

radiate from calice centers over the walls and continue as costae on perithecal areas. Principal costae
fuse with those of adjacent calices. Septal and
costal margins feel slightly rough to the touch.

Skeleton
Septa are in cycles, only the 12 of the first two
cycles reaching the columella. Paliform lobes are
not well developed. Costae drop down to the
trough between corallites and the larger ones usually fuse with those of neighboring calices. Smaller
ones may be discontinuous. Margins of both septa
and costae are finely serrated. The columella is
broad and spongy in appearance.

SIMILARITIES
The rounded, regular calices in *Montastraea*
easily distinguish this genus from *Favia,* in which
the calices are distinctly irregular in shape. *M. annularis,* with its small calices, can be confused with
Solenastrea or *Stephanocoenia. Solenastrea* is
identified by the non-fusion of costae on perithecal
areas. Costae are also absent in *Stephanocoenia,*
and the calices are separated by a faint line or wider
groove. In addition, *Stephanocoenia* has smooth
septal margins, a solid columella and a distinctive
ring of paliform lobes.

DISTRIBUTION AND ECOLOGY   (Map #9)
Montastraea is a common and extremely important reef-building coral in the western Atlantic.
Colonies are often large and may dominate certain
areas. There are probably four species.

Solenastrea Milne-Edwards & Haime, 1848
(Gr: *solen,* channel; Gr: *aster,* star.
Possibly relating to the gap between the
calices.)

DESCRIPTION
Living coral
Solenastrea forms massive colonies that are
usually rounded or hemispherical. It is usually
brown or greenish in color, and polyps are
retracted during the day. Corallites are distinct,
with separate walls, and are separated by a narrow
gap. They are rounded, about 2 to 3 mm in
diameter and usually raised by about a millimeter
from the surface of the coral.

Solenastrea hyades (X 3). Florida. BM(NH) 1928.9.1.256.

Septa are visible as they radiate from calice centers on to the walls. They run down the outside of the corallite walls but do not fuse with costae of adjacent calices. Septal margins are slightly rough to the touch.

Skeleton

Septa are in cycles, and the larger ones reach the columella. Paliform lobes are very weak or absent. Costae of adjacent corallites do not meet, and perithecal areas are uneven or blistered. Septal margins are finely serrated. The columella is small and spongy.

SIMILARITIES

Solenastrea can be mistaken for *Montastraea annularis* but is distinguished by the short costae, discontinuous over perithecal areas.

Solenastrea also resembles *Stephanocoenia,* and in some cases diagnosis underwater is difficult. The skeleton of *Stephanocoenia* is readily identified by the smooth septal margins, solid columella and exsert primary septa.

DISTRIBUTION AND ECOLOGY (Map #10)

Solenastrea seldom forms colonies greater than 25 cm in diameter and apparently prefers deeper waters. It may replace *Montastraea annularis* below depths of about 20 m. There are two species: *Solenastrea bournoni* Milne-Edwards & Haime (calices 2 to 2.5 mm in diameter; costae extend on

to perithecal areas) and *Solenastrea hyades* (Dana) (calices 3 to 3.5 mm in diameter; costae do not extend beyond the corallite wall).

Favia Oken, 1815
(L: *favus,* honeycomb. Relating to the appearance of the corallites.)

DESCRIPTION
Living coral (Col. pl. p. 96)

Favia forms small spherical or encrusting colonies. The corallum is yellow or brownish in color, and polyps are normally extended only at night. Calices are rounded or irregular in shape and usually between 4 and 7 mm in diameter. They are generally monocentric but may have two or three centers when in the process of asexual reproduction (intratentacular). Corallites are crowded closely together, but the walls are distinct and slightly raised.

Septa are clearly visible as they radiate from the calice centers. They run over the walls and continue as costae on perithecal areas. Costae and septa are slightly rough to the touch.

Skeleton

Septa are numerous and arranged in cycles. Their margins bear prominent irregular spines, and paliform lobes may be present. The columella is well developed and spongy. Costae are well defined, and the larger ones are often continuous between adjacent corallites. Others are separated by a slight gap.

Favia fragum (X 2.2). Jamaica.

SIMILARITIES

Favia bears a superficial resemblance to *Montastraea* but is readily distinguished by the small size of the corallum and the irregular rather than rounded corallites.

Favia could also be mistaken for *Dichocoenia,* but the latter is identified by its tendency to form series of corallites, by the nondentate septa and by the absence of costae on perithecal areas.

DISTRIBUTION AND ECOLOGY   (Map #11)

Favia is unimportant in the western Atlantic in terms of reef-building. Colonies are always small (less than 30 cm in diameter) and are generally restricted to shallow reefs. A single species, *Favia fragum* (Esper, 1795), occurs in the Caribbean. Two species are reported from Brazilian waters: *Favia gravida* Verrill 1868, which often has elongate calices, and *Favia leptophylla* Verrill 1868, with round or slightly irregular calices and vesicular exotheca.

Diploria Milne-Edwards & Haime, 1848
Brain coral
(Gr: *diplon,* fold; Gr: *oros,* mountain. Presumably describing the massive corallum and the longitudinal ridges or folds that cover its surface.)

DESCRIPTION

Living coral   (Col. pl. pp. 97, 100, 101)

Diploria is usually massive and rounded but may be flattened or encrusting according to depth and exposure. Colonies are yellow, brown, greenish or gray-brown in color, and sometimes the valleys contrast in color with the rest of the colony.

Calices are united in longitudinal series, and their fused walls form ridges across the surface of the corallum. Polyp mouths are visible in the valleys as rounded or slit-like apertures. Tentacles are retracted during the day but expand at night and line the valleys. The shape of the walls and the width and depth of the valleys vary from one species to another as well as among coralla of the same species. Width from mid-ridge to mid-ridge is generally between 5 and 15 mm. *Diploria labyrinthiformis* is distinctive because there is always a groove along the top of the wall. It may be narrow but in some cases is wider than the polyp-bearing

Diploria labyrinthiformis BM(NH)1957.8.24.8

valley. Other species may have a faint line along the top of the wall.

Septa are clearly visible as parallel lines running over the walls. There are between 15 and 45 per cm, depending on species. The septa are slightly rough to the touch, and small teeth can just be seen beneath the mantle of living tissues.

Skeleton

Septa are slightly exsert as they pass over the walls. They usually run uninterrupted between adjacent valleys but in some cases are separated by a narrow gap or groove. There are sharp, often ragged, teeth along the septal margins and sharp teeth on the septal sides. Small paliform lobes may be present. The columella is continuous and plate-like, with spongy calice centers.

SIMILARITIES

Some *Diploria* species with wide valleys can be confused with other meandrine corals, but in most cases this is a distinctive genus (see Table 1 for comparisons).

DISTRIBUTION AND ECOLOGY   (Map #12)

Diploria species are found in a variety of biotopes from shallow to deep water but are probably most successful at depths of around 10 to 15 m. Colonies are often several meters in diameter and contribute substantially to reef-building. As many as 12 species have been reported, but probably only three or four are valid.

Manicina Ehrenberg, 1834
Rose coral

(Gr: *manos,* wide, loose; Gr: *kineo,* to move. Possibly relating to the wide, spongy columella that runs along the center of the valleys.)

DESCRIPTION
Living coral   (Col. pl. pp. 101, 109)

Manicina is a spherical to oval-shaped coral that seldom exceeds 20 cm in diameter. It is either attached by a short stem or lies free on soft substrates. Calices are united and generally form only a single valley system. The main valley runs along the length of the corallum and gives off shorter valleys to either side. The valleys are deep (7 to 10 mm), and the width of the meanders from mid-ridge to mid-ridge is about 10 to 20 mm. Mouths are visible in the valleys as rounded or slit-shaped apertures. Polyps are generally retracted during the day.

Septa run over the walls and into the valleys,

Manicina areolata (X 1.4). Jamaica.

	Colony form	Diameter mid-wall to mid-wall	Form of valley	Number of septa per cm	Paliform lobes	Septal ornamentation
Diploria	Large, massive	4-15 mm	Meandering, short or long	13-45	If present then small	Margins with sharp, sometimes ragged teeth. Sides with sharp teeth.
Manicina	Small & may be unattached	10-20 mm	Usually one main valley system only	11-14 (large + small ones between)	Large and prominent	Margins with sharp, often ragged teeth. Spines on septal sides.
Colpophyllia	Large, massive	13-20 mm	Meandering, short or long	9-12	Large and prominent	Small fine teeth on margins. Sides smooth, minutely ridged, or with small spines.
Meandrina	Large, massive	10-15 mm	Meandering, short or long	6-8 (large, may be smaller ones between)	Absent	Septal margins and sides smooth.
Goreaugyra	Small, columnar	6-15 mm	Long, meandering and laterally separated.	6-8	Absent	Septal margins mostly smooth, costae partly dentate. Septal sides minutely granulated.
Dendrogyra	Large, columnar	5-6 mm	Meandering, short or long	6-7 (large, may be smaller ones between)	Absent	Septal margins and sides non-dentate.

Table 1. Some comparisons between meandrine corals from the western Atlantic. Other distinguishing features are given in the text.

where they can be seen passing to the calice centers. The number per centimeter that is visible is about 14, but this is variable because some are small and cannot be distinguished under the mantle of living tissue. Septal margins are slightly rough to the touch. There is generally a distinct line along either side of the valley that corresponds to the notch between the paliform lobes and the rest of the septa. There may also be a groove along the top of the walls.

Skeleton
There are 11 to 14 large septa per cm and smaller ones between. These smaller ones do not reach the columella. Septal margins have well developed spines that themselves bear lateral teeth. Paliform lobes are large, with spiny margins, and are separated from the main part of the septum by a notch. The columellar is wide and spongy (trabecular).

SIMILARITIES
Manicina has a characteristic growth form and valley system and is unlikely to be confused with other meandrine corals (also see Table I).

DISTRIBUTION AND ECOLOGY   (Map #13)
Manicina may be attached to hard substrates but is often free-living in muddy or sandy areas such as lagoons or reef slopes. These colonies are able to right themselves by inflating the polyp. There is a single species: *Manicina areolata* (Linnaeus, 1758).

Colpophyllia Milne-Edwards & Haime, 1848
(Gr: *kolpodes,* sinuous; Gr: *phyllon,* leaf. Referring to the prominent winding valleys.)

DESCRIPTION
Living coral   (Col. pl. pp. 81, 97, 104)
Colpophyllia is a massive coral that forms rounded or flattened colonies. In *C. natans* most calices are joined to form long and sinuous meanders. In *C. breviserialis* calices are single or form short series. Mouths are visible and often contrast in color with the rest of the living tissues; the valleys (or fossa) may also be a different color from the walls. Colors range from whitish to yellow, brown or green.

Single calices are wide and shallow, sometimes reaching 30 mm in diameter. They are rounded, polygonal or slightly elongate. Valleys are usually wide (mid-ridge to mid-ridge about 10 to 25 mm) and have gently or steeply sloping walls. Septa are prominent and widely spaced (9 to 12 per cm) and their margins are slightly rough to the touch. They are parallel on the walls but curve and run to calice centers in the valleys. They are interrupted by a distinct groove along the top of the wall. There is also a line along either side of the valley that corresponds to the notch between the paliform lobes and the septa.

Skeleton
Septa are exsert by several millimeters, except at the top of the wall where they are interrupted by a notch. However, the basal parts of the septa are continuous between adjacent valley systems. Septal margins are uneven or have small, regular teeth; septal sides are smooth, minutely ridged or have small spines. Paliform lobes are wide and are separated from the rest of the septum by a notch. Their margins are also minutely toothed. The columella at calice centers is spongy, but linkage between centers is plate-like (lamellar).

SIMILARITIES
Colpophyllia is usually readily recognized by the

Colpophyllia natans (nat. size). Jamaica.

shape and size of its calices and valleys. Useful diagnostic characters are shown in Table 1.

DISTRIBUTION AND ECOLOGY (Map #14)

Colpophyllia occurs on most reefs from shallow to deep water and can form heads over a meter in diameter. There are two species: *Colpophyllia natans* (Houttuyn, 1772), with long sinuous valleys; and *Colpophyllia breviserialis* Milne-Edwards & Haime, 1849, with single calices or short series.

FAMILY FLABELLIDAE

Gardineria Vaughan, 1907
(Named for J. Stanley Gardiner.)

DESCRIPTION
Living coral

Gardineria is a solitary ahermatypic coral that is tympanoid to cylindrical in shape. Calices are round and seldom exceed 5 mm in diameter. Polyps may be partially extended during the day and are pale pinkish in color. Septa are just visible.

Skeleton

There are 12 septa in two cycles. Septal margins are smooth and the sides are spinulose. Paliform lobes may be present. The columella consists of small pinnacle-like protrusions. Costae are absent.

SIMILARITIES

The small size of *Gardineria,* the absence of costae and the small number of septa distinguish this coral from other solitary forms.

DISTRIBUTION AND ECOLOGY

Gardineria is found in caverns and on the undersurface of rocks and corals but is easily overlooked. There are two species that occur in shallow waters in the western Atlantic. The genus *Monomyces* may also be found in relatively shallow waters; it differs from *Gardineria* in lacking a columella.

FAMILY RHIZANGIIDAE

DESCRIPTION
Living coral (Col. pl. p. 105)

Rhizangiids are small ahermatypic (non-reef-

Phyllangia mouchezii (X 3). Mediterranean. BM(NH) 1978.2.5.411.

building) corals that may be found in shallow waters. Corallites are rounded and cylindrical, with a diameter of about 5 mm (*Astrangia*) to 10 mm (*Phyllangia*). Corallites in *Phyllangia* generally occur in small groups connected at their bases by stolon-like expansions that creep over the substrate. *Astrangia* may be solitary or form colonies in the same way. These small corals are brownish or reddish in color, sometimes with the mouth paler. Polyps are normally retracted during the day, but septa are numerous and clearly visible.

Skeleton

Septa are numerous and in cycles, and their margins are irregularly dentate. The columella is occasionally absent, usually feebly developed and spongy, rarely solid. Costae are present and have granulated margins.

SIMILARITIES

Rhizangiids can be confused with other ahermatypic corals such as *Caryophyllia* and *Balanophyllia*, which have a similar growth form. In general, rhizangiids are smaller and less brightly colored. Also, they have dentate rather than smooth septal margins, the septa are never joined and the columella is only feebly developed.

DISTRIBUTION AND ECOLOGY

Rhizangiid corals tend to grow under ledges and rocks in both shallow and deep waters. This cryptic habit, together with their small size, means that they are readily overlooked. There are probably four or five species that occur on shallow reefs in the western Atlantic and others that are more widely distributed in the temperate waters of North and South America.

FAMILY OCULINIDAE

Oculina Lamarck, 1816

(L: *oculus,* eye; L: *-ina,* suffix denoting likeness. Presumably relating to the eye-like appearance of the calices.

DESCRIPTION

Living coral (Col. pl. p. 105)

Oculina forms loosely branched colonies that are straggly and bushy; they are usually pale yellowish in color. The tentacles are pale or transparent, but are extended only at night.

The main branches seldom exceed 1 cm in diameter, and side branches are delicate and about half this width. Corallites are distinct, separate and

Oculina diffusa (nat. size). Jamaica.

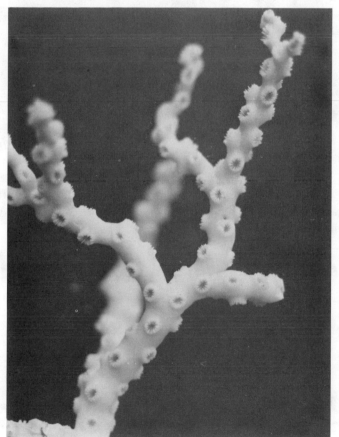

usually widely spaced, although sometimes crowded toward the branch tips. They are raised by about a millimeter and may lie perpendicular or at a slight angle to the branch axis. Calices are about 3 to 4 mm in diameter. Septa are visible but do not continue outside the calices, and perithecal areas appear smooth.

Skeleton

The 12 septa of the primary cycle are slightly exsert and are more prominent than intermediate ones. They drop steeply to the fossa, and their margins are minutely dentate. The columella is broad and papillose. An examination of perithecal areas reveals that costae are present but are often greatly reduced and consist of little more than ill-defined ridges. The corallum is dense.

SIMILARITIES

It is possible to confuse *Oculina* with *Cladocora*, but the latter does not have a bushy form and does not have branches with calices along its length. Instead, each branch in *Cladocora* represents a single corallite.

DISTRIBUTION AND ECOLOGY (Map #15)

Oculina is common in areas of high sedimentation such as lagoons, back reefs and sheltered reef slopes. It is usually absent from areas of vigorous coral growth on more exposed sites. Colonies grow to about 30 cm in diameter. There are probably about ten species, but this includes ahermatypic species that grow in deep water. The common shallow-water species found in the Caribbean is *Oculina diffusa* Lamarck, 1816.

FAMILY MEANDRINIDAE

Dichocoenia Milne-Edwards & Haime, 1848

(Gr: *dicha,* divided into two; Gr: *koinos,* shared. Possibly relating to the tendency of calices to divide and form a series within a single valley.)

DESCRIPTION

Living coral (Col. pl. pp. 108, 109)

Dichocoenia forms massive colonies that are either rounded or flattened. They are whitish, yellow or brown in color, and the tentacles are normally retracted during the day. Corallites are

Dichocoenia stokesi (X 3). Caribbean. BM(NH) 1843.5.12.2.

separate and have distinct walls. They are monocentric to polycentric and correspondingly are either rounded, oval or elongate. Diameter is usually between 3 and 4 mm, but valleys may be as much as 5 cm in length and sometimes branch.

Corallites protrude by several millimeters and are separated by a gap of about 2 mm. Septa are clearly visible in the calices, but they stop at the top of the wall and the perithecal areas appear smooth.

Skeleton

Septa are usually in two cycles, and their margins are smooth. Paliform lobes are absent. The columella consists of short or long vertical plates and is continuous between calice centers in the valleys. Perithecal areas are non-costate and slightly irregular, usually with low tubercles or granules.

SIMILARITIES

Dichocoenia is distinctive and is unlikely to be confused with any other genus, except possibly *Favia*. *Dichocoenia* is recognized by the larger corallum, presence of elongate or Y-shaped corallites, the non-costate perithecal areas and smooth septal margins.

DISTRIBUTION AND ECOLOGY   (Map #16)

Dichocoenia does not usually form colonies over about 50 cm in diameter but is a fairly common coral, especially on deeper reefs. There are two species: *Dichocoenia stokesi* Milne-Edwards &

Haime, 1848, forms rounded heads, has rounded, elongate or Y-shaped calices and the valleys are less than 5 cm in length; *Dichocoenia stellaris* Milne-Edwards & Haime, 1849, forms flattened heads, has rounded or elongate calices, seldom Y-shaped and the valleys may reach 12 cm in length.

Meandrina Lamarck, 1801
(Gr: *maiandros,* winding; L: *-ina,* like. A reference to the winding valley.)

DESCRIPTION

Living coral   (Col. pl. pp. 108, 109)

Meandrina forms rounded or flattened colonies that may be attached to hard substrates or be free-living on sand and rubble. Colonies are usually yellowish or pale brown in color, and a mass of white-tipped tentacles may be partially extended during the day. At night they cover the corallum.

Corallites are joined in series to form a system of valleys and ridges. The distance from mid-ridge to mid-ridge is about 10 to 15 mm, and the valleys may be 10 mm deep. Septa are prominent and run to calice centers. The larger septa are widely spaced (about 7 per cm), and smaller intermediate ones can sometimes be seen. The margins of the septa are uneven but smooth. There is a distinct line along the top of the wall to which the septa join.

Skeleton

Paliform lobes are absent. The columella is

Meandrina meandrites (nat. size). Jamaica.

plate-like and lies deep in the fossa. It is spongy at calice centers.

SIMILARITIES
Meandrina can be distinguished from other meandrine corals by the leafy, widely spaced septa and smooth septal margins (also see Table 1).

DISTRIBUTION AND ECOLOGY (Map #17)
Attached colonies grow to a meter or more in diameter and are found in a variety of habitats. Free-living ones are smaller and restricted to soft substrates. There are two species. The common Caribbean species is *Meandrina meandrites* (Linnaeus, 1758), which forms broad, low colonies and has a complex system of meanders. *Meandrina braziliensis* (Milne-Edwards & Haime, 1849) is small and unattached, with a simple valley system resembling that of *Manicina*.

Goreaugyra Wells, 1973
(Named for Thomas F. Goreau; Gr: *gyros*, round.)

DESCRIPTION
Living coral (Col. pl. p. 112)
Goreaugyra is massive and forms columnar or pillar-like growths. The colonies discovered so far have consisted of a single pillar usually less than 50 cm tall. It is brown or greenish in color, and the tentacles may be partially extended during the day.

Calices are united in longitudinal series to form long meanders. The valley walls are not fused laterally with neighboring meanders, but are separated by a prominent groove. The grooves are 6 to 15 mm wide and 5 to 8 mm deep. The width of the calice-bearing valleys is 5 to 7 mm. Septa are prominent, exsert and widely spaced (about 6 to 8 per cm). Their margins are smooth to the touch. Costae are visible as low ridges.

Skeleton
Septa alternate in size, but all are thick and exsert. Their margins are smooth, except toward the apex of the colony where they may be weakly dentate. Their sides are minutely granulated. Major septa join to a spongy (trabecular) columella. Linkage between calice centers is plate-like (lamellar). Costae become reduced in size as they pass down the outside of the valley wall, and they cross the grooves as low ridges. Costal margins are toothed at the top of the wall and granular on the parts of the costae that run across the grooves.

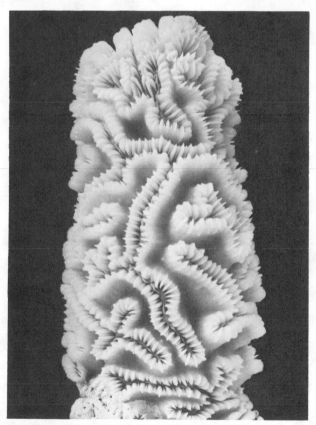

Goreaugyra memorialis (X 0.75). Holotype. USNM 45703.

Goreaugyra memorialis (X 1.5). Holotype. USNM 45703.

SIMILARITIES

Goreaugyra resembles *Dendrogyra* in its growth form but is readily identified by the prominent leafy septa and the large inter-calice groove. The closely related *Meandrina* is distinguished by lateral fusion of the walls of the meanders (see Table 1).

DISTRIBUTION AND ECOLOGY   (Map #18)

Goreaugyra has been discovered relatively recently and is not a well-known coral. It appears to be restricted to deep water (20 to 30 m). There is a single species: *Goreaugyra memorialis* Wells, 1973.

Dendrogyra **Ehrenberg, 1834**
Pillar coral
(Gr: *dendron,* tree; Gr: *gyros,* round. Presumably relating to the rounded but columnar growth form.)

DESCRIPTION
Living coral   (Col. pl. pp. 112, 113)

Dendrogyra is a massive coral that grows in a distinctive columnar or pillar-like form. The colony may be 2 or 3 meters high and about the same width across the base. The surface of the corallum

Dendrogyra cylindrus (X 3). Cayman Islands. BM(NH) 1976.4.14.35.

is covered by a mass of pale brown tentacles that are about 5 mm in length and retract rapidly when touched.

There are a few monocentric calices, but most are joined in short or long series. The valleys are narrow and sinuous, the shared walls wide and prominent. The distance from mid-ridge to mid-ridge is about 5 mm, and the ridges are flat-topped or grooved. Septa are clearly visible as they pass over the walls; there are about 6 or 7 large ones per cm, with smaller ones between. Septal margins are smooth to the touch.

Skeleton

Septa from adjacent valley systems are separated on the walls by a narrow groove. Septal margins are smooth and non-dentate. The columella is well developed and plate-like (lamellar).

SIMILARITIES

Dendrogyra has a distinctive growth form unlike any other coral except *Goreaugyra* (see Table 1).

DISTRIBUTION AND ECOLOGY   (Map #19)

Dendrogyra usually occurs on gentle slopes on the shallow fore reef. It is not a particularly common coral, but where colonies do occur they are often of a large size. There is a single species: *Dendrogyra cylindrus* Ehrenberg, 1834.

FAMILY MUSSIDAE

Scolymia **Haime, 1852**
(Gr: *skolymos,* artichoke. Presumably relating to the growth form of this coral.)

DESCRIPTION
Living coral   (Col. pl. pp. 109, 113)

Scolymia is rounded, disc-like and attached to the substrate by a broad or narrow stem. It is flat, concave or convex. The corallum is usually about 5 cm in diameter but may be larger. It is a solitary coral, and there is a single rather fleshy polyp, dark green or brownish in color. The tentacles are only extended at night.

Septa are prominent and radiate from the center of the corallum to the outer edge. Septal margins have prominent sharp teeth that can easily be felt beneath the fleshy mantle. Costae are also visible and have spiny margins.

Scolymia lacera (X 1.2). Cayman Islands. BM(NH) 1976.4.14.37.

Skeleton

Septa are arranged in cycles, and the large ones radiate from the columella to the perimeter. Smaller, shorter ones lie between. The teeth on the septal margins are several millimeters long and have a stout base. They are also present on the outside wall, although the costae themselves are reduced and do not extend to the base of the wall.

SIMILARITIES

Scolymia is a distinctive coral and is unlikely to be confused with any other genus.

DISTRIBUTION AND ECOLOGY   (Map #20)

Scolymia is fairly common on deep reefs but is seldom found in areas of dense coral growth in shallow areas. There are three Atlantic species, two in the Caribbean: *Scolymia lacera* (Pallas, 1776), with triangular septal teeth; and *Scolymia cubensis* (Milne-Edwards & Haime, 1849), with smaller, awl-shaped septal teeth. These were originally considered as a single species until differences in aggressive behavior were discovered (Lang, 1971). There is a third species, *Scolymia wellsi* Laborel, 1967, which occurs on Brazilian reefs.

Mussismilia Ortmann, 1890
(Etymology obscure.)

DESCRIPTION
Living coral

Mussismilia forms massive colonies of a relatively small size. Corallites are distinct but vary in arrangement according to species. *Mussismilia hartii* (Verrill, 1868) has separate corallites arising from a common base (phaceloid growth form). In the remaining species the corallites are tightly packed with their walls closely appressed, separated only by a narrow groove. *Mussismilia hispida* (Verrill, 1868) has relatively large calices, usually well over 10 mm in diameter. *Mussismilia braziliensis* (Verrill, 1868) has calices approximately 8 to 10 mm in diameter. In all three species calices are rounded, irregular or slightly elongate, with one to several centers.

Septa are visible, and their margins are rough and spiky to the touch. The outer wall in *M. hartii* is also spiny, due to underlying spines on the costal margins.

Mussismilia hartii (X 2.5). Brazil. BM(NH) 1928.3.1.113.

59

Skeleton

In all species of *Mussismilia* the septa are stout and exsert by several millimeters as they pass over the walls. In cerioid species there is a narrow groove separating adjacent corallites, but many of the septa are continuous. In *M. hartii,* which has a phaceloid growth form, the septa continue as costae or rows of spines. Septal and costal margins bear slender, sharply pointed and often ragged teeth. Septa are porous. The columella is generally well developed (reduced in *M. braziliensis*) and is formed from twisted trabeculae.

SIMILARITIES

Mussismilia (also referred to as *Protomussa*) is a rather poorly known coral that has clear affinities with several other mussid genera. It is, however, restricted to Brazilian waters and so is geographically separated from *Mussa, Isophyllia* and other Caribbean forms. In addition, it is characterized by its slender rather than triangular teeth, porous septa and well defined wall.

DISTRIBUTION AND ECOLOGY (Map #21)

Mussismilia occurs in a variety of reef habitats but is a relatively small coral with a restricted range, so it is not often encountered. There are three species: *M. hartii, M. braziliensis* and *M. hispida.*

Mussa Oken, 1815
(L: *mus,* mouse. Etymology obscure.)

DESCRIPTION
Living coral (Col. pl. pp. 116, 117)

Mussa forms massive, usually rounded, colonies that consist of a clump of large corallites rising from a common base. The corallites are monocentric to tricentric and as a result are either rounded, irregular or slightly elongate. They are separated by a gap of at least 5 mm, but this is often obscured by the coral polyp. The polyp usually combines shades of pink, purple, red, green or brown and is so fleshy that it extends beyond the corallite boundary and makes contact with adjacent polyps. A fringe of small tentacles appears at night.

Corallites are about 4 to 10 cm in diameter, and the stalks from which they arise are about 10 to 20 cm in length. The septa are just visible beneath the

Mussa angulosa (X 1.1). Barbados. BM(NH) 1886.6.14.14.

polyps, and there are numerous fleshy warts that correspond to the position of the septal spines. The spines themselves can be felt but not seen. The outer wall of the corallites is also spiny.

Skeleton

Small and large septa alternate, and all are exsert. Their margins have strong, sharp teeth several millimeters tall. The columella is spongy (trabecular).

SIMILARITIES

Mussa, with its separate stalked calices and fleshy polyps, is unlikely to be confused with any other coral genus (also see *Mussismilia*).

DISTRIBUTION AND ECOLOGY (Map #22)

Occasional, of moderate size and occurring in most reef habitats, there is but a single species: *Mussa angulosa* (Pallas, 1766).

Isophyllastrea Matthai, 1928
Rough star coral
(Gr: *isos,* equal; Gr: *phyllon,* leaf; Gr: *aster,* star. Referring to the shared, polygonal calices.)

DESCRIPTION
Living coral (Col. pl. p. 117)

Isophyllastrea rigida (nat. size). Jamaica.

Isophyllastrea is massive and forms hemispherical or flattened colonies. Corallites are united by their walls and are polygonal, occasionally irregular when dividing. Tentacles are retracted during the day but the polyps are large and their fleshy margins are pressed together, forming a line along the top of the corallite wall. The polyp margins are brown, green, purple or pinkish in color, the oral discs white or pale. There is usually a single mouth in each calice, sometimes two or three, and these are visible as small rounded apertures. Calice diameter is usually between 10 to 20 mm.

The position of the septa can just be seen through the mantle of living tissue. In some cases they appear as rows of small warts which correspond to the spines on the septal margins. These are strong and sharp and can be felt through the overlying polyp.

Skeleton

Septa rise steeply from the fossa and are exsert by several millimeters as they pass over the walls and fuse with septa of adjacent calices. The spines on the septal margins are large and sharply pointed. The columella appears to be formed by a mass of interlocking spines.

SIMILARITIES

Isophyllastrea is readily distinguished from other members of its family by the polygonal calices and fused walls, which usually enclose a single polyp.

DISTRIBUTION AND ECOLOGY   (Map #23)

Isophyllastrea is small (seldom exceeding 20 cm in diameter) and is generally found in relatively shallow water. There is a single species: *Isophyllastrea rigida* (Dana, 1846).

Isophyllia Milne-Edwards & Haime, 1851
(Gr: *isos,* equal; Gr: *phyllon,* leaf. Probably a reference to the shared, leafy walls.)

DESCRIPTION

Living coral   (Col. pl. p. 120)

Isophyllia is massive and forms rounded, hemispherical colonies. Corallites are joined in longitudinal series to give a distinct pattern of ridges and valleys. The valleys are elongate, Y-shaped or irregular. The polyps and tentacles are only fully extended at night, but during the day a fleshy mantle covers the skeleton. There is usually a distinct line along the top of the wall where polyps from adjacent valleys meet. Living tissues are brown, green, bluish, purple or yellow, often with the valleys and walls different shades. Mouths are visible in the valleys, but there are not usually

Isophyllia sinuosa (nat. size). Jamaica.

61

more than three per valley. Distance from mid-ridge to mid-ridge may be anything from 10 to 30 mm.

Septa are scarcely visible, but the position of septal spines is indicated by rows of small warts. The spines are strong and sharp and can be felt through the living tissue.

Skeleton

The valleys are deep and have steep sides. Septa run from the calice centers and are exsert by several millimeters as they pass over the walls. They are usually continuous between adjacent valleys but in some cases are notched at the top of the wall. Septal margins bear strong, long and sharp spines. The columella is spongy (trabecular).

SIMILARITIES

Isophyllia is distinguished from other meandrine corals by the fleshy mantle and prominent septal spines. It is unlikely to be confused with related mussids because none have the distinctive pattern of continuous ridges enclosing valleys.

DISTRIBUTION AND ECOLOGY   (Map #24)

Isophyllia is a fairly common coral, with colonies seldom exceeding 20 cm in diameter. It usually occurs in relatively shallow water on the back or fore reef. There are two species: *Isophyllia sinuosa* (Ellis & Solander, 1786), with valleys about 25 to 35 mm in width and 8 to 10 mm deep; and *Isophyllia multiflora* Verrill, 1901, with valleys about 10 to 20 mm wide and 5 to 10 mm deep.

Mycetophyllia Milne-Edwards & Haime, 1848

(Gr: *myketos,* knobbed; Gr: *phyllon,* leaf. Relating to the appearance of this coral, with its leaf-like form and rough, uneven surface.)

DESCRIPTION

Living coral   (Col. pl. p. 117)

Mycetophyllia may form massive, flattened heads, but more often it is encrusting with broad, leafy extensions. The living tissue is slightly fleshy and is green, bluish or brown in color. Often calice centers and ridges are paler, white or a contrasting color. Tentacles are not extended during the day.

Calices are separate and are spread over the surface of the corallum; the distance between calice

centers is usually between 5 to 15 mm. Calices are often superficial but may appear slightly raised due to the exsert spiny septa. Septa are continuous and appear as lines or as rows of warts linking adjacent calice centers. The warts correspond to the spines on the septal and septo costal margins.

The surface of the corallum is sometimes flat and even, but in many cases collines are present. These vary from low (a few mm) and rounded to high (2 cm) and leafy. They may be widely spaced or enclose only a single row of calices. In general the collines radiate from the center of the colony toward the margin but are discontinuous and do not form an unbroken pattern of valleys and ridges. The only exception to this is *Mycetophyllia ferox*. In this species, not only do the ridges tend to be continuous, but cross-walls are formed so that the calices may be completely enclosed.

Skeleton

Septa are prominent and continue as septocostae between calice centers. Their margins have spines that are tall, strong and sharply pointed. The columella is small and spiny.

SIMILARITIES

Mycetophyllia is readily identified as a mussid by the covering of large, sharp spines. It can usually

Mycetophyllia aliciae (X 1.1). Jamaica.

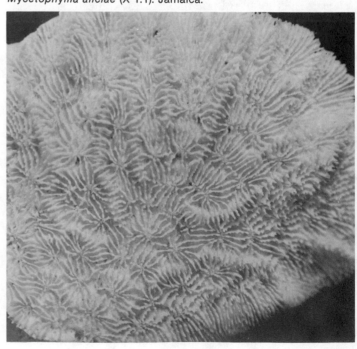

be distinguished from *Isophyllia* and *Isophyllastrea* by its large flattened corallum and by the lack of continuous unbroken walls. The only exception is *Mycetophyllia ferox,* in which some coralla have calices that are completely enclosed. This species is distinguished from the other genera by the relatively small calices (less than 1 cm diameter) and narrow walls (2 mm diameter).

DISTRIBUTION AND ECOLOGY (Map #25)

Mycetophyllia occurs mainly along the fore reef and is especially common in deeper water. Colonies may reach a meter in diameter and make an important contribution to reef-building. There are probably five species.

FAMILY CARYOPHYLLIIDAE

DESCRIPTION
Living coral (Col. pl. p. 120)

Several solitary caryophylliids occur in coral reef areas, even though they do not contribute to reef-building. These corals are cylindrical to trochoid in shape and are seldom more than 1 cm in diameter. They are often pale in color with transparent polyps. Septa are visible, and the larger ones are slightly or distinctly exsert. They have smooth margins.

Skeleton

Septa are in cycles, and higher cycles unite to lower. The corallite wall is solid. Costae may run a short way down the outside of the corallite wall. Septal and costal margins are smooth. The columella is well developed.

SIMILARITIES

There are several other solitary corals that can be mistaken for caryophylliids. Rhizangiids are distinguished by the non-exsert septa and dentate septal margins. Dendrophylliids resemble caryophylliids in having smooth septal margins, and it may be difficult to distinguish between the two underwater. An examination of the skeleton reveals that dendrophylliids have fused septa (Pourtales plan) and porous walls. *Gardineria* (family Flabellidae) is smaller than most caryophylliids (less than 5 mm diameter) and has fewer septa (12).

DISTRIBUTION AND ECOLOGY

Solitary caryophylliids occur to depths of thousands of meters, but there are some that are found in caverns and underhangs on shallow reef slopes. They are often overlooked because of their small size and cryptic habits. *Thalamophyllia riisei* (Duchassaing & Michelotti, 1860) is probably the commonest species, and there are also several species of *Caryophyllia*. Caryophylliids are widely distributed throughout temperate and tropical waters.

Eusmilia Milne-Edwards & Haime, 1848
Flower coral
(Gr: *eu-,* true; Gr: *smilion,* knife; Gr: *leios,* smooth. Presumably relating to the form and structure of the septa.)

DESCRIPTION
Living coral (Col. pl. pp. 117, 120, 121)

Eusmilia forms rounded colonies of prominent, well spaced corallites. The corallites are on long

Eusmilia fastigiata (X 2.4). Jamaica.

Eusmilia fastigiata (X 1.8). Jamaica.

FAMILY DENDROPHYLLIIDAE

Balanophyllia Wood, 1844
(Gr: *balanos,* acorn; Gr: *phyllon,* leaf. Referring to the growth form of this coral.)

DESCRIPTION
Living coral

Balanophyllia is a solitary coral that is cylindrical to trochoid in shape. Corallites are about 1.0 to 1.5 cm tall and around 1 cm wide at the top. They may appear grayish in deep water but brilliant orange or red toward the surface. A ring of tentacles is sometimes partially extended during the day.

The position of the larger septa is visible beneath the living tissues and their margins are smooth to the touch. Fine ridges run down the outside of the corallite wall.

Skeleton

Septa are numerous and drop steeply to a well developed spongy columella. They are arranged in cycles, and the inner ends of some of the cycles are curved and fused to their neighbors (Pourtales plan). Septal margins are smooth or granular, occasionally weakly dentate. Costal margins have small teeth. The corallum is porous, with the walls and septa pierced by small holes.

SIMILARITIES

There are several other solitary corals with which *Balanophyllia* could be confused. *Gardineria* (flabellid) is smaller, has a pinnacle-like columella and has fewer septa (12). Caryophylliids do not have the septa arranged according to the Pourtales plan and have a solid skeleton. Rhizangiids have dentate septal margins and a solid skeleton.

DISTRIBUTION AND ECOLOGY

Balanophyllia is a small, rare coral which is easily overlooked and generally prefers deeper water. It can occur at depths exceeding 1,000 meters. As many as 50 species have been described (worldwide), but it is probable that only about half this number are valid. Solitary dendrophylliids are widely distributed throughout temperate and tropical waters.

stalks arising from a common base (phaceloid growth form). The upper part of the colony expands as new corallites are produced. When corallites divide they normally give rise to separate corallites, but they may remain united and form elongate, sinuous calices (flabellate form). Single calices are rounded and about 1.5 cm in diameter. Polyps and tentacles are retracted during the day but expand at night to cover the skeleton. The corallum is yellowish, brown or bluish, and the tentacles are colorless.

Septa are prominent and leafy, and their margins are smooth. Costae are visible on the outside walls and are slightly rough to the touch.

Skeleton

Septa are numerous and in cycles. Septal margins are smooth. The smaller septa are not exsert, but larger ones are leafy and protrude by about 5 mm. They continue down the outside of the corallite wall as costae and have crenulated or minutely dentate margins. A small columella is present.

SIMILARITIES

Eusmilia is distinctive and unlikely to be confused with any other coral.

DISTRIBUTION AND ECOLOGY   (Map #26)

Eusmilia is fairly common and forms colonies to about 50 cm in diameter. It occurs in a variety of

Close-up of a polyp of the solitary coral *Balanophyllia bairdiana*. Photo by Keith Gillett from *Australian Seashores in Colour*.

Tubastraea Lesson, 1834

(L: *tubus,* tube; Gr: *aster,* star. Referring to the tube-like calices.)

DESCRIPTION

Living coral (Col. pl. pp. 121, 124)

Tubastraea forms low-growing clumps of corallites that arise from a common base. Polyps are sometimes partially extended during the day, and at night the corallum is hidden by a ring of bright yellow tentacles. The rest of the polyp is orange or red in color.

Corallites are cylindrical or turbinate, and the diameter across the top is about 1 cm. They are well separated (except where newly budded), and intervening perithecal areas appear smooth or faintly ridged. Living tissues are fleshy and obscure the smaller septa, but the major ones are just visible.

Skeleton

Septa are numerous and arranged in cycles. In young calices the inner ends of smaller septa curve and unite with their neighbors, but in mature calices they are free and normal. Septal margins are smooth or finely and irregularly dentate. Costae are present as low ridges. The skeleton is porous.

SIMILARITIES

Tubastraea has a characteristic growth form and color and is unlikely to be confused with other corals.

Tubastraea coccinea (× 2). Jamaica.

DISTRIBUTION AND ECOLOGY

Tubastraea has a restricted distribution and in general is absent from areas of dense coral growth. It prefers underhangs, drop-offs and the sides of boulders, and in these situations it may be common. It can grow in shallow water in current or wave-exposed sites, but also occurs in deeper water. There is only one species in the western Atlantic: *Tubastraea coccinea* Lesson, 1834. This species has a world-wide distribution throughout the tropics.

CLASS HYDROZOA

FAMILY MILLEPORIDAE

Millepora Linnaeus, 1758
Fire coral
(L: *mille,* thousand; L: *porus,* pore. A reference to the numerous small pores that cover the surface of the coral.)

DESCRIPTION

Living coral (Col. pl. pp. 124, 125, 128)

Millepora forms branched, plate-like, massive and encrusting colonies. Branches are rounded or flattened; the plates are upright and often fused with each other to form a box-like structure. *Millepora* is white, yellow or brown in color, and the surface of the coral appears smooth and structureless.

White hair-like tentacles are extended during the day, and these have a powerful and irritating sting. There are also stinging cells on the coenosteum, and thus *Millepora* has earned itself the name fire coral. A close examination reveals minute pores scattered over the surface of the coral.

Skeleton

The largest pores are about 0.1 mm in diameter and are referred to as gastropores. It is through these that the feeding polyps (gastrozooids) are extended. Around each gastropore are five to seven smaller pores known as dactylopores, which contain dactylozooids (defensive polyps). The surface of the coral is finely granulated and may be pitted with shallow cups. These are ampullae, receptacles for the reproductive medusae. The skeleton is pale yellow or yellow-brown.

SIMILARITIES

Millepora is readily distinguished from stony

(scleractinian) corals by the presence of minute featureless pores on the coral surface and the lack of corallites and septa. It is larger and more robust than its relative *Stylaster* and is never purple or red in color.

DISTRIBUTION AND ECOLOGY (Map #27)

Millepora is an important coral in terms of reef-building and is especially successful in shallow fore reef areas where it may form large tracts or colonies several meters in diameter. *Millepora* occurs in sheltered and exposed sites and thrives in both shallow and deep water. It can make use of other substrates apart from the reef itself; for example, it often forms encrustations over sea fans and sea whips. *Millepora* is the only coral to produce medusae, tiny "jellyfish" that contain the gametes.

There are probably three species, but the main differences are in growth form, so some authors consider that they are ecomorphs, *i.e.,* their morphological variations are produced simply as a result of environmental conditions.

FAMILY STYLASTERIDAE

Stylaster Gray, 1831

(Gr: *stylos,* style; Gr: *aster,* star; referring to the pillar-like structure in the center of each gastropore.)

DESCRIPTION

Living coral (Col. pl. p. 125)

Stylaster forms fragile branched colonies that do not exceed 10 cm in height. The branches are oriented in one plane, and the colonies are fan-like in shape. They are usually pink, purple or red, occasionally white. Minute white tentacles are sometimes visible.

Skeleton

There are larger gastropores (0.1 mm diameter) and smaller dactylopores scattered over the surface (see the description of *Millepora*). The gastropores have a style in the center that is visible under high magnification. The surface of the coral is pitted or granulated, and the pores are often slightly exsert.

SIMILARITIES

Stylaster is a distinctive coral that is unlikely to be confused either with scleractinians or with its close relative *Millepora*.

DISTRIBUTION AND ECOLOGY (Map #28)

Stylaster is generally restricted to caves and crevices on reef slopes but is occasionally found on the sides of boulders in shallower water. The common Caribbean species is *Stylaster roseus* (Pallas, 1766). *Stylaster duchassaingi* Pourtales is reported from Brazilian waters.

Indo-Pacific Reef Corals

LIST OF INDO-PACIFIC CORALS IN SEQUENCE COVERED

SCLERACTINIANS

FAMILY ASTROCOENIIDAE
    Stylocoeniella
FAMILY POCILLOPORIDAE
    Seriatopora
    Pocillopora
    Stylophora
    Palauastrea
    Madracis
FAMILY ACROPORIDAE
    Acropora
    Montipora

    Anacropora
    Astreopora
FAMILY AGARICIIDAE
    Pavona
    Gardineroseris
    Leptoseris
    Pachyseris
    Coeloseris
FAMILY SIDERASTREIDAE
    Siderastrea
    Pseudosiderastrea

Small islands off the west coast of Borneo, showing the development of fringing reefs.

Northwest Island on the Great Barrier Reef of Australia. It is surrounded by an extensive back reef (Photo: W. Deas).

The fore reef rim around Sumilon Island, Philippines. It supports luxuriant growths of coral and attracts many fish.

A shallow water "coral garden" or reef flat on a fringing reef off the coast of Borneo.

Corals grow in many forms and provide microhabitats for fish and other marine animals.

Coral blocks taken from reefs in Malaysia. The limestone is crushed and used as a basic material in the construction of roads and buildings.

A lime kiln in Indonesia. Coral is collected and fired to produce quicklime, a constltuent of cement.

Corals and shells for sale to tourists in Thailand. Such trade causes concern among conservationists.

Damaged reefs often fail to regain their former glory. This coral has been shattered by a fish bomb, and the fragments are now overgrown by algae.

Large gorgonian sea fans on the reef slope. Here they overshadow the hard corals, which can be seen at the bottom of the photograph. Philippines, 12 m depth.

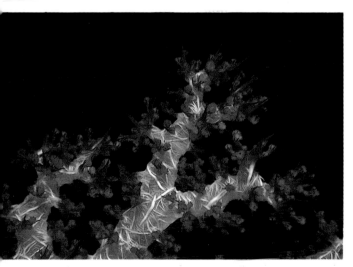

The soft coral *Dendronepthya* (class Alcyonaria). Around the polyps and embedded in the wall of the colony are sharp calcareous spinules. Sabah, Malaysia, 10 m depth.

Sarcophyton (class Alcyonaria) is one of the commonest soft corals on Indo-Pacific reefs. The upper surface of the fleshy colony is covered with long polyps which bear eight feathery tentacles.

69

Anomastrea
Coscinaraea
Horastrea
FAMILY THAMNASTERIIDAE
  Psammocora
FAMILY FUNGIIDAE
  Key to free-living fungiids
  Cycloseris
  Diaseris
  Fungia
  Heliofungia
  Herpetoglossa
  Herpolitha
  Polyphyllia
  Halomitra
  Sandalolitha
  Zoopilus
  Lithophyllon
  Podabacia
FAMILY PORITIDAE
  Goniopora
  Porites
  Alveopora
FAMILY FAVIIDAE
  Caulastrea
  Bikiniastrea
  Favia
  Favites
  Goniastrea
  Platygyra
  Leptoria
  Oulophyllia
  Hydnophora
  Plesiastrea
  Montastraea
  Diploastrea
  Oulastrea
  Leptastrea
  Cyphastrea
  Echinopora
  Moseleya

FAMILY TRACHYPHYLLIIDAE
  Trachyphyllia
  Wellsophyllia
FAMILY MEANDRINIDAE
  Ctenella
  Gyrosmilia
FAMILY FLABELLIDAE
FAMILY RHIZANGIIDAE
FAMILY OCULINIDAE
  Galaxea
  Acrhelia
FAMILY MERULINIDAE
  Merulina
  Clavarina
  Scapophyllia
FAMILY MUSSIDAE
  Blastomussa
  Cynarina
  Scolymia
  Acanthastrea
  Lobophyllia
  Symphyllia
FAMILY PECTINIIDAE
  Echinophyllia
  Oxypora
  Mycedium
  Physophyllia
  Pectinia
FAMILY CARYOPHYLLIIDAE
  Solitary and ahermatypic caryophylliids
  Euphyllia (Euphyllia)
  Euphyllia (Fimbriaphyllia)
  Catalaphyllia
  Plerogyra
  Physogyra
FAMILY DENDROPHYLLIIDAE
  Solitary Dendrophylliids
  Dendrophyllia
  Tubastraea
  Turbinaria

NON-SCLERACTINIANS

FAMILY MILLEPORIDAE
  Millepora
FAMILY STYLASTERIDAE
  Stylaster
  Distichopora

FAMILY HELIOPORIDAE
  Heliopora
FAMILY TUBIPORIDAE
  Tubipora

CLASS ANTHOZOA
FAMILY ASTROCOENIIDAE

Stylocoeniella Yabe and Sugiyama, 1935
(Gr: *stylos,* pillar; Gr: *koinos,* shared; L: *ellus,* suffix denoting diminutive. Relating to the small pillar that occurs on the shared walls.)

DESCRIPTION
Living coral
(Col. pl. p. 128)

Stylocoeniella generally forms brown-red or greenish encrustations that are seldom more than a few centimeters in diameter. Small knobby and columnar colonies have been reported from the Great Barrier Reef (Veron and Pichon, 1976). A ring of 12 small pale brown tentacles may be extended during the day.

The corallites are crowded closely together or separated by coenosteum covered with minute spines. Calices are round, about 0.5 to 1.0 mm in diameter and are not raised above the coral surface. The septa are barely visible.

Stylocoeniella armata. Bali, Indonesia, 20 m depth.

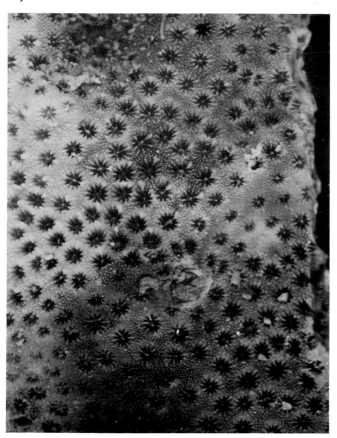

Skeleton

There are 12 septa arranged in two cycles of six. In the great majority of cases the upper outer edge of one of the primary septa is raised into a styliform (calicular) pillar. This is situated on the calice wall and is less than one millimeter in height. Septal margins are finely serrated. A pinnacle-like columella is present.

SIMILARITIES

The growth form of the colony and the size and arrangement of calices can cause *Stylocoeniella* to be mistaken for *Montipora, Porites* or *Pocillopora.* The most reliable way of identifying *Stylocoeniella* is to examine the surface of the corallum for styliform pillars that can just be made out underwater. These are different in appearance from the hoods associated with the corallites in *Stylophora.*

Useful diagnostic features for *Stylocoeniella* are shown in Table 2.

DISTRIBUTION AND ECOLOGY
(Map #29)

Stylocoeniella is an inconspicuous coral and is readily overlooked among other larger and more exotic reef corals. It often grows in crevices or on the undersides of rocks or corals and may be fairly common in certain localities.

There are two species: *Stylocoeniella armata* (Ehrenberg, 1834), with the second cycle of septa approximately the same size as the first cycle, found from the Maldives to Enewetak; and *Stylocoeniella guentheri* (Bassett-Smith, 1890), with the second cycle of septa only weakly developed, found from the Red Sea to Tahiti.

FAMILY POCILLOPORIDAE

Seriatopora Lamarck, 1816
(L: *seriatus,* arranged in series; L: *porus,* pore. Relating to the arrangement of the calices.)

DESCRIPTION
Living coral
(Col. pl. p. 128)

Colonies are always branched, and it is common for branches to cross and coalesce. In most cases the branches are narrow, about 5 mm in diameter and taper to a fine, delicate point. Occasionally they are stouter and sturdier, with the tips of the

One Tree Island, Great Barrier Reef. The shallow reef flat is well developed and drops away to deep water beyond the island (Photo: F. Talbot).

Oeno Atoll in the Pitcairn group (central Pacific). A circle of shallow coral reefs and small islands encloses a lagoon, and to the outside are deep oceanic waters (Photo: G. Allen).

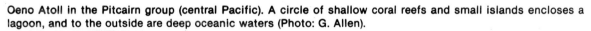

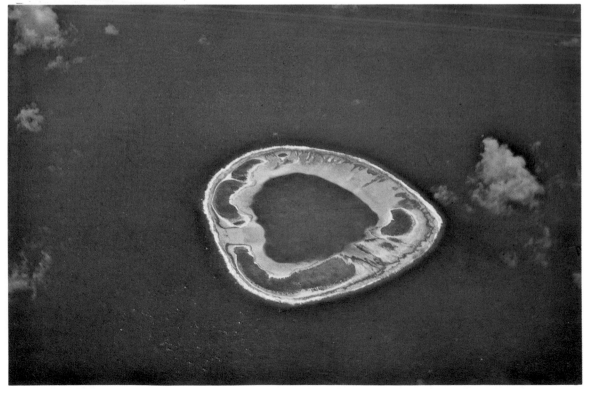

A variety of species and growth forms of corals can be seen in this view of a western Pacific reef. Photo by Michio Goto, from *Marine Life Documents*.

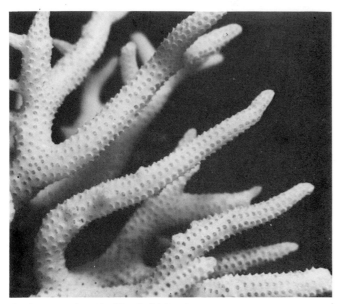

Seriatopora hystrix (X 1.6). Malaysia.

Veron and Pichon (1976) recognize two from the Great Barrier Reef: *Seriatopora hystrix* Dana, 1846 ("an extremely polymorphic species") and *Seriatopora caliendrum* Ehrenberg, 1834.

The branches in *S. hystrix* are usually tapering, with finely pointed ends; occasionally they end abruptly. Diameter toward the tip is between 1.5 and 4.5 mm, and the angle of the branches is between 30° and 80°. The branches in *S. caliendrum* do not taper and usually have blunt ends. Diameter toward the tip is between 3 and 8 mm, and the average angle of branching is between 60° and 80°. The two species are not easy to distinguish, and comparisons should always be made between specimens from the same biotope.

branches rounded. The majority of colonies are pink or white, but shades of brown and green occur. Often the tips of the branches are paler.

Calices are small (0.5 to 1.5 mm diameter) and rounded. They are arranged in straight or slightly spiralling rows along the branches. They do not protrude, although hoods (as in *Stylophora*) may occasionally be present. A ring of tiny simple tentacles is sometimes visible.

Skeleton

The intervening surface between calices is covered with minute tubercles. A styliform columella is present, and there are six often poorly developed septa and sometimes rudiments of a second cycle.

SIMILARITIES

Seriatopora can usually be identified by its characteristic growth form; other distinguishing features are shown in Table 2.

DISTRIBUTION AND ECOLOGY   (Map #30)

Seriatopora is widespread and common, but colonies are usually isolated and there is less tendency to form large tracts than there is in *Pocillopora*. The most delicate, finely branched forms are found on sheltered reef slopes, the sturdier forms in more exposed areas.

About 28 species have been described, but probably only five or six can be considered true species.

Pocillopora Lamarck, 1816
(L: *pocillum,* cup or bowl; L: *porus,* pore. Presumably relating to the appearance of the calices, which look like tiny, shallow cups.)

DESCRIPTION
Living coral   (Col. pl. pp. 128, 129)

Most *Pocillopora* colonies are arborescent, but occasionally massive or encrusting growth forms are found. Branches usually have rounded tips, but

Pocillopora verrucosa (X 1.8). Malaysia.

Genus	Growth form	Calice arrangement	Coenosteum	Corallite wall	Verrucae	Septa	Skeleton
Seriatopora	Slender branches with fine branch tips; branches may fuse	In rows; usually well spaced	Where present covered with minute tubercles (invisible underwater)	Rarely with small hoods	Not present	Usually 6 poorly developed septa	
Pocillopora	Usually branched and with stout branch tips; occasionally massive or encrusting	Not in rows; may be crowded		No projections	Usually present	12 poorly developed septa	Imperforate
Stylophora				With hood arched over calice	Not present	Usually 12 septa, 6 of which are well developed	
Palauastrea	Moderately stout branches with rounded or slightly knobbed ends			May be circle of granules		12 septa: 6 broad & well developed	
Madracis	Encrusting, submassive or branched			Well formed from ridge of fused granules		Usually 10 well developed septa	
Stylocoeniella	Usually encrusting, occasionally semi-massive	Not in rows; may be crowded or well spaced	Minute spines	No hood, but often a small pillar between the calices		6 or 12 well developed septa	
Montipora	Usually leafy, encrusting or semi-massive; may be branched	Not in rows; may be crowded	Smooth or with prominent tubercles that obscure the calices	No projections		Small or rudimentary	Perforate

Table 2. Features that assist in the diagnosis of pocilloporids, *Stylocoeniella* and *Montipora*, corals with small superficial calices and other features in common.

there is a great deal of variation in overall dimensions of the branches. Color varies through shades of green, brown and yellow, but pink is probably the most common. Each polyp has a ring of 12 small tentacles that may be extended during the day. These may be colorless or colored, sometimes with the tip a different shade. When the tentacles are retracted the calice is outlined by a fine dark ring.

Calices are small (0.5 to 1.0 mm diameter), rounded or angular and do not protrude. They are often so crowded that the corallite walls touch. This occurs especially at the branch tips. In many cases the corallites are borne on rudimentary branchlets called verrucae, which protrude from the main corallum.

Skeleton

Corallite walls and intervening surfaces are armed with tiny tubercles that make the surface slightly rough to the touch. Septa are in two cycles but are usually rudimentary. The columella is absent or present as a low blunt spine.

SIMILARITIES

Pocillopora can be mistakenly identified as *Stylophora* or *Seriatopora*, both of which are com-

An antipatharian or black coral (class Ceriantipatharia) with slender branches strengthened by an internal skeleton of horny material. When large enough, the basal portion of the colony is exploited for jewelry. Bahamas, 24 m depth (Photo: P. Colin).

The black coral *Antipathes pennacea* may grow 1.5 m high and has a series of feather-like branches with lateral pinnules. These bear tiny polyps with unbranched tentacles. Puerto Rico, 27 m depth (Photo: P. Colin).

The gorgonian *Eunicea*, with closely set polyps covering the branches. Bahamas, 12 m depth (Photo: P. Colin).

The corallimorpharian *Ricordia florida* (class Zoantharia). This "false coral" grows in low clumps and the polyps have rings of short, unbranched tentacles. There is no skeleton. Puerto Rico, 1 m depth (Photo: P. Colin).

mon on most reefs. Differences are shown in Table 2. There are two other close relatives, *Palauastrea* and *Madracis*, but *Madracis* is seldom found on reefs while *Palauastrea* has a restricted range and prefers muddy substrates. These two genera are also included in Table 2.

DISTRIBUTION AND ECOLOGY   (Map #31)

Pocillopora is common on most reefs, especially along the reef front, where it may occur in dense banks. An examination of the branch tips often reveals cage-like structures that are occupied by the gall crab *Hapalocarcinus marsupialis*.

Thirty-five species have been described since 1758, but intraspecific variation is so great that probably fewer than ten are valid species.

Stylophora Schweigger, 1819
(Gr: *stylos*, style or pillar; Gr: *phero*, to bear. Probably referring to the hooded corallites characteristic of the genus.)

DESCRIPTION
Living coral   (Col. pl. pp. 129. 192)

Growth form in *Stylophora* varies from branched to massive. Branches have rounded tips and are generally at least 1 cm in diameter. Colonies are usually pale brown with the tips of the

Stylophora pistillata (X 1.8). Malaysia.

branches paler, sometimes pink or purplish with the branch ends white. Each polyp has a single ring of tiny tentacles that are sometimes extended during the day.

The surface of the corallum is slightly rough to the touch because most or all of the calices are hooded. The hood is a delicate arched structure just visible to the naked eye and corresponds to part of the corallite wall. Calices are small (about 0.6 to 1.5 mm in diameter) and either round or polygonal. The area between calices appears smooth. The depth of the fossa is variable, and calices situated toward the branch tips are generally deeper than those lower down the colony.

Skeleton

There are six main septa that unite with a styliform columella. A second cycle of six septa may also be present. Costae are not present. Perithecal areas are covered with minute tubercles.

SIMILARITIES

See Table 2 and the comments for *Pocillopora*, which also apply to *Stylophora*.

DISTRIBUTION AND ECOLOGY   (Map #32)

Occasional; usually found along the reef front rather than the back reef or reef slope. There is considerable range in growth form, but in general the quieter the water the more branched the colony.

Over ten species have been described for this genus, but it appears that there is a great deal of growth form variation and that there are only a few polymorphic species. Veron and Pichon (1976) describe only *Stylophora pistillata* (Esper, 1797) from the Great Barrier Reef in Australia.

Palauastrea Yabe & Sugiyama, 1941
(Named after the location where this genus was first discovered, the Palau Islands in the western Pacific; Gr: *aster*, star.)

DESCRIPTION
Living coral

Palauastrea forms branched colonies that may be up to 30 cm tall. The branches taper gradually and usually have a rounded or slightly knobby extremity. In some colonies the branches fuse

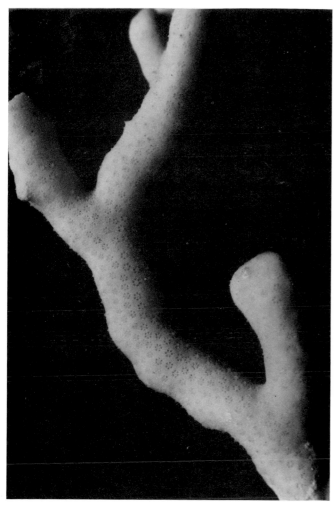

Palauastrea ramosa (X 1.8). Malaysia.

together, a feature characteristic of *Seriatopora*. The coral is light brown or pinkish in color with a yellow oral disc. There are 12 yellow to pinkish brown tentacles.

Calices are round and regular, approximately 0.6 to 0.8 mm in diameter and do not protrude. They are usually about 1 mm apart but are more crowded toward the branch tips. The calices do not have a distinct wall, but a circle of granules may be present that gives the impression of a wall.

Skeleton

Perithecal areas are covered with small spines. Six broad septa of the first cycle reach the columella. Septa of the second cycle are less well developed and may be very small. Septal margins are beaded. The columella is well developed and projects as a distinct spine from a broad base.

SIMILARITIES

Palauastrea can be confused with *Stylophora*

and other seriatoporids and also has affinities with *Stylocoeniella* (see Table 2).

DISTRIBUTION AND ECOLOGY (Map #33)

Palauastrea occurs in relatively shallow water on sheltered coral reef slopes covered with a layer of fine deposits. It may be common in such areas, and the colonies are frequently unattached. There is a single species: *Palauastrea ramosa* Yabe & Sugiyama, 1941.

Madracis Milne-Edwards & Haime, 1849
(Ital: *madre,* mother; Gr: *akis,* point. Possibly a reference to the small spines that surround the calices and form the wall.)

DESCRIPTION
Living coral

Madracis forms small encrusting, submassive or branched colonies. These are usually green to pinkish in color, sometimes with the oral discs green. There are about 20 tentacles arranged in two rows.

Madracis kirbyi (X 2.8). Malaysia.

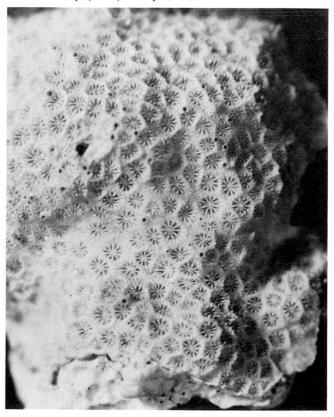

79

The polyps of alcyonarians are readily recognized by the ring of eight feathery tentacles. This unidentified soft coral was photographed in the Red Sea (Photo: M. Melzac).

A zeniid soft coral (class Alcyonaria), whose tentacles open and close rhythmically every few seconds. Sabah, Malaysia, 15 m depth.

The anemone-like polyps of a zoanthid. The polyps are united by creeping stolons and have a ring of tiny tentacles around the edge of the oral disk. Sabah, Malaysia, 5 m depth.

The scleractinian coral *Euphyllia*, in which the tentacles protrude from calcareous "cups" (corallites). These are easily felt beneath the thin covering layer of tissue (coenosarc). Sabah, Malaysia, 6 m depth.

Tiny flatworms live in association with some corals, but little is known about the relationship between the two organisms. These small brown worms are creeping on the expanded vesicles of the "bubble" coral, *Plerogyra*. Sabah, Malaysia, 30 m depth.

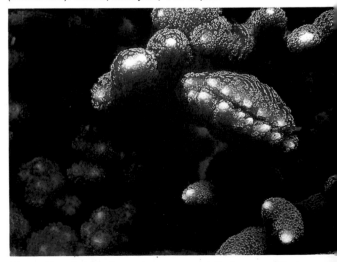

The gall crab *Hapalocarcinus marsupialis* has modified the tip of a branch of the coral *Pocillopora* to form a cage-like structure in which it is trapped. Sabah, Malaysia, 6 m depth.

The zoanthid *Palythoa caribbea* is sometimes mistaken for a true coral. It is distinguished by the fleshy rather than calcareous base in which the polyps are embedded. Puerto Rico, 1.5 m depth (Photo: P. Colin).

The goby *Gobiosoma illecebrosum* on the coral *Colpophyllia natans*. Various fish, especially gobies, spend their entire lives in association with a particular species and colony of coral. Colombia (Photo: C. Roessler).

Madracis kirbyi (X 5). Malaysia.

Calices are small, superficial and often crowded but may be separated by coenosteum. They are rounded or polygonal and about 2 mm in diameter, occasionally 3 mm. Corallites are usually bounded by a narrow ridge that is just visible underwater. A ring of septa can also be seen.

Skeleton

There are usually ten septa, but occasionally smaller calices are found with only eight and larger ones with 18 to 20. Eight to ten septa reach the columella, which is styliform and well developed. Septa are narrow and have smooth or finely spinulose margins with one or two prominent lobes. Each corallite is bounded by a ring of spines or granules that may be united into a ridge.

SIMILARITES

Madracis is distinguished from other members of its family by the possession of ten rather than six or 12 septa. Further details and comparisons are shown in Table 2.

Madracis also bears a superficial resemblance to *Porites* because both genera have small, crowded calices. In the living coral the corallite wall and septa are more prominent in *Madracis* than in *Porites*.

The skeleton is easily distinguished because it is porous in *Porites*, solid in *Madracis*.

DISTRIBUTION AND ECOLOGY   (Map #34)

Madracis is probably widely distributed but apparently is nowhere abundant and is generally uncommon on reefs. Several species are ahermatypic (non-reef-building), and there are probably eight or ten species world-wide. *Madracis kirbyi* Veron & Pichon, 1976, occurs on shallow Indo-Pacific reefs.

FAMILY ACROPORIDAE

Acropora Oken, 1815

(Gr: *akron,* extremity or summit; L: *porus,* pore. Relating to the presence of a corallite at the tip of each branch.)

DESCRIPTION

Living coral   (Col. pl. pp. 129, 132)

Branched *Acropora* colonies are abundant and show infinite variety, even within species. Massive or encrusting colonies are rarely seen. Among the branched forms it is possible to recognize staghorns, clusters, plates and tables, and between them lie many intermediates. The branches of staghorn *Acropora* are usually over 10 cm in length and may be 1.5 cm or more in width. They arise from a single main stem and rarely fuse. Clusters consist of profusely divided branches that form a thicket of branchlets. The latter are usually less than 5 mm in diameter and may interlock. Plates and tables have a short, stout stem attached by a spreading base. Branches arise from the top of the stem and spread in a horizontal rather than a vertical direction, often fusing together. The closely set and interlocking branches form a roughly circular plate sometimes two or three meters in diameter. Young colonies do not fall into these categories because virtually all are encrusting or knobby. *Acropora* species are among the most brightly colored corals on the reef. Often they are blue, green, purple or pink, sometimes cream, yellow, brown or red. The branch tips are usually paler. Each polyp has six or 12 slender tentacles that when extended may be 3 or 4 mm long. They are often white.

Acropora is easily recognized by the shape and general characteristics of the corallites. In branched colonies the corallites are of two types.

At the branch tip is a symmetrical and usually larger axial corallite, and down the length of the branches are many smaller asymmetrical ones. These radial corallites have been budded off from the axial corallite, and any of the radial polyps have the capacity to take up this reproductive role. Lobed or semi-massive colonies have scattered axial corallites, but they are scarcely more prominent than the others.

Corallites are round in cross section and protrude several millimeters from the surface. Radial corallites often protrude only on one side because they lie at an angle to the branch. The size of corallites varies even in a single specimen, but their width is around 1.5 to 2.5 mm. It is common for the corallite wall to be fairly thick and the fossa relatively small. Calices are often crowded with the walls touching.

Skeleton

The coenosteum is usually pitted or porous and covered with tiny blunt spines. There are normally 12 septa, but these are small and may be poorly developed. There is no columella.

SIMILARITIES

Semi-massive *Acropora* colonies can be mistaken for *Astreopora*. In this genus, however, the corallites are distinctly cone-shaped and the lip of the corallite wall is not expanded as it often is in *Acropora*. Additionally, there are no axial corallites in *Astreopora*.

DISTRIBUTION AND ECOLOGY (Map #35)

Acropora is an extremely important genus in terms of both species diversity and general abundance. Over 300 species have been described throughout the world, but it is thought that many of these can sensibly be grouped together, bringing the true total down to at least half that number.

Throughout its range, *Acropora* can be found on any stretch of reef and is often the dominant coral, especially along the reef front. Staghorn and plate forms flourish in sheltered areas, whereas clusters and semi-massive types can withstand more exposed conditions. Species that occur from the reef top to the reef slope become gradually more flattened with depth.

Most *Acropora* colonies provide shelter for fishes, especially juveniles, and are also a source of food for butterflyfishes and others. *Acropora* species grow rapidly because of their porous

skeleton and branched habit and will re-establish themselves readily if damaged.

Montipora de Blainville, 1830
(L: *mons,* mountain; L: *porus,* pore. Presumably relating to the tubercles that are often a feature of the corallum and which sometimes bear calices.)

DESCRIPTION

Living coral (Col. pl. pp. 133, 192)

Montipora may form leafy, encrusting, plate-like, branching or semi-massive colonies, and there are numerous intermediates. Color variation is equally wide, and colonies may be blue, brown, yellow, green, pink, purple or red. Polyps are small and may be retracted or extended during the day. The tentacles are small and often white in color.

Calices are round, about 0.5 mm in diameter, rarely more than 1 mm. They may be well separated or crowded together, but in either case the calice wall is indistinct. They are often difficult to distinguish because of a tendency for the coral surface to be covered with papillae, tubercles or ridges. These protuberances may separate calices, or calices may be borne on their sides or summits. The calices themselves do not protrude.

Skeleton

Septa are small or rudimentary, and the col-

Montipora sp. (X 2.8). Malaysia.

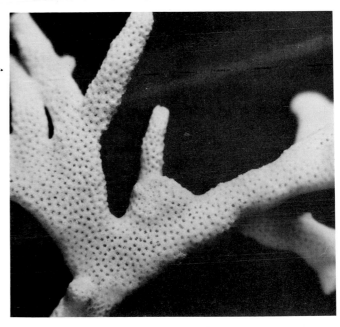

The two branches of spiralling tentacles belong to the tube-worm *Spirobranchus giganteus*. In this case the body of the worm is buried within the skeleton of the coral *Porites*, but it has been found in association with a great many other corals in both the Caribbean and Indo-Pacific. Sabah, Malaysia, 3 m depth.

A number of molluscs make corals their permanent home. Some bore into the skeleton and remain hidden from view, but the giant clam (*Tridacna*) always exposes its brightly colored mantle and so is readily seen. Sabah, Malaysia, 4 m depth.

The predatory crown-of-thorns starfish, *Acanthaster planci*, feeds on coral polyps. Where it occurs in "plague" proportions it can cause considerable damage to reefs. Sabah, Malaysia, 5 m depth.

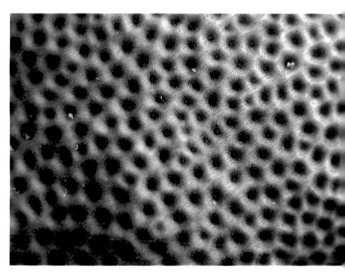

Siderastrea siderea. Jamaica, 15 m depth.

Stephanocoenia michelinii. Jamaica, 18 m depth.

Stephanocoenia michelinii. Jamaica, 18 m depth.

Acropora cervicornis. Bahamas, 9 m depth (Photo: P. Colin).

Acropora prolifera. Bahamas, 12 m depth (Photo: P. Colin).

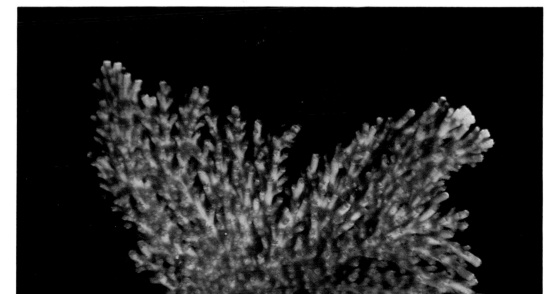

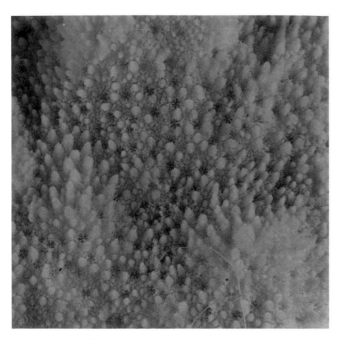

Montipora sp. (X 4). Malaysia.

umella is rarely developed. The skeleton of *Montipora* is highly porous, and perithecal areas are formed by a network of small spines and trabeculae. Species that lack surface projections are termed glabrous.

SIMILARITIES

Foliaceous *Montipora,* generally known as lettuce corals, are usually unmistakable, but some of the branched and encrusting colonies can be confused with other genera. This confusion arises especially with species that lack the highly ornamented coral surface described above. In these cases *Montipora* may be mistaken for *Porites, Stylocoeniella* or occasionally for members of the family Pocilloporidae. *Porites* can be identified by its larger calices (1.0 to 1.5 mm diameter), shared corallite walls and moderately well developed septa and columella. Differences between *Montipora* and the other genera are shown in Table 2.

DISTRIBUTION AND ECOLOGY (Map #36)

Montipora is common and widespread and often contributes significantly to overall coral cover. Some foliaceous colonies may grow well over one meter in diameter. These forms in particular provide shelter for such animals as featherstars and crabs that creep among the leaves. Barnacles and fanworms often inhabit the massive or encrusting forms.

At least 45 species have been described, but there is a great deal of variation within species, and it is possible that less than half are true species.

Anacropora Ridley, 1884
(Gr: *an-*, without; Gr: *akron,* extremity or summit; L: *porus,* pore. Relating to the absence of a leading or axial corallite at each branch tip.)

DESCRIPTION
Living coral
This delicate coral forms small branched colonies that seldom reach 10 cm in height. The branches may be clustered or more widely spreading and sometimes fuse together. They are less than 5 mm in width and usually taper to a fine point.

Calices are rounded and between 0.5 and 1.0 mm in diameter. They are raised by less than 1 mm from the coral surface and are well spaced. In *Anacropora spinosa* most corallites lie at the base of a sharp spine several millimeters in length.

Perithecal areas appear smooth or faintly granular. Septa are scarcely visible.

Skeleton
There are usually six main septa and additional secondary ones, but in some cases the septa are poorly developed. The coenosteum between the calices is porous and covered with small tubercles, some of which join to form a reticulate structure.

Anacropora spinosa (X 4.7). Malaysia.

Anacropora spinosa (X 2.2). Malaysia.

SIMILARITIES

Anacropora is distinguished from *Acropora* by the lack of axial corallites and by its well spaced, almost superficial calices. These last two features also prevent it from being confused with other corals such as *Seriatopora, Porites* and their relatives.

DISTRIBUTION AND ECOLOGY (Map #37)

There are few records for this coral, and it is difficult to give detailed information on its distribution. It is not necessarily particularly rare but may easily be overlooked because of its small size and superficial resemblance to *Acropora*. It is generally found on soft substrates of lower reef slopes in clear or slightly turbid water. In certain areas it may occur in extensive tracts. There are probably five species.

Astreopora de Blainville, 1830
(Gr: *aster,* star; L: *porus,* pore. Presumably relating to the appearance of this coral with its prominent corallites.)

DESCRIPTION
Living coral (Col. pl. pp. 133, 136)

Astreopora forms rounded heads or encrusting colonies. Leafy extensions may grow from the lat-ter, especially if the colony is growing on a sheltered reef slope. Yellow, brown, green and pink are probably the commonest colors, but blue and purple colonies are also found. Often the calice rims are a different color from the rest of the colony. Tentacles are tiny and are seldom seen during the day.

Corallites are distinct and separate. They are round in cross section, and most protrude a few millimeters in the shape of a truncated cone. The diameter across the base of the cone is usually about 3 to 4 mm, but the width at the top is often less than half that. The corallite walls are thick, and the fossa is only about 1 mm in diameter. Septa are not visible. The area between corallites has a slightly rough, granular appearance.

Skeleton

The skeleton of *Astreopora* is porous, and between the corallites the surface has a reticulate appearance. There are numerous tiny spines that produce the rough appearance of the living coral. Septa are extremely poorly developed.

SIMILARITIES

Astreopora has a similar appearance to the faviid coral *Cyphastrea*, but the two are easily distinguished by examining the corallites. They appear as empty pits in *Astreopora*, while in *Cyphastrea* the cavity is crossed by well developed

Astreopora ocellata (X 2.2). Malaysia.

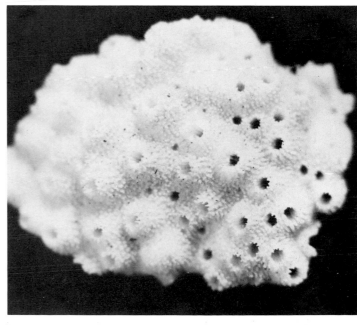

Agaricia agaricites. Bahamas, 8 m depth (Photo: P. Colin).

Agaricia tenuifolia. Puerto Rico, 15 m depth (Photo: P. Colin).

Madracis mirabilis. Jamaica, 18 m depth.

Madracis mirabilis. Jamaica, 6 m depth.

Agaricia agaricites. Jamaica, 19 m depth.

Agaricia sp. Jamaica, 20 m depth.

Porites astreoides. Jamaica, 18 m depth.

Porites porites. Jamaica, 10 m depth.

septa that reach the central columella. *Astreopora* is distinguished from its close relative *Acropora* by its growth form, lack of axial corallites, and larger corallite size.

DISTRIBUTION AND ECOLOGY (Map #38)

Astreopora is found at all depths and on most reefs but is much less common than its relatives *Acropora* and *Montipora*. Colonies are often small but may grow to half a meter or more in diameter. At least 20 species have been described, but the true number is probably considerably fewer.

FAMILY AGARICIIDAE

Pavona Lamarck, 1801

(L: *pavo,* peacock. Presumably relating to the arrangement of the septa that have an attractive appearance similar to the pattern of feathers on a peacock's tail.)

DESCRIPTION

Living coral (Col. pl. pp. 136, 137)

Pavona forms foliaceous, encrusting or massive colonies. Foliaceous types may have fronds that are entire and flat or twisted and fused together. In general, calices are on both sides of vertically growing fronds or plates but on the upper face only of horizontal folia. Most colonies are pale brown. Some show shades of gray, pink, purple, green or yellow, and often the tops of the collines are paler or white. In some cases the calices are a different color from the rest of the coral. Tiny tentacles less than a millimeter in length are sometimes extended during the day.

Calices are round, polygonal or oval. In many species hillocks called collines are present between the calices. These are usually acute and may be elongate. Some enclose a single calice, but most surround a short series, giving a complicated system of ridges and grooves. In *Pavona clavus* there are low walls between the calices. These are usually shared, but occasionally calices are separated, each with its own wall. Calice diameter is usually between 2 and 3 mm.

Septa are visible as fine lines running from one calice center to the next, continuing uninterrupted over walls and collines. Often they form characteristic star-shaped patterns over the surface of the corallum. They are extremely fine, and the coral is smooth to the touch.

Pavona maldivensis (X 3.5). Malaysia.

Skeleton

The septa are in cycles, and not all reach the columella. In some cases the columella lies deep within the fossa or is poorly developed. The septal edges are smooth or extremely finely serrated.

SIMILARITIES

Pavona can be confused with other agariciids, particularly *Gardineroseris* and *Leptoseris* and also with species belonging to the family Siderastreidae. Features that help to distinguish these corals are shown in Table 3.

DISTRIBUTION AND ECOLOGY (Map #39)

Pavona is a fairly common coral that is found in most reef habitats. Some of the massive colonies are large, and the foliaceous ones may form extensive tracts.

At least 53 species have been described, including species of the subgenera *Polyastra* and *Pseudocolumnastraea*. Recent studies (Veron and Pichon, 1980) have indicated that there is great variability within species. These authors recognize only eight species from the eastern Australian region, and it seems possible that only around 12 to 15 occur within the Indo-Pacific region as a whole.

Gardineroseris Scheer & Pillai, 1974
(For J. Stanley Gardiner; Gr: *seris*, lettuce.)

DESCRIPTION
Living coral (Col. pl. p. 137)
Colonies are usually massive and columnar but may be encrusting or partially foliaceous. They are pale to dark brown in color but occasionally purplish. The tentacles are not extended during the day.

Calices are polygonal, irregular or elongate, their diameter between 2 and 5 mm. They are closely packed, and the corallite walls are shared, narrow and prominent. There may be several centers enclosed within one wall. The walls are several millimeters high, and the septa dip down steeply to the fossa. Septa are visible as numerous fine lines that run from the center of the calice over the walls to adjacent calices. The coral surface is smooth to the touch.

Skeleton
Septa are arranged in cycles, and only the larger ones run from one calice to the next. They are usually slightly expanded at their inner ends, and their upper margins are smooth or granular. The columella is a small pinnacle.

SIMILARITIES
Gardineroseris is occasionally mistaken for *Pavona* but can readily be distinguished by its larger calice size and by the high walls that enclose the calices. It also has features in common with other agariciids, which are indicated in Table 3.

DISTRIBUTION AND ECOLOGY (Map #40)
Gardineroseris can be found in most reef habitats but is not a particularly common coral. There is a single species, *Gardineroseris planulata* (Dana, 1846), that was originally described as *Agaricia planulata* and has also been referred to as *Agaricia ponderosa* Gardiner, 1906.

Leptoseris Milne-Edwards & Haime, 1849
(Gr: *leptos,* slender; Gr: *seris,* lettuce. Referring to the leafy form of this coral.)

DESCRIPTION
Living coral (Col. pl. p. 137)
Most *Leptoseris* colonies have an encrusting base with extensive lateral folia or ascending leafy scrolls and crests. Some species are encrusting. They are brown, green, dark red or gray, often with the tips of the scrolls and crests paler or white. Tentacles are not generally extended during the day.

Calices are present only on the upper surfaces of the folia but on both sides of vertical scrolls. They are often swollen and protuberant. The undersides of folia are smooth or faintly ridged. Calicular boundaries are often indistinct because septa are continuous between adjacent calice centers. This arrangement makes it difficult to assess calice diameter with accuracy, but it lies approximately between 2 and 5 mm (and may reach 12 mm).

Collines may be present, especially in encrusting forms. They are usually high and distinct, enclose a series of mouths, and are about 1 to 3 mm wide. In other forms the calices are more widely spaced. Septocostae are visible as fine lines running over the surface of the coral between calices. The surface of the coral is smooth or slightly rough to the touch.

Gardineroseris planulata (X 4.8). Malaysia.

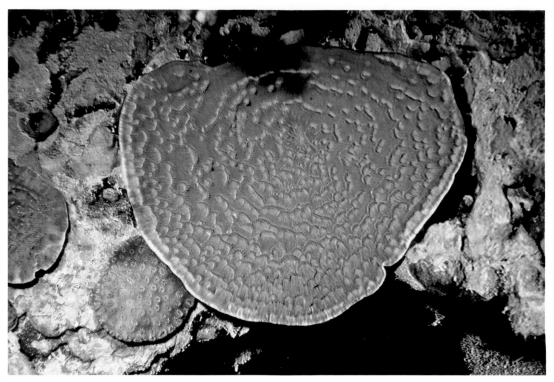

Leptoseris cucullata. Jamaica, 18 m depth (Photo: P. Colin).

Porites astreoides. Bahamas, 15 m depth (Photo: P. Colin).

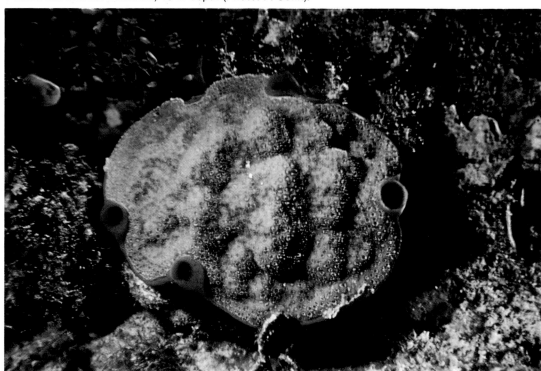

Porites porites. Bahamas, 10 m depth (Photo: P. Colin).

Cladocora arbuscula. Puerto Rico, 9 m depth (Photo: P. Colin).

Skeleton

Septa and septocostae are numerous and closely packed. Most run uninterrupted from one calice center to the next, but there are sometimes a few smaller, shorter ones between. Septocostal margins are granular or finely to coarsely serrated. Often the serrations are well spaced. Septocostae are perforate or imperforate. The columella is weakly to well developed, sometimes absent.

SIMILARITIES

In many cases *Leptoseris* is readily identified by its thin, leafy corallum. In this respect it can resemble certain pectiniids (*e.g., Oxypora, Mycedium*), but it lacks the sharp and prominent septal and septocostal spines. *Leptoseris* is distinguished from its close relative *Pavona* by the larger, usually more protuberant and widely spaced calices. In addition, the septocostal margins in *Leptoseris* are more coarsely serrated, and the septa and septocostae comparitively stouter. However, as pointed out by Dinesen (1980), "the distinction between *Leptoseris* and some unifacial *Pavona* species is still somewhat uncertain." For example, she considers *Pavona yabei* as a *Pavona*, while Veron and Pichon (1980) believe it is a *Leptoseris*. *Leptoseris mycetoseroides* is another problematical species which has clear affinities with *Pavona*.

DISTRIBUTION AND ECOLOGY   (Map #41)

Leptoseris is not a particularly common coral. It

Leptoseris hawaiiensis (X 2.8). Malaysia.

is often concealed in slightly shaded places on the reef slope, such as the sides of boulders or in caverns and underhangs. It often occurs in deep water and is reported from 470 m at Hawaii (Vaughan, 1907).

Twenty-eight species have been described, but *Leptoseris* shows a great deal of natural variation, and a revision by Dineson (1980) has shown that there are only nine valid Indo-Pacific species.

Leptoseris glabra (X 2). Malaysia.

Pachyseris Milne-Edwards & Haime, 1849

(Gr: *pachys,* thick; Gr: *seris,* lettuce. Relating to the lettuce-like growth form seen in some colonies.)

DESCRIPTION

Living coral   (Col. pl. p. 140)

Pachyseris is a distinctive coral that forms leafy,

94

Pachyseris rugosa (X 2.6). Malaysia.

encrusting or massive colonies. *P. rugosa* is encrusting or plate-like, often with vertical plates, ridges or columns. In larger colonies these may branch and join (Veron & Pichon, 1980). *P. speciosa* has a similar basic form, but the folia are generally horizontal or sloping and are thin and delicate.

Colonies are pale to dark brown in color and their upper surfaces are covered with closely packed ridges and valleys. These are arranged in neat concentric rows in leafy or flat forms (condition typical of *P. speciosa*), but are shorter and more haphazard in encrusting, irregularly shaped or massive colonies (condition typical of *P. rugosa*). The ridges are usually steep-sided, often come to an acute point and are 1 to 2 mm high. Distance from mid ridge to mid-ridge is usually around 3 mm but may be more. Calices are present in the valleys but are indistinct because of the arrangement of the septa. These are fine, numerous and regular in appearance. They run across the valleys at right angles to the ridges, over which they pass uninterrupted.

Skeleton
Septal margins bear extremely fine serrations. The columella is well formed in *P. rugosa* but absent or rudimentary in *P. speciosa*.

SIMILARITIES
Pachyseris is a distinctive coral that is not easily confused with other genera. The parallel arrange-

ment of the septa and the absence of distinct calice centers are particularly diagnostic.

DISTRIBUTION AND ECOLOGY   (Map #42)
Pachyseris prefers shallow, sheltered waters and reef slopes but can also be found in most other reef habitats. Colonies may be several meters in diameter, and some of the foliaceous ones are loosely attached and fragile.

There are 12 nominal species of *Pachyseris,* but Veron and Pichon (1980) suggest that many of these can be included in *P. rugosa* (Lamarck, 1801), which shows considerable variation in growth form and skeletal characters. There may be a third species in addition to *P. speciosa* (Dana, 1846), but Ditlev (1980) suggests that only *Pachyseris rugosa* is valid.

Coeloseris Vaughan, 1918
(Gr: *koilos,* hollow; Gr: *seris,* lettuce. Presumably relating to the deep fossa characteristic of the genus.)

DESCRIPTION
Living coral   (Col. pl. pp. 140, 141)
Coeloseris forms massive rounded colonies, pale brown, green or yellow in color. Calices are rounded or polygonal with distinct shared walls. In the living coral the wall appears wider than the fossa and the top of the wall is rather flattened and has a

Coeloseris mayeri (X 2.4). Malaysia.

Montastraea cavernosa. Bahamas (Photo: P. Colin).

Favia fagrum. Jamaica, 5 m depth (Photo: P. Colin).

Montastraea cavernosa. Jamaica, 15 m depth.

Montastraea cavernosa. Jamaica, 18 m depth.

Montastraea annularis. Jamaica, 3 m depth.

Competing colonies of *Diploria labyrinthiformis* (left) and *Diploria strigosa* (right). Jamaica, 15 m depth.

Colpophyllia natans. Jamaica, 6 m depth.

Colpophyllia natans. Jamaica, 6 m depth.

Coeloseris mayeri (X 4). Malaysia.

characteristic "reticulate" appearance. Corallite diameter is between 2 and 5 mm, usually 4 to 5 mm.

Septa are numerous and clearly visible as they run from the fossa onto the walls. The fossa is several millimeters deep, and the polyp is usually retracted during the day.

Skeleton

There are usually 20 to 30 septa per calice (diameter 3 mm), arranged in cycles. They are slightly exsert and leafy as they pass over the walls and their margins are smooth or have a few very small teeth. The septa join to the top of the wall, which is also thin and leafy and circles the calices. The columella is absent or small and pinnacle-like.

SIMILARITIES

Coeloseris can be mistaken underwater for a faviid, particularly *Leptastrea*, but the two genera can be distinguished as follows. In *Coeloseris* the fossa is small and deep and the walls wide and flat-topped with a characteristic sculptured appearance. In *Leptastrea* the calices are shallower and the walls narrower, and there is usually a distinct dark line along the midline of the wall. An examination of the skeleton reveals several major differences between the genera. Most obvious is the lack of a columella in *Coeloseris* (if present, then pinnacle-like) and the absence of well developed spines on the septal margins.

Coeloseris can also be confused with other members of its family. Some diagnostic characters are shown in Table 3.

DISTRIBUTION AND ECOLOGY (Map #43)

Coeloseris has a scattered distribution on most

reefs, but is most likely to be found along the reef top and rim. There is a single species: *Coeloseris mayeri* Vaughan, 1918.

FAMILY SIDERASTREIDAE

Siderastrea de Blainville, 1830
(Gr: *sideris*, star; Gr: *aster*, star. Presumably relating to the regular star-like arrangement of the calices.)

DESCRIPTION
Living coral

Siderastrea forms encrusting or massive colonies that are usually small in size. Tentacles are tiny and seldom seen. Calices are crowded, with shared walls. They are rounded and regular, with the fossa appearing as a fairly deep pit. The corallite walls are wider than the fossa and have flattish, smooth tops. There may be a faint mark along the midline of the wall, and using this as a guide, calice diameter is usually between 2 and 4 mm. Septa are visible as fine lines radiating from the center of the calice over the walls.

Skeleton

Septa are numerous and in cycles. There are often over 40 in an average sized calice (3 mm diameter), of which half reach the columella. They meet septa of adjacent calices at the top of the wall and are usually confluent with them. Synapticulae link the septa by their lateral walls, and distinct synapticular rings may be formed. Septal margins are armed with extremely small spines. These are often simple, but are occasionally bifurcated. Septa are perforated. New calices are added by extratentacular budding.

SIMILARITIES

Siderastrea can be distinguished from other members of its family by its rounded, regular calices and wide calice walls. Other features are shown in Table 3.

Siderastrea also resembles *Coeloseris*, but the two genera are geographically separated, *Siderastrea* in the western Indian Ocean, *Coeloseris* in the eastern Indian Ocean and western Pacific. It is unlikely to be confused with other agariciids that occur within its range (see differences in Table 3).

DISTRIBUTION AND ECOLOGY (Map #44)

Siderastrea is uncommon, inconspicuous and is

Genus	Form and size of colony	Calice arrangement	Walls/collines	Septal and septocostal arrangement and features
Pavona	Great variation in growth form and colony size.	Round, oval or elongate polygonal; 2-3 mm dia.	Walls lacking or present. Collines may enclose several calices.	Septa narrow, continuous between centers. Margins smooth or with very fine serrations. Synapticulae absent or present.
Gardineroseris	Massive and often columnar.	Polygonal, irregular or elongate; 2-5 mm dia.	Walls high and prominent. No midline.	Septa in cycles, about 50 in a calice 3 mm in diameter. Margins smooth or granular. Inner ends of septa broad. Synapticulae absent.
Leptoseris	Often leafy, may be encrusting. Colonies small to medium size.	Outline indistinct. Approx 2-10 mm dia.	Collines may be present, enclosing a series of mouths.	Numerous and run uninterrupted between centers. Margins with fine or coarse serrations. Synapticulae absent or a few present.
Pachyseris	Foliaceous to massive, often large.	Calices in series. 2-5 mm across valleys.	Distinct collines with calices in the valleys.	Numerous and parallel, about 40-50 per cm. Margins finely serrated. Synapticulae absent.
Coeloseris	Massive, rounded colonies of medium to large size.	Rounded or polygonal. 2-5 mm dia.	Distinct shared walls.	Well spaced and in cycles. Some run over walls, some join to narrow ridge along midline. 20-30 in calice 3 mm in diameter. Margins smooth or with a few fine spines. Synapticulae absent.
Siderastrea	Small massive or encrusting colonies.	Rounded and regular. 2-4 mm dia.	Walls shared, wide and often with midline.	Numerous and in cycles. 35-45 in a calice 3 mm in diameter. Margins with small either simple or dentate spines. Synapticulae present. Septa often fuse. Septa perforated.
Pseudosiderastrea	Encrusting or massive colonies usually less than 10 cm diameter.	Rounded, irregular or angular. 2-4 mm dia.	Shared wall a narrow ridge, no midline. Calice wide and shallow.	Septa in cycles, usually about 30 in calice 3 mm in diameter, up to 48 in larger calices. Margins with small dentate spines. Synapticulae present. Septa often fuse in calices. Septa rarely perforated.
Anomastrea	Encrusting or massive, usually less than 10 cm diameter.	Rounded, angular or irregular. 2-4 mm dia.	Shared wall a narrow ridge, no midline. Fossa wide and fairly deep.	About 30 septa in a calice 3 mm in diameter. Margins with small dentate spines. Synapticular links rarely formed. Fusion of septa is common. Septa may be partially perforated.
Coscinaraea	Massive, encrusting or partly foliaceous. Seldom larger than 30 cm diameter.	Rounded, irregular, elongate or in series. 2-7 mm dia. or across valley.	High or low walls or collines around the calices. Walls may be wide, but no midline.	About 20-30 septa in a calice 3 mm in diameter. Margins with dentate spines. Synapticulae present. Occasional fusion of septa in calices. Septa perforated.
Psammocora	Great variation in growth form and colony size.	Rounded, with indistinct outline. About 2 mm dia.	No walls, but collines often enclose single or several calices.	Septa often branch and ramify, giving a petaloid appearance. Seldom more than 10 reach the columella. Margins with granular protuberances that are usually minutely branched. Synapticular rings usually well developed. Septa do not fuse in calices.

Table 3. Features of corals from the families Agariciidae, Siderastreidae and Thamnasteriidae. Some of the genera are easily confused underwater, and a careful examination of the skeleton is required for positive identification.

Diploria labyrinthiformis. A non-polyp-bearing groove runs along the top of the walls. Bahamas, 10 m depth (Photo: P. Colin).

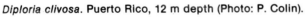

Diploria clivosa. Puerto Rico, 12 m depth (Photo: P. Colin).

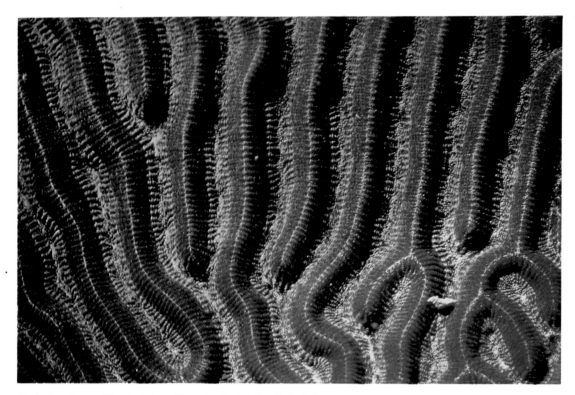

Diploria clivosa. Puerto Rico, 12 m depth (Photo: P. Colin).

Manicina areolata. Puerto Rico, 18 m depth (Photo: P. Colin).

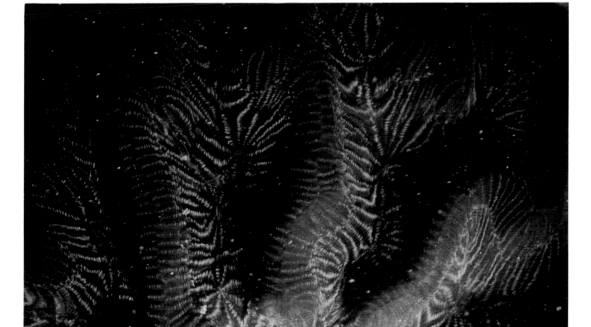

easily overlooked on Indian Ocean reefs. This contrasts with the situation in the western Atlantic, where *Siderastrea* is common and readily found. There is probably only a single species in the Red Sea and western Indian Ocean: *Siderastrea savignyana* Milne-Edwards & Haime, 1850.

Pseudosiderastrea Yabe & Sugiyama, 1935

(Gr: *pseudes,* false; Gr: *sideris,* star; Gr: *aster,* star. Presumably relating to the affinity of this coral with *Siderastrea.)*

DESCRIPTION

Living coral (Col. pl. p. 141)

Pseudosiderastrea forms encrusting or massive colonies that are generally less than 10 cm in diameter and are unlikely to exceed 15 cm. They are pale brown, gray or pinkish in color, with the corallite walls paler or white. Corallites are crowded, with shared walls. They are polygonal or rounded but may be irregular in shape when in the process of budding. Diameter is generally between 2 and 4 mm. The fossa is shallow, and the walls appear as a narrow ridge without a midline. Septa are closely packed and visible as fine lines running between adjacent calice centers.

Pseudosiderastrea tayamai (X 5). Malaysia. BM(NH) 1979.9.25.12.

Skeleton

Septa are numerous and in cycles, with about 30 in a calice 3 mm in diameter, nearly 50 in larger calices. The larger septa reach the columella and often fuse by their lateral margins to their smaller neighbors. The septa are slightly exsert as they run over the walls and join with septa of adjacent calices. There are dentate spines or granules on the septal margins and small spines on the sides. Septa are rarely perforated. Synapticular links between the lateral faces of adjacent septa are usually present but are irregular and do not form complete rings. A pinnacle-like columella is present. New calices are produced by extratentacular budding (contrast *Anomastrea*).

SIMILARITIES

Pseudosiderastrea is unlikely to be confused with *Siderastrea* because the calices in the two genera have a different appearance (see Table 3), but it is more readily confused with *Anomastrea*. A reliable distinction is the presence of synapticular links, which are absent or rare in *Anomastrea*. In addition, the mode of budding is different.

TAXONOMIC NOTE

Pseudosiderastrea was created for a new species discovered by Yabe and Sugiyama (1935) that they considered closely allied to *Anomastrea* and particularly close to *Siderastrea*. It was later referred to as a subgenus of *Anomastrea* (Vaughan & Wells, 1943; Wells, 1956), and it is only recently (Veron & Pichon, 1980) that further studies have reconfirmed that *Pseudosiderastrea* is closer to *Siderastrea* than *Anomastrea* and should be considered as a genus in its own right.

DISTRIBUTION AND ECOLOGY (Map #45)

Pseudosiderastrea may be easily overlooked because of its small size and inconspicuous growth form. Even so, it is not a common coral. There is a single species: *Pseudosiderastrea tayamai* Yabe & Sugiyama, 1935.

Anomastrea von Marenzeller, 1901

(Gr: *anomos,* irregular, unequal; Gr: *aster,* star. Probably a reference to the irregular calices formed during budding.)

DESCRIPTION
Living coral
This coral is encrusting or massive, but colonies are generally less than 10 cm in diameter. Calices are crowded with shared walls and are hexagonal, circular, elongate or irregular in shape. Calice diameter varies within and between colonies but is usually between 2 and 4 mm. The fossa is shallow, and the walls are a narrow ridge without a midline. Septa are visible as fine lines radiating from the calice centers over the walls.

Skeleton
Septa are numerous, and the main ones reach the columella. Intermediate ones often fuse with their longer neighbors. There are about 25 to 30 septa in a calice 3 mm in diameter. They are slightly exsert as they run over the walls and join with septa of adjacent calices. Septal margins are armed with dentate spines. Septa may be partially perforated. Synapticular links between the lateral faces of adjacent septa are rarely seen. New calices are produced by intratentacular budding.

SIMILARITIES
Anomastrea is similar in appearance to *Pseudosiderastrea,* but a close examination of the skeleton reveals that it lacks synapticular links between the septa. These are present in *Pseudosiderastrea.* Other distinguishing features of *Anomastrea* are shown in Table 3.

Anomastrea irregularis (X 2.5). Western Indian Ocean. BM(NH) 1961.7.17.68.

Anomastrea irregularis (X 5). Western Indian Ocean. BM(NH) 1961.7.17.68.

DISTRIBUTION & ECOLOGY   (Map #46)
This small coral is uncommon and easily overlooked. There is a single species: *Anomastrea irregularis* von Marenzeller, 1901.

Coscinaraea Milne-Edwards & Haime, 1848
(Gr: *koskinos,* sieve; Gr: *araios,* thin, porous. Referring to the septa, which are perforated by small holes.)

DESCRIPTION
Living coral   (Col. pl. p. 141)
Colonies are massive or encrusting, sometimes with plate-like extensions, and seldom exceed 30 cm in diameter; they are brown or greenish in color. The tentacles are small and seldom seen during the day. Calices are crowded and have shared walls. These walls or collines sometimes surround a single calice but often enclose several or a series. There tends to be variation in size and shape of calices and valleys even within a single specimen. Calice diameter or valley width may reach 7 mm but is usually 2 to 5 mm. The walls may be steep and acute or flatter and more crowded, but they are generally wide and distinct. Septa are clearly

Colpophyllia natans. Bahamas (Photo: P. Colin).

Colpophyllia breviserialis. Jamaica, 18 m depth (Photo: P. Colin).

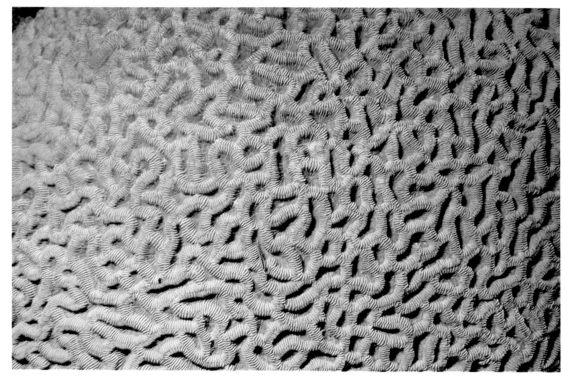

Astrangia solitaria. Puerto Rico, 1 m depth (Photo: P. Colin).

Oculina diffusa. Puerto Rico, 6 m depth (Photo: P. Colin).

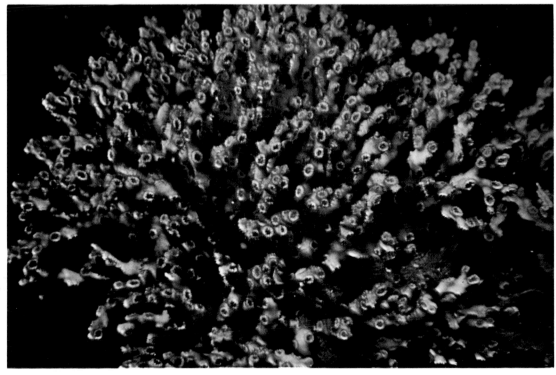

visible as they run over the walls or collines into the calices.

Skeleton

There are between 20 and 30 septa in a calice 3 mm in diameter. Most reach the columella, but some fuse with their neighbors. Septal spines are prominent and minutely dentate, and those along the top of the wall may fuse together. Synapticulae are also present, joining the lateral walls of the septa. Septa are perforated. The columella is papillose.

SIMILARITIES

Many *Coscinaraea* species have calices joined in longitudinal series, and this readily distinguishes them from other members of the family. Those species with single or slightly elongate calices can generally be identified by their larger calice diameter, but in some cases dimensions and shape overlap with other genera. Diagnosis underwater may be difficult because such features as the presence of synapticulae and the fusion and perforation of septa are seen only in cleaned specimens (see Table 3).

A difficult species is *Coscinaraea exesa* (Dana), which is similar in many respects to *Psammocora* and has often been placed in this genus. It has a larger calice size (5 mm) than is expected of *Psammocora* (2 to 3 mm), and some of the septa fuse in the calices, which in *Psammocora* is unusual. A

Coscinaraea columna (X 2.8). Aldabra. BM(NH) Unreg.

Coscinaraea monile (X 2.8). Arabian Gulf. BM(NH) 1978.2.2.118.

full description of this species is given by Veron and Pichon (1980).

There are several forms of *Coscinaraea* that have a well developed system of valleys and ridges and resemble small brain corals of the family Faviidae. *Coscinaraea* species can be identified by a number of features, including the crowded septa, presence of synapticulae, complex spines on the septal margins and poorly developed columella.

DISTRIBUTION AND ECOLOGY   (Map #47)

Coscinaraea is a relatively small, inconspicuous coral that appears in general to be uncommon. About 14 species have been described, but Veron and Pichon (1980) consider that only about seven are valid.

Horastrea Pichon, 1971
(Hora: a Malagasy word meaning coral or coral reef; Gr: *aster,* star.)

DESCRIPTION
Living coral

Horastrea forms massive subhemispherical colonies that are small in size. The polyps are pale brown with a pale gray-blue oral disc. Corallites are separate and distinct, usually raised several millimeters above the general coral surface. They are rounded or irregular, and the largest have as many as 7 centers. Most calices are between 8 and 10 mm in diameter, but valleys may reach 4 cm in length. The fossa is several millimeters deep.

Septa are clearly visible and closely packed. Their margins are slightly rough due to the presence of numerous small spines. The septa continue over the corallite wall and are visible on perithecal areas as low costal ridges.

Skeleton

Septa are numerous, with as many as 80 arranged in five cycles. Synapticulae are present, septa may be perforated, and some fuse to their neighbors. Septal margins are slightly irregular and armed with numerous closely set, often compound teeth. Septal sides are also spiny. Costae are usually continuous and have small teeth along their margins. The columella is distinct and papillose in appearance. Reproduction is primarily intratentacular.

SIMILARITIES

Horastrea bears a superficial resemblance to *Favia*, but close examination reveals several non-faviid characters such as fused septa, papillose columella, compound spines on the septal margins and low, crowded costae. *Horastrea* appears to be

Horastrea indica (X 3.8). Madagascar. BM(NH) 1973.9.17.1.

most closely related to *Coscinaraea* but is easily distinguished by its plocoid form and well developed peritheca.

DISTRIBUTION AND ECOLOGY (Map #48)

Horastrea has been found from depths of 0 to 40 m but apparently prefers reef slopes. It is relatively common within its known range but has probably been overlooked in the past because of its small size. Thus its geographical distribution may be wider than indicated at present. There is a single species: *Horastrea indica* Pichon, 1971.

FAMILY THAMNASTERIIDAE

Psammocora Dana, 1846
(Gr: *psammos,* sand; Gr: *kore,* pupil of the eye. Presumably relating to the surface features of the coral, which has a texture like fine sandpaper.)

DESCRIPTION
Living coral (Col. pl. p. 141)

Psammocora forms branching, encrusting, leafy or massive colonies that are usually green or brown in color. Polyps are usually extended during the day, forming a dense cover over the corallum. The tentacles are about 1 to 2 mm long and retract when touched.

The surface of the coral is smooth or faintly granular to the touch and in most cases is covered with small hillocks (collines). These are a few millimeters high but of variable length, and they may be low and rounded or high and acute. They enclose one or more calices, but these are difficult to distinguish underwater because of their small size. They are approximately 2 mm in diameter, closely packed and superficial.

Septa are numerous and just visible to the naked eye. They converge toward the center of each calice, forming intricate patterns as they do so. In some cases they split into two or three branches (septo-costae) that surround short, wide costae. Both septo-costae and costae may end in a wide, blunt monticule, giving a flower-like appearance.

Skeleton

Close examination reveals that septo-costae may be broken into rows of minute tubercles. Septal margins have small granular protuberances that themselves are usually minutely branched. The col-

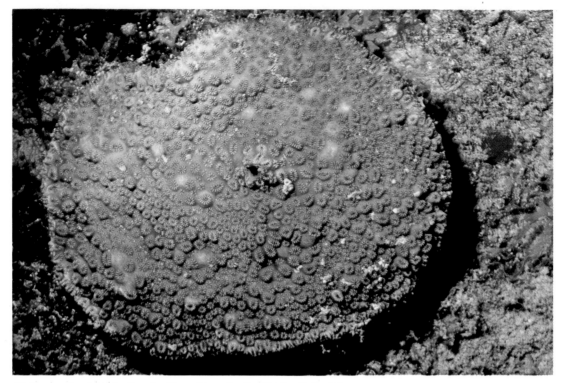

Dichocoenia stellaris. Puerto Rico, 24 m depth (Photo: P. Colin).

Meandrina braziliensis. Puerto Rico, 12 m depth (Photo: P. Colin).

Manicina areolata. Jamaica, 6 m depth.

Phyllangia americana. Jamaica, 18 m depth.

Dichocoenia stokesi. Jamaica, 15 m depth.

Dichocoenia stokesi. Jamaica, 15 m depth.

Meandrina meandrites. Jamaica, 15 m depth.

Scolymia lacera. Jamaica, 40 m depth.

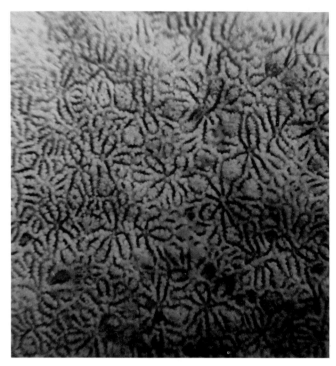

Psammocora digitata (X 5.5). Malaysia.

umella is usually small and pinnacle-like, but may be reduced to a few papillae or be almost absent. Synapticulae connect the lateral walls of the septa and are usually arranged in rings. The corallite wall is absent or weak.

SIMILARITIES

Psammocora resembles *Pavona* and other agariciids but can usually be distinguished by its short, stout septa that form characteristic petaloid patterns as they ramify over the surface of the coral. In agariciids the septa are finer and usually run uninterrupted between calices.

Psammocora also has features in common with *Coscinaraea*, especially with *C. exesa*, which for many years was referred to as *Psammocora exesa* (see discussion in Veron and Pichon, 1980). Both genera have petaloid septa, similarly ornamented septal margins and synapticulae. However, corallite size is different (seldom over 2 mm in *Psammocora*, 2 to 7 mm in *Coscinaraea*), and the corallite wall in *Coscinaraea* is more solid.

Useful diagnostic features for *Psammocora* are shown in Table 3.

TAXONOMIC NOTE

Vaughan and Wells (1943) subdivided the genus *Psammocora* and introduced the subgenera *Stephanaria* Verrill, 1867 and *Plesioseris* Duncan, 1884. These names are occasionally still used in present-day literature but are generally considered to confuse the taxonomy of the group.

DISTRIBUTION AND ECOLOGY   (Map #49)

Psammocora can be found on most reefs, especially along the reef front. Colonies are usually isolated, but small, leafy forms may grow in profusion. There are at least seven species, possibly more.

FAMILY FUNGIIDAE
KEY TO FREE-LIVING FUNGIIDS

The fungiids described in this key are attached as juveniles but subsequently become detached and live free on soft or rubble substrates. There are other fungiids that remain attached throughout their lives, and these are included in the main key to genera rather than the key below.

1. Solitary corallum: a single polyp with a distinct rounded or elongate mouth...............2
   Colonial corallum: several or many mouths, either scattered or a central rounded or elongate mouth with a series of smaller lateral ones....................................4
2. Corallum rounded, to 20 cm or more in diameter; living coral always with long finger-like tentacles extended during the day; spines on septal and costal margins prominent but non-dentate; corallite wall perforate.........
   ....*Heliofungia*
   Corallum rounded or elongate, to 50 cm or more in length or diameter; living coral with tentacles retracted during the day; spines on septal and costal margins small to large, either smooth-edged, granulose, spinulose or distinctly branched; corallite wall perforate.....
   ....*Fungia*
   Corallum rounded or wedge-shaped, less than 10 cm in diameter; living coral with tentacles retracted during the day; spines on septal and costal margins small; corallite wall imperforate; small septa of highest cycle perforate.3
3. Corallum rounded and entire......*Cycloseris*
   Corallum wedge-shaped or rounded but split into wedge-shaped segments.........*Diaseris*

4. Corallum elongate, with distinct groove running along length of coral................5
   Corallum elongate or rounded, without central groove................................6
5. Several mouths in central furrow, but no lateral mouths; septal margins with large triangular spines; costal spines smaller....*Herpetoglossa*
   Several mouths in central furrow, and few to many lateral mouths; septal margins with small spines; costal spines small.......*Herpolitha*
6. Corallum rounded; lateral calices few and indistinct; septa long, some sweep in distinct arc from top of coral to outer margin; corallum light in weight...................*Zoopilus*
   Corallum rounded or elongate; lateral calices numerous and distinct; septa short and radiate between calice centers; corallum heavy......7
7. Corallum elongate; tentacles extended during day, forming dense mat over corallum; calices closely packed and with distinct petaloid appearance; septa short and thick, only slightly exsert.......................*Polyphyllia*
   Corallum rounded or slightly elongate; tentacles not extended during day; calices closely packed but not petaloid in appearance; septa exsert, arching up between calice centers....8
8. Septal spines serrated; costal spines usually branched....................*Sandalolitha*
   Septal spines smooth; costal spines finely spinulose......................*Halomitra*

Cycloseris Milne-Edwards & Haime, 1849

(Gr: *kyklos,* circle; Gr: *seris,* lettuce. Relating to the growth form of this genus.)

DESCRIPTION
Living coral   (Col. pl. pp. 141, 144)

Juvenile *Cycloseris* are attached by a narrow stem, but this later becomes detached, leaving a small scar on the underside of the coral. The corallum is in the form of a rounded or slightly oval disc that can reach 10 cm in diameter but is usually much less. Small specimens are flat, some of the larger ones strongly domed. They are brown or greenish in color, and small tentacles may be visi-

Cycloseris costulata (nat. size). Malaysia.

ble. The central mouth is often elongate, but there are no lateral mouths.

Septa are clearly visible as they radiate from the center of the corallum to its outer edge. Septal margins are spiny. The septa are usually continued on the underside of the corallum as costal ridges, but these may be feebly developed. The margins of these ridges vary from smooth to rough.

Skeleton

Septa are arranged in cycles; those of the primary cycle are larger, wider and slightly exsert, and between them are smaller, lower ones of higher cycles. Septal margins have small, sharp teeth or dentate spines. Costal margins are smooth, granular or armed with extremely small blunt spines. The upper parts of the septa of higher cycles are fenestrate (penetrated by small holes). The undersurface of the corallum, which represents the wall, is solid and imperforate.

SIMILARITIES

Cycloseris may be confused with *Fungia,* and the two genera are difficult to distinguish underwater. *Cycloseris* rarely exceeds 6 cm in diameter, while *Fungia* is larger, but the main characters used to define the genus are concerned with the structure of the wall, septa and costae. The wall in *Cycloseris* is imperforate, while in *Fungia* it is perforated. In *Cycloseris* the upper parts of the smaller septa are

111

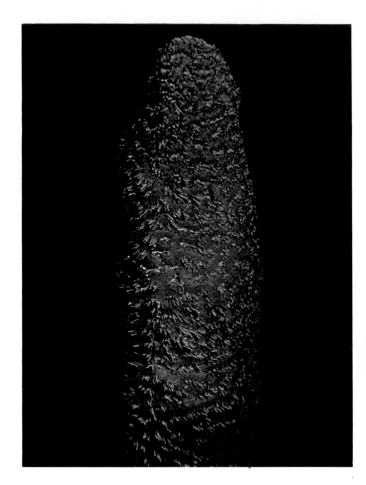

Goreaugyra memorialis.
Bahamas, 15 m depth (Photo:
P. Colin).

Dendrogyra cylindrus. Jamaica, 15 m depth (Photo: P. Colin).

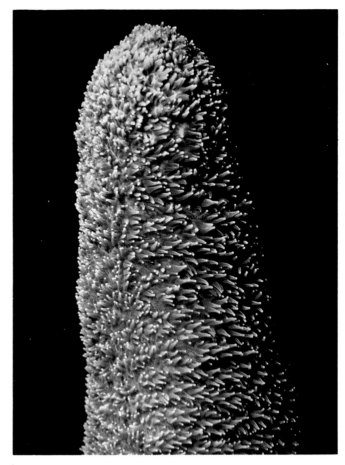

Dendrogyra cylindrus.
Jamaica, 15 m depth (Photo:
P. Colin).

Scolymia (Photo: P. Colin).

113

fenestrate, but in *Fungia* this condition is less well developed and seen only in the highest cycle. Costae in *Cycloseris* are usually developed, but their margins are smooth, granular or with feeble, non-denticulate spines. In *Fungia* the costae have prominent spines on their margins or are represented by rows of spines or dentate tubercles.

For comparisons with *Diaseris,* see that genus.

DISTRIBUTION AND ECOLOGY (Map #50)

Probably widespread and fairly common, preferring sandy or rubble-strewn areas at the bottom of the reef slope. Possibly about ten species.

Diaseris Milne-Edwards & Haime, 1849
(Gr: *dia-,* across, through; Gr: *seris,* lettuce. Probably a reference to the segmented nature of the corallum.)

DESCRIPTION
Living coral
Diaseris is a small discoid to wedge-shaped coral that is attached as a juvenile by a short stem but lies free as an adult. The corallum is flat or slightly domed, and the adult is seldom more than 6 cm in diameter. It may be wedge-shaped, or is rounded but partially split into wedge-shaped segments. The formation of these segments is a method of asexual reproduction characteristic of the genus. Various stages of division are usually visible, with the split restricted only to the edge of the corallum or extending all the way to the center. Complete separation results in the production of a new, initially wedge-shaped, corallum. There is usually a single center to each corallum, but occasionally several centers may develop. The corallum is generally brown or yellowish, sometimes with tinges of green.

Septa are numerous and clearly visible as they radiate to the center of the corallum. Their margins are smooth or slightly rough to the touch. Fine lines are also visible on the underside of the coral, which again is slightly rough to the touch.

Skeleton
Septa are thick, and the larger ones are slightly exsert and may fuse distally with septa of higher cycles. There are small spines or granules along the septal margins, which may be simple or minutely dentate. The costae on the underside of the coral are fine and their margins have delicate spines. The corallite wall is solid and imperforate.

SIMILARITIES
Diaseris may be confused with *Cycloseris,* but the form of the corallum in the two genera is distinctive. In *Cycloseris* the disc is rounded and entire. In *Diaseris* it is either wedge-shaped or rounded but split into wedge-shaped segments. This continual production of regularly shaped pieces can readily be distinguished from regeneration that occurs as a result of damage. Most

Diaseris distorta (X 2.5). Philippines. BM(NH) 1880.11.25.137.

114

fungiids, including *Cycloseris,* are capable of regeneration that may result in the formation of an irregularly shaped corallum. However, such a corallum is irregular rather than segmented.

DISTRIBUTION AND ECOLOGY

Diaseris is usually found on soft substrates and reef slopes away from areas of vigorous coral growth. It is very mobile and is capable of both climbing and digging hollows in the sand in order to right itself (Hubbard, 1972). There are probably three species with a distribution similar to *Cycloseris.*

Fungia Lamarck, 1801
Mushroom corals
(L: *fungus,* mushroom. Describing the mushroom-like appearance of most specimens.)

DESCRIPTION
Living coral   (Col. pl. p. 144)
Juveniles occur as tiny, solitary discs attached to dead coral or rocks by a short stem. These discs seldom remain attached when over about 4 cm in diamcter unless they are in a well protected place. A scar on the underside of the free-living coral indicates the position of the stem. Some adult species are flat, others convex. They may be round or elongate, but those that have been damaged at some time are often irregular in outline. They may reach 50 cm in diameter but are usually less. All are solitary, with the mouth clearly visible at the center of the colony. In elongate types the mouth forms a long groove. Many specimens are pale brown in color, but shades of pink, purple, blue and green are frequently seen. In most individuals the tentacles are completely withdrawn during the day, but in others they can be seen lying in a series of rings between the septa.

Septa are numerous and conspicuous. They radiate out from the central fossa or groove, and their edges are uneven or armed with teeth. On the underside of the coral the costae are normally well developed, appearing as radiating ridges with rough margins.

Skeleton
Septa are in cycles and often arch up between the center of the corallum and the perimeter. Their

Fungia concinna (nat. size). Malaysia.

margins are indented or have small to large teeth. Costae have prominent spines on their margins or are represented by rows of dentate tubercles. The corallite wall is perforate but the septa are imperforate, except in some cases those of the highest cycle.

SIMILARITIES
Juvenile or small *Fungia* can be mistaken for *Cycloseris;* the differences between these two genera are explained under genus *Cycloseris.* The corallum of *Fungia* is also very similar to that of *Heliofungia,* but the latter is easily distinguished by the prominent tentacles of the living coral (see the discussion under *Heliofungia*).

TAXONOMIC NOTE
Species of *Fungia* fall into distinct categories based on the shape of the corallum and features of the septa and costae. Five subgenera are recognized: *Pleuractis, Ctenactis, Verrillofungia, Danafungia* and *Fungia* (for further details see Wells, 1966; Ditlev, 1980).

Mussa angulosa. Jamaica, 18 m depth (Photo: P. Colin).

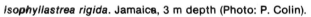

Isophyllastrea rigida. Jamaica, 3 m depth (Photo: P. Colin).

Mussa angulosa. Jamaica, 18 m depth.

Isophyllastrea rigida. Jamaica, 6 m depth.

Isophyllastrea rigida. Jamaica, 6 m depth.

Mycetophyllia lamarckana. Jamaica, 16 m depth.

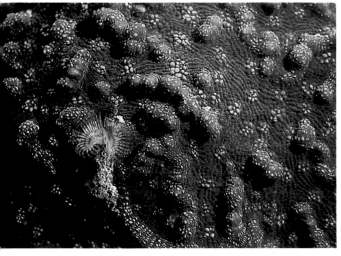

Mycetophyllia aliciae. Jamaica, 18 m depth.

Eusmilia fastigiata. Jamaica, 16 m depth.

117

DISTRIBUTION AND ECOLOGY (Map #51)

Juveniles are often found in crevices or other sheltered places. Adults are rare to abundant, depending on the type of reef. Rubble-strewn slopes are often densely populated with fungiids, but few are found in areas where there are dense growths of attached corals. *Fungia* and other fungiids are adept at removing sediment from their surfaces. Small *Fungia* can also move efficiently by using the tentacles at the edge of the corallum. There are probably 15 to 20 species of *Fungia*.

Heliofungia Wells, 1966

(Gr: *helios,* sun; L: *fungus,* mushroom. Describing the shape of the coral and the prominent tentacles, resembling rays of the sun.)

DESCRIPTION

Living coral (Col. pl. p. 144)

The corallum in *Heliofungia* is rounded, heavy and free-living. It is often slightly domed and may be 20 cm in diameter. The living coral is easily recognized by its prominent tentacles. These are always extended during the day and cover the corallum in a thick mat. They are usually over 5 cm long and are gray, blue or green in color with a slightly inflated, often paler colored tip.

Septa are hidden in the living coral, but costae are visible on the undersurface if the coral is turned over. They form ridges running from the center of the corallum to the periphery, and their edges are uneven or spiny.

Skeleton

Septa are numerous and arranged in cycles. Their margins are armed with pointed or rounded spines, and the septa themselves are imperforate. Costal margins are scalloped or bear low, blunt teeth. The corallite wall (*i.e.,* the underside of the coral) is perforated.

SIMILARITIES

The living coral is unmistakable, but the skeleton can be confused with *Fungia* species. It is distinguished from these by the characteristically

Heliofungia actiniformis (X 3). Malaysia.

Heliofungia actiniformis (nat. size). Malaysia.

low, smooth costal spines and the prominent non-dentate septal spines.

TAXONOMIC NOTE

The name *Heliofungia* was introduced by Wells (1966) to describe *Fungia actiniformis* but was used until recently only as a subgenus. Veron and Pichon (1980) believe that *Heliofungia* is sufficiently distinct for it to be treated as a separate genus.

DISTRIBUTION AND ECOLOGY (Map #52)

This coral has a similar distribution to other free-living fungiids, preferring reef slopes and other areas where the substrate is soft. There is a single species: *Heliofungia actiniformis* (Quoy & Gaimard, 1833).

Herpetoglossa Wells, 1966
(Gr: *herpo,* to creep; Gr: *glossa,* tongue. Referring to the low, elongate shape of this coral.)

DESCRIPTION
Living coral

Herpetoglossa is an elongate, colonial, free-living fungiid. It may be flat or arched and is often over 30 cm in length. There is a furrow running along the length of the coral in which are several mouths. There are no secondary lateral centers. The corallum is brownish in color, and the tentacles are retracted during the day.

Septa are numerous and alternate large and small. Long septa run from the central fossa to the edge of the corallum, and there are shorter, higher ones between. On the undersurface of the corallum the costae are reduced to rows of small spines.

Skeleton

The upper margins of the long septa have large triangular spines that themselves have serrated edges. The shorter septa have smaller, lower teeth. The small spines on the undersurface of the coral are granular or finely serrated.

SIMILARITIES

Herpetoglossa resembles *Fungia echinata* but can be distinguished by the presence of several mouths rather than a single mouth in the central groove. In addition, the septal spines in *Herpetoglossa* are triangular rather than rounded.

Herpetoglossa can also be confused with *Herpolitha,* but the latter typically has lateral as well as axial mouths and smaller septal and costal teeth.

DISTRIBUTION AND ECOLOGY (Map #53)

As with other fungiids, *Herpetoglossa* prefers soft substrates and protected or semi-protected sites. There is a single species: *Herpetoglossa simplex* (Gardiner, 1905).

Herpolitha Eschscholtz, 1825
(Gr: *herpo,* to creep; Gr: *lithos,* stone. Referring to the elongate, flattened appearance of this coral.)

DESCRIPTION
Living coral (Col. pl. p. 144)

Herpolitha is an elongate, colonial coral that lives free on the bottom. Some specimens are irregular due to regeneration and may have more than two ends. The upper side of the coral is convex, the lower side concave, and the corallum may

119

Isophyllia sinuosa. Puerto Rico, 15 m depth (Photo: P. Colin).

Thalamophyllia riisei. Jamaica, 30 m depth (Photo: P. Colin).

Eusmilia fastigiata. Puerto Rico, 5 m depth (Photo: P. Colin).

Eusmilia fastigiata. Bahamas, 15 m depth (Photo: P. Colin).

Tubastraea aurea. Puerto Rico, 5 m depth (Photo: P. Colin).

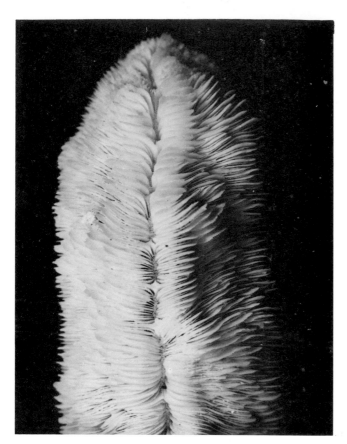

Herpolitha limax (nat. size). Malaysia.

edges have small, regular teeth that may themselves be minutely dentate. Costal spines also have fine spinules on their margins. The lower surface of the coral is perforated.

SIMILARITIES

Herpolitha is distinguished from elongate *Fungia* species by the series of mouths in the central groove. In this respect it resembles *Herpetoglossa*, but *Herpolitha* typically has lateral as well as axial mouths and also has smaller septal and costal teeth.

DISTRIBUTION AND ECOLOGY   (Map #54)

Herpolitha is fairly common and has a similar habitat preference to other unattached fungiids. There are two species: *Herpolitha limax* (Houttuyn, 1772) and *Herpolitha weberi* (van der Horst, 1921). *H. limax* has lateral centers but short principal septa; *H. weberi* has few or no lateral centers and long principal septa.

reach a length of 50 cm. There is a central groove on the upper surface, along which is a series of conspicuous slit-like mouths. To either side are usually smaller, less obvious mouths visible as discrete centers from which the septa radiate. The mouths are sometimes green and contrast with the rest of the coral, which is brownish. Polyps are confluent and indistinguishable from each other. Short, stubby tentacles can usually be seen lying between the septa; there is apparently a single one associated with each secondary center (Veron & Pichon, 1980).

There is a distinct set of high, short septa in *Herpolitha limax* that do not extend all the way from the central groove to the perimeter. These are followed in this species by slightly lower ones that may or may not reach the outer edge. In *Herpolitha weberi* the principal septa run directly from the central groove to the perimeter. On the underside of both species the costal ridges are represented by small spines that are arranged in rows or crowded and irregular.

Skeleton

The septa alternate thick and thin, and their

***Polyphyllia* Quoy & Gaimard, 1833**
(Gr: *polys,* many; Gr: *phyllon,* leaf. A reference to the numerous calices with their leaf-like appearance.)

DESCRIPTION
Living coral   (Col. pl. p. 144)

Polyphyllia is a free-living colonial coral that may be extremely elongate. It may be flat or arched

Polyphyllia talpina (X 2.6). Malaysia.

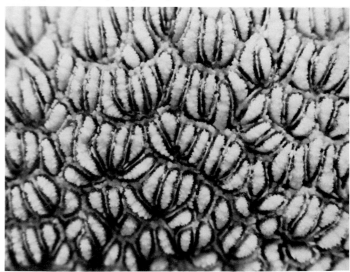

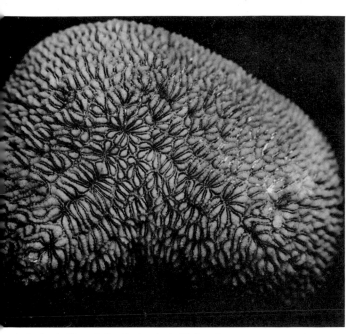

Polyphyllia talpina (nat. size). Malaysia.

and occasionally is crescent-shaped or tri-radiate. Polyps are confluent, and the tentacles are usually extended during the day, forming a dense carpet over the skeleton. Overall color is brown, although sometimes the tentacles are paler.

The central groove may be indistinct, but there is usually a row of calices running longitudinally along the corallum. Lateral calices are numerous and closely packed, giving a regular leaf-like or petaloid appearance. Septa are short and thick, and their margins are spiny. On the underside of the coral the costae are represented by tall pillars, making the surface rough and uneven to the touch. These may form into rows around the perimeter of the coral, but toward the center they become crowded and irregular.

Skeleton

The septa may radiate from one calice center to the next but often are interrupted by cross walls. These are formed from fused septa that run at right angles to the central axis. The septal margins are toothed, and these teeth have spinules or granules on their upper edges. The costal pillars are also spinose.

SIMILARITIES

Polyphyllia is a distinctive coral that is readily distinguished from other free-living fungiids by the prominent tentacles and the characteristic petaloid appearance of the calices.

TAXONOMIC NOTE

Veron and Pichon (1980) point out that there is considerable intraspecific variability in *Polyphyllia* and that as a result it has been described as eight different species belonging to three different genera (*Polyphyllia, Cryptabacia* and *Lithactinia*). It is now generally agreed that all the past names are synonyms of the single species, *Polyphyllia talpina.*

DISTRIBUTION AND ECOLOGY (Map #55)

Found in similar habitats to other fungiids, but generally less common. A single species: *Polyphyllia talpina* (Lamarck, 1801).

Halomitra Dana, 1848
(Gr: *halos,* sea; Gr: *mitra,* cap. Relating to the hat-like shape of this coral.)

DESCRIPTION
Living coral (Col. pl. p. 144)

This fungiid is colonial, free-living and rounded. It is usually strongly domed and about 20 cm in diameter but can grow to 60 cm. The corallum is brownish, and the mouths may show tints of gray, green or blue. Frequently the perimeter of the coral is blue or purple. Tentacles are not generally extended during the day.

There is a central calice that is often larger than

Halomitra pileus (X 4.4). Malaysia.

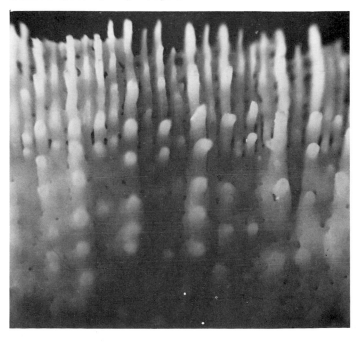

123

Tubastraea aurea. Puerto Rico, 2 m depth (Photo: P. Colin).

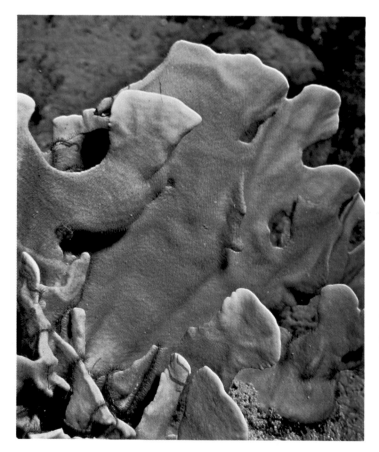

Millepora complanata. Puerto Rico, 6 m depth (Photo: P. Colin).

Millepora alcicornis. Bahamas, 10 m depth (Photo: P. Colin).

Stylaster roseus. Jamaica, 18 m depth (Photo: P. Colin).

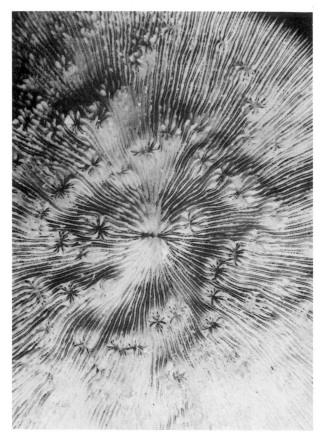

Halomitra pileus (nat. size). Malaysia.

Calice arrangement in *Halomitra* is similar to *Podabacia* and *Lithophyllon,* but these two genera are always attached whereas *Halomitra* is invariably free-living.

DISTRIBUTION AND ECOLOGY   (Map #56)
Rare to occasional, often in protected areas or on soft substrates. There are possibly two species, although Veron and Pichon (1980) consider that only *Halomitra pileus* (Linnaeus, 1758) is valid.

Sandalolitha Quelch, 1884
(Gr: *sandalon,* flat-fish; Gr: *lithos,* stone. Describing the growth form and shape of this coral.)

DESCRIPTION
Living coral   (Col. pl. p. 145)
Sandalolitha is colonial, free-living and rounded to elongate in shape. It is flat to dome-shaped and may be 50 cm in length. There is a central corallite that may not be distinct. Few to numerous secondary centers are scattered over the upper surface of the coral. The corallum is brownish, and the

Sandalolitha robusta (nat. size). Malaysia.

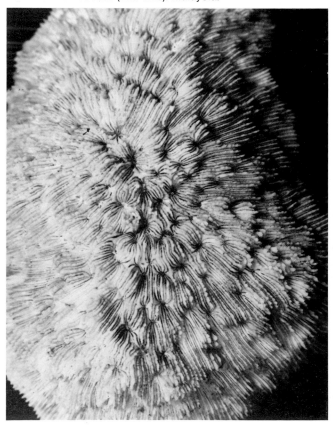

the secondary ones. The latter are usually numerous and arranged radially but may be few in number and scattered irregularly over the surface. The calices lack walls and their diameter is difficult to determine, but calice centers are often 0.5 to 1.0 cm apart. Septa converge on the calice centers and are closely packed, with thick and thin ones alternating. They usually arch upward between one calice and the next, giving the coral surface a lumpy appearance. Occasionally they run uninterrupted from the central corallite to the edge of the colony. The underside of the coral is rough to the touch due to the presence of costal spines.

Skeleton
Septal margins are armed with strong, smooth triangular spines up to 3 mm high. Costal spines are tall and have finely spinulose tips. They are arranged in rows or clusters.

SIMILARITIES
Halomitra can be confused underwater with its close relative *Sandalolitha.* The latter is distinguished by its serrated septal spines and branched costal spines.

126

perimeter is often a bluish brown. Tentacles are not generally extended during the day.

Septa are closely packed and alternate thick and thin. Most are short and run between adjacent calice centers, but some are longer. As in *Halomitra,* the septa usually arch upward between calices, giving the coral surface a lumpy appearance. Both the upper and the lower surfaces are rough and spiny.

Skeleton

Septal margins have rounded or triangular spines with granular or finely serrated margins. On the underside of the corallum are numerous spinose or granulose spines. These are arranged in rows or clusters.

SIMILARITIES

Sandalolitha is homeomorphic with *Halomitra,* and thus the two corals can easily be confused underwater. The only way to distinguish between the two genera is to examine the septal and costal spines. In *Sandalolitha* the septal spines are ser-

Sandalolitha robusta (undersurface) (X 4). Malaysia.

rated (smooth in *Halomitra*) and the costal spines are usually branched (finely spinulose in *Halomitra*).

TAXONOMIC NOTE

The original description of *Sandalolitha* was based on a specimen from Tahiti where "some morphological deviation from the normal western Pacific range of variation might be expected" (Veron & Pichon, 1980). These and other authors (Mergner and Scheer, 1974; Pillai & Scheer, 1976) believe that the genus *Parahalomitra,* described by Wells in 1937 from the central Indo-Pacific region, is synonymous with *Sandalolitha.* Thus the earlier name has been re-introduced (Veron & Pichon, 1980).

DISTRIBUTION AND ECOLOGY (Map #57)

Rare to occasional, especially on reef slopes and in rubble-strewn areas. There are probably two species: *Sandalolitha dentata* (Quelch, 1884), with few secondary centers, and *Sandalolitha robusta* (Quelch, 1886), with numerous secondary centers.

Sandalolitha robusta (X 2.8). Malaysia.

Millepora alcicornis. Jamaica, 6 m depth.

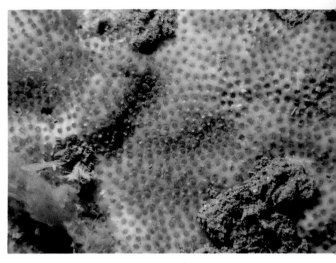

Stylocoeniella armata. Bali, Indonesia, 20 m depth.

Seriatopora hystrix. Sabah, Malaysia, 6 m depth.

Seriatopora hystrix. Sabah, Malaysia, 6 m depth.

Seriatopora. Sabah, Malaysia, 8 m depth.

Pocillopora. Sabah, Malaysia, 5 m depth.

Pocillopora. Sabah, Malaysia, 5 m depth.

Stylophora pistillata, with *Acropora*. Sabah, Malaysia, 4 m depth.

Stylophora pistillata. Sabah, Malaysia, 5 m depth.

Stylophora. Red Sea (Photo: M. Melzac).

Acropora, a tabular colony in which the stout "stem" is hidden from view. Sabah, Malaysia, 7 m depth.

Tabular *Acropora* in competition with a massive colony of *Porites*. Sabah, Malaysia, 6 m depth.

129

Zoopilus Dana, 1846

(Gr: *zoon*, animal; L: *pilus*, hair. Presumably relating to the distinctive arrangement of septa over the surface of the corallum, like hair on a head.)

DESCRIPTION

Living coral   (Col. pl. p. 145)

Zoopilus is free-living, either rounded or slightly elongate and usually about 20 to 30 cm in diameter. The corallum is strongly domed and light in weight. It is brownish in color and lacks the bluish colored margin characteristic of *Halomitra* and *Sandalolitha*. Tentacles are not extended during the day.

Zoopilus is colonial, with a central calice and a few irregularly placed lateral centers. These are small and indistinct in the living coral. Septa are prominent and arranged in a distinctive pattern over the surface of the coral. Some sweep in a widening arc starting slightly off-center, while others radiate out from the top of the coral. The principal septa run from the center of the corallum to the perimeter without arching up, as they do in some related fungiids. The top and undersurface of the corallum are spiny and rough to the touch.

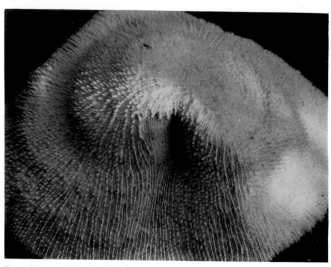

Zoopilus echinatus. Malaysia.

Skeleton

Septal margins are armed with well-spaced spines that themselves have serrated edges. The costae have strongly branched spines.

SIMILARITIES

Zoopilus is a distinctive fungiid that is readily identified by the arrangement of the septa, light-weight corallum and indistinct calice centers.

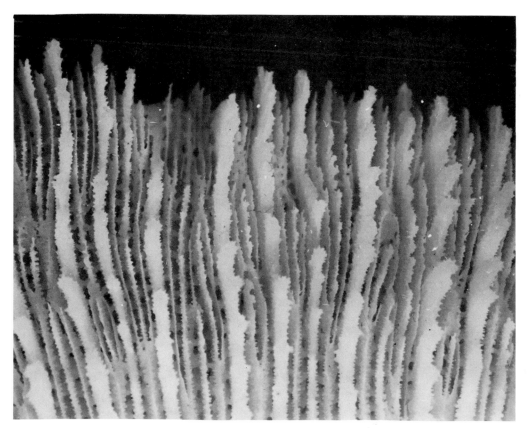

Zoopilus echinatus (X 4.7). Malaysia.

DISTRIBUTION AND ECOLOGY   (Map #58)

In general this is a relatively uncommon coral unless conditions are particularly suitable. Like other free-living fungiids it prefers soft substrates and reef slopes. There is a single species: *Zoopilus echinatus* Dana, 1846.

Lithophyllon Rehberg, 1892
(Gr: *lithos,* stone; Gr: *phyllon,* leaf. Presumably relating to the growth form of the genus.)

DESCRIPTION
Living coral

Lithophyllon forms small encrusting, semi-encrusting or foliaceous colonies. These are attached to the substrate and are brownish in color. Tentacles are not generally extended during the day.

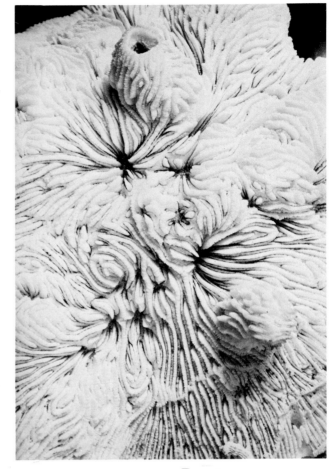

Lithophyllon cf. *edwardsi* (X 1.9). Great Barrier Reef.

Lithophyllon cf. *edwardsi* (X 5). Great Barrier Reef.

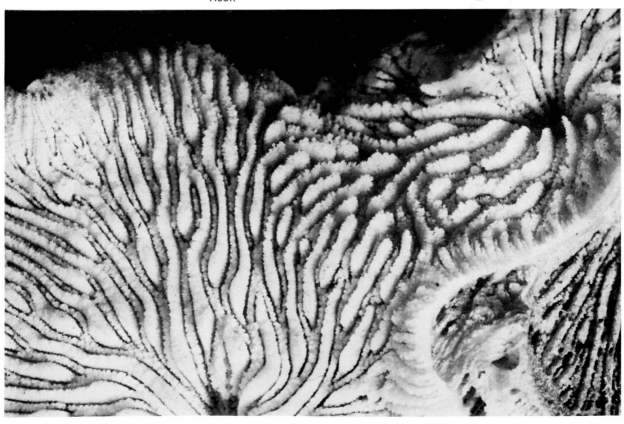

Acropora. Sabah, Malaysia, 10 m depth.

A semi-massive species of *Acropora*, on top of which is growing a second species. Sabah, Malaysia, 6 m depth.

Acropora. Sabah, Malaysia, 8 m depth.

Tabular *Acropora*. Sabah, Malaysia, 6 m depth.

Semi-massive *Acropora*. Sabah, Malaysia, 7 m depth.

Staghorn *Acropora*. Sabah, Malaysia, 7 m depth.

Foliaceous *Montipora*. Sabah, Malaysia, 10 m depth.

Leafy and plate-like *Montipora* species. Sabah, Malaysia, 6 m depth.

Branching *Montipora*. Sabah, Malaysia, 15 m depth.

Montipora, with the polyps extended. Sabah, Malaysia, 6 m depth.

Anacropora spinosa. Sabah, Malaysia, 10 m depth.

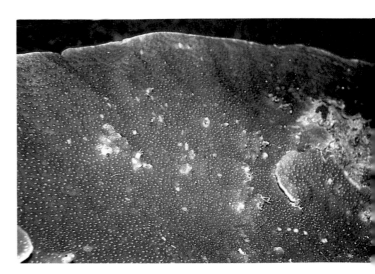

Astreopora. Sabah, Malaysia, 10 m depth.

A central calice is often visible, and there are numerous lateral calices packed closely together. They lack distinct walls, and the septa run from one calice to the next, arching up slightly as they do so. The septa are short, and this radial arrangement gives the surface of the coral a rather uneven appearance. High and low septa alternate, and their margins are toothed. The undersides of foliaceous parts of the corallum are covered with inconspicuous, low, rounded costae that are slightly rough to the touch.

Skeleton

Septal margins in *Lithophyllon* are granular or minutely spinulose. Costal margins are granular or have small rounded or pointed teeth. The corallum is solid and non-perforate.

SIMILARITIES

The size and arrangement of calices in *Lithophyllon* are similar to *Podabacia,* but growth form is a useful guide to the genera. *Lithophyllon* is usually encrusting, with the upper surface convex, but may have large lobe-like lateral folia. *Podabacia* generally grows upward from the substrate as a strong plate, with only the basal part attached. A more reliable distinction is that the corallum in *Podabacia* is pierced by many slits or pores, whereas in *Lithophyllon* it is solid. In addition the septal margins in *Lithophyllon* are granular or minutely spinulose, whereas in *Podabacia* they are strongly dentate.

DISTRIBUTION AND ECOLOGY   (Map #59)

Generally uncommon, this coral probably prefers deeper water on the reef slope. There is possibly only a single species: *Lithophyllon edwardsi* (Rosseau, 1850).

Podabacia Milne-Edwards & Haime, 1849

(Gr: *podos,* foot; L: *baca,* rounded, like a berry. Possibly relating to the mode of attachment of the corallum.)

DESCRIPTION

Living coral   (Col. pl. pp. 145, 148)

Podabacia is attached by its base and grows upward as a strong plate-like or foliaceous growth. It may sometimes occur in the shape of a large bowl,

exceeding one meter in diameter. Occasionally it is encrusting. The corallum is brownish in color, and tentacles are not visible during the day.

Calices are numerous and are present only on the upper surface of the corallum. They are arranged radially, and there is no distinct central calice. Calices are usually about 3 to 5 mm in diameter, but dividing walls are not formed. Septa converge on the calice centers and are closely packed with thick and thin ones alternating. In *Podabacia crustacea* they usually arch strongly upward between one calice center and the next. In *Podabacia formosa* they tend to be flatter and broader. Costal ridges are present or reduced to rows of spines.

Skeleton

Septal margins are adorned with dentate or serrated spines. Costal ridges are usually well developed in *Podabacia crustacea* and have spines along their margins that are granulose or branched. Costal ridges tend to be reduced in *Podabacia formosa* and represented by small, well spaced, simple or compound spines. In both species the corallum is pierced by numerous small pores or slits.

Podabacia crustacea (X 3). Malaysia.

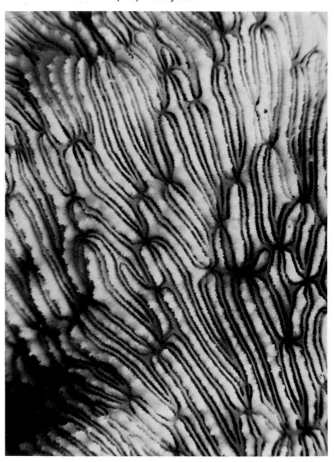

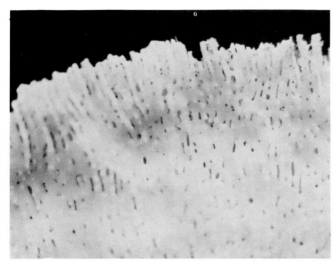

Podabacia crustacea (undersurface) (X 3). Malaysia.

SIMILARITIES

The arrangement of calices in *Podabacia* is similar to several other fungiids, but most are detached and the only confusion likely to arise is with *Lithophyllon*. The latter is attached but is generally encrusting rather than foliaceous. Positive identification is made by examining the corallum for small slits or pores. These are present in *Podabacia*, absent in *Lithophyllon*.

Podabacia could possibly be mistaken for an agariciid (*e.g., Leptoseris*) but can be identified by its growth form, the presence of costae or costal spines on the underside of the corallum and the stout, often exsert septa.

DISTRIBUTION AND ECOLOGY   (Map #60)

Rare to occasional and often preferring reef slopes, there are probably two species: *Podabacia crustacea* (Pallas, 1776) and *Podabacia formosa* Yabe & Sugiyama, 1932.

FAMILY PORITIDAE

Goniopora de Blainville, 1830

(Gr: *gonia,* an angle; L: *porus,* pore. Presumably relating to the angular shape of the calices.)

DESCRIPTION

Living coral   (Col. pl. p. 148)

Most *Goniopora* colonies are massive and rounded and a few are encrusting, but it is rare to find branched forms. The polyps are nearly always extended during the day, and the polyp column alone may be several centimeters long. At its upper end is a ring of about 24 simple tentacles that are typically spread out in a flower-like pattern. The polyps retract rapidly when touched to reveal the skeleton below. The polyps and corallum may be brown, gray, green or blue. Sometimes the peristome (within the ring of tentacles), the polyp column and the tentacles are all different colors.

Calices are rounded or hexagonal with a diameter of 1 to 3 mm and occasionally as much as 5 mm. Walls are shared and prominent.

Skeleton

There are usually 24 septa arranged in three cycles, but the number may be reduced in some species. Septal margins are pitted or spiny, and the skeleton is porous.

SIMILARITIES

Some *Goniopora* species have small corallites similar in size to those of *Porites*, which can cause confusion between the two genera. *Goniopora* can be distinguished underwater by the long polyps and

Goniopora sp. (X 3.3). Malaysia.

135

Astreopora. Sabah, Malaysia, 10 m depth.

Astreopora. Sabah, Malaysia, 12 m depth.

Astreopora. Sabah, Malaysia, 9 m depth.

Pavona decussata. Sabah, Malaysia, 7 m depth.

Pavona clavus. Sabah, Malaysia, 6 m depth.

Pavona venosa. Sabah, Malaysia, 10 m depth.

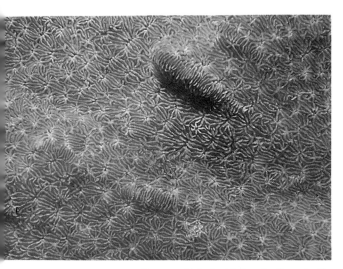

Pavona. Sabah, Malaysia, 7 m depth.

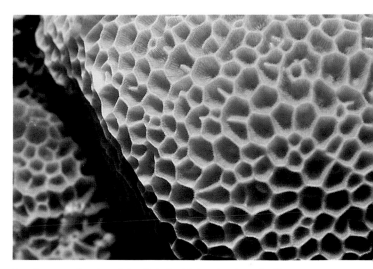

Gardineroseris planulata. Sabah, Malaysia, 4 m depth.

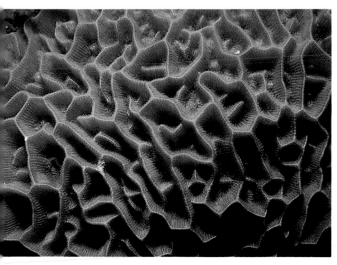

Gardineroseris planulata. Sabah, Malaysia, 6 m depth.

Gardineroseris planulata. Sabah, Malaysia, 7 m depth.

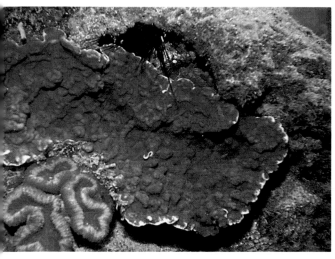

Leptoseris. Sabah, Malaysia, 12 m depth.

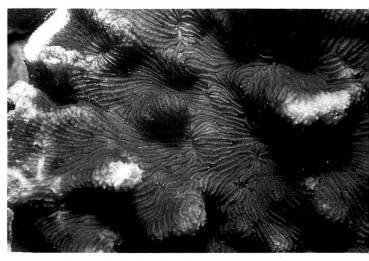

Leptoseris. Sabah, Malaysia, 10 m depth.

137

prominent tentacles. A close examination of the skeleton reveals that *Porites* has fewer septa (usually 12) than *Goniopora* (usually 24).

DISTRIBUTION AND ECOLOGY (Map #61)

Goniopora occurs over a wide range of habitats and thrives especially on reef slopes. Many colonies are small, but some may grow to a considerable size. There are probably between 20 and 30 species.

Porites Link, 1807
(L: *porus,* pore; Gr: *–ites,* suffix denoting likeness. Relating to porous nature of the corallum.)

DESCRIPTION

Living coral (Col. pl. pp. 148, 149)

Porites forms massive, branched or encrusting colonies. Most are brown in color, but green, blue, pink and purple are not uncommon. The polyps are often retracted during the day. If extended they can just be seen as a ring of tiny tentacles each less than a millimeter in length.

The surface of the coral is smooth or slightly granular to the touch. Calices are about 1.0 to 1.5 mm in diameter, round or polygonal and usually closely united by their walls or coenosteum. This arrangement gives a characteristic honeycomb ap-

Porites sp. (X 4.5). Malaysia.

pearance. In the subgenus *Synaraea* the calices are more widely spaced.

Skeleton

There are usually 12 septa, with paliform lobes at their inner ends. Septal edges are uneven or granular, and the skeleton is porous.

SIMILARITIES

Some *Montipora* and *Porites* species are confused underwater because of similarities in growth form, corallite arrangement and calice dimensions. In general, *Porites* can be identified by the lack of spiny tubercles or protrusions on the surface of the corallum and the regular, crowded corallites. Positive identification is made by examining the calices for septa, paliform lobes and columellae. In *Montipora* there may sometimes be as many as 12 septa, but they are poorly developed and often little more than ridges on the calice wall. Paliform lobes are absent, and a columella is rarely developed. In *Porites* there are generally 12 well formed septa with paliform lobes and a pinnacle-like columella.

Porites can also resemble its close relatives *Goniopora* and *Alveopora* but can generally be identified underwater because it lacks the highly elongate polyps characteristic of these two genera. Other differences are explained under the relevant generic descriptions.

DISTRIBUTION AND ECOLOGY (Map #62)

Porites is usually common on all reefs and may dominate certain areas. Branched colonies sometimes form large tracts along the reef front,

Porites sp. (X 3). Malaysia.

while encrusting forms tend to grow on the reef slope or at exposed sites. *Porites* heads are generally found along the reef rim and upper slopes and may grow to several meters in diameter. They provide a refuge for fishes and vantage points for the growth of other organisms. Often the living colonies are inhabited by brightly colored fanworms. The tops of massive forms (micro-atolls) in shallow back reef areas may be killed by overheating and emersion and the bare limestone colonized by clams (*Tridacna*) and other animals. *Porites* species are among the hardiest of corals and often survive in highly turbid areas.

At least 100 species of *Porites* (including the subgenus *Synaraea*) have been described, but a complete revision of the genus would probably reveal that only about half of these species were valid. It is unfortunate that a coral of such ecological importance is so difficult to identify (to species) underwater.

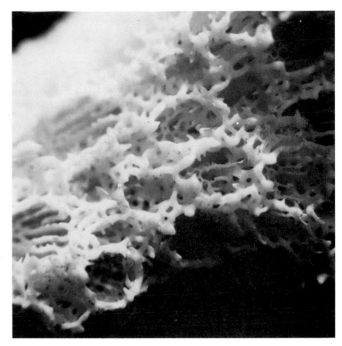

Alveopora sp. (X 4.5). Malaysia.

Alveopora de Blainville, 1830
(L: *alveolus,* small hollow; L: *porus,* pore. Relating to the small calices with their porous walls.)

DESCRIPTION
Living coral   (Col. pl. p. 149)
Alveopora forms massive, plate-like or branched

Alveopora sp. (X 4.5). Malaysia.

colonies. The polyps are small, but both column and tentacles protrude as they do in *Goniopora*. There are 12 tentacles. Corallum and tentacles are brown or bluish.

Calices are usually about 1 mm in diameter but may exceed 2 mm, and are either rounded or polygonal. They are crowded and closely united by their walls. The walls are narrow, and there is no intervening peritheca. There are no signs of septa in the living coral.

Skeleton
There are usually 12 to 24 septa, but these are reduced to small spines projecting inward from the corallite wall. The shared wall is pierced by numerous pores that give the wall a lace-like appearance. The corallum is extremely light due to its highly porous nature.

SIMILARITIES
The skeleton of *Alveopora* is unmistakable, but the living coral can occasionally be mistaken for *Goniopora* or *Porites*. The polyps in *Alveopora* are intermediate between the two genera, neither as long or large as in *Goniopora* but not as short as in *Porites*. Calices may be of a similar size to those in *Porites* but are usually smaller than in *Goniopora*. The corallite walls in *Alveopora* are always narrow and have a fragile appearance.

Pachyseris speciosa. Sabah, Malaysia, 7 m depth.

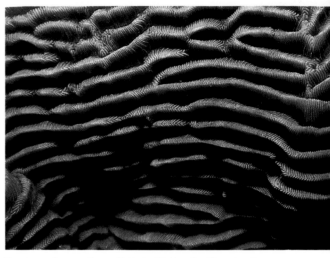

Pachyseris speciosa. Sabah, Malaysia, 7 m depth.

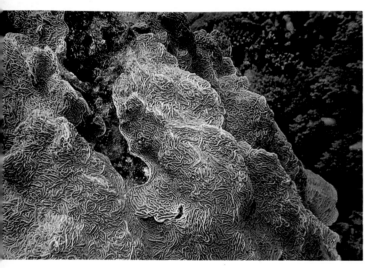

Pachyseris rugosa. Sabah, Malaysia, 8 m depth.

Pachyseris rugosa. Sabah, Malaysia, 10 m depth.

Coeloseris mayeri. Sabah, Malaysia, 8 m depth.

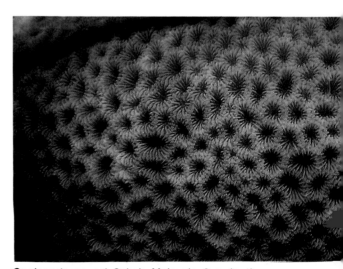

Coeloseris mayeri. Sabah, Malaysia, 8 m depth.

Coeloseris mayeri. Sabah, Malaysia, 6 m depth.

Pseudosiderastrea tayamai. Bali, Indonesia, 15 m depth.

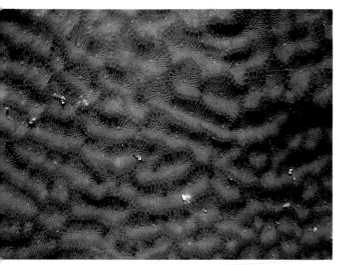

Coscinaraea columna. Sabah, Malaysia, 10 m depth.

Psammocora digitata. Sabah, Malaysia, 6 m depth.

Psammocora digitata. Sabah, Malaysia, 6 m depth.

Cycloseris. Great Barrier Reef, Australia (Photo: W. Deas).

141

DISTRIBUTION AND ECOLOGY (Map #63)

Alveopora is the least common member of its family. It is not often found in shallow regions, but tends to be restricted to the reef slope. There are probably about eight species.

FAMILY FAVIIDAE

Caulastrea Dana, 1848

(Gr: *kaulos,* cabbage stalk; Gr: *aster,* star. Probably relating to the projecting corallites and the star-like arrangement of septa.)

DESCRIPTION

Living coral (Col. pl. pp. 149, 152)

Colonies are usually low-growing, projecting less than 10 cm from the substrate. Occasionally they form low, rounded heads. The corallites branch freely and are separate from each other, rising up as parallel or nearly parallel branches (phaceloid growth form). Most calices are round, but they may be oval or irregular if in the process of asexual division. The diameter is around 1 cm but may reach 2 cm. The corallites are well separated at their upper ends, sometimes by a gap that exceeds the calice diameter. This feature may be obscured in live specimens by the soft tissue that extends over the top of the walls. The living mantle is usually some shade of brown, gray, green or blue. It is common for the color of the peristomal region (around the mouth) to contrast with that of the rest of the colony. A green center against brown is often seen. Each polyp has a ring of small simple tentacles that are normally retracted during the day.

Septa are numerous, and the larger ones are visible as distinct ridges under the soft tissue. Costae are present but can only just be seen in the living coral.

Skeleton

Septa are in cycles, and the larger ones are slightly exsert, projecting a few millimeters above the top of the wall. Septal margins are toothed. Costae are continuous with the septa and run from the top of the wall down the outside of the corallite. The extent to which they are developed varies, and they are most clearly seen at the upper ends of the branches.

SIMILARITIES

Caulastrea is easily distinguished from other faviids by its long, freely branching corallites. This type of growth form is similar to that in some *Euphyllia* species, but *Caulastrea* can be readily identified by its small, delicate tentacles and by the serrated septal margins. *Euphyllia* has prominent tentacles and smooth septa.

TAXONOMIC NOTE

The poorly known coral *Astraeosmilia* Ortmann, 1892, may be synonymous with *Caulastrea.* It has only been reported from East Africa and is described as similar to *Caulastrea* but subplocoid, with the corallites partly united by epitheca. Until further specimens are found, its status remains obscure.

DISTRIBUTION AND ECOLOGY (Map #64)

Caulastrea is an uncommon coral that generally prefers reef slopes. It often forms small colonies

Caulastrea furcata (X 2). Malaysia.

less than 20 cm in diameter but can grow in broad tracts over a meter in diameter. There are probably five or six species.

Bikiniastrea Wells, 1954
(*Bikini,* first found on Bikini Atoll; Gr: *aster,* star.)

DESCRIPTION
Living coral

Bikiniastrea forms rounded heads from a few centimeters to half a meter or more in diameter. The corallites protrude about 1 cm from the surface and are well separated, except where budding occurs and small clumps of corallites are produced. These compact clumps occur at intervals over the surface of the corallum. Calices are circular, and mature ones are about 1 cm in diameter. Polyps do not extend fully during the day, but a ring of small tentacles may just be visible. Colony color is usually brown or greenish.

Septa are prominent and numerous, with rough margins. The major septa rise gently or steeply from the central fossa and are slightly exsert as they pass over the walls. Costae run down the outside of the corallites to the perithecal areas, where they are clearly visible as low ridges.

Skeleton

The margins of both septa and costae are serrated. There is a well formed columella. New corallites are formed by intratentacular division.

SIMILARITIES

Bikiniastrea can be mistaken for *Caulastrea,* but the corallites in *Bikiniastrea* are distinctly shorter and are clumped rather than freely branching. The polyps in *Caulastrea* are also fleshier than in *Bikiniastrea* and tend to obscure the corallum.

Bikiniastrea may also be confused with *Favia,* but examination of the corallum reveals that the corallites in *Bikiniastrea* are considerably taller than in *Favia,* are more widely separated and in places are produced into distinctly branched clumps (see also note below).

TAXONOMIC NOTE

There are differing opinions as to the validity of this genus. *Bikiniastrea* was first described by Wells in 1954, but more recent workers claim that it is simply a plocoid *Favia* converted to the subdendroid form by environmental conditions, *i.e.,* an ecomorph of *Favia.* It has been placed in the "*Favia amicorum* complex" by Veron, Pichon & Wijsman-Best (1977). They suggest that the branching corallites appear to be "largely a result of deposition of sediment within and around colonies, allowing only exsert corallites and protruding parts of colonies to grow."

There is, in addition to *Bikiniastrea,* another coral called *Barabattoia* Yabe & Sugiyama, 1941, that may or may not be a valid genus. It has corallites that rise about 1 cm from the surface of the corallum but do not form small clumps as in *Bikiniastrea.* Veron *et al.* (1977) consider that *Bikiniastrea laddi, Barabattoia mirabilis* and *Favia amicorum* may be closely related species or, as claimed by Wijsman-Best (1972), just a single species (*Favia amicorum*). They admit, however, that they have insufficient specimens to resolve the problem. The present author has studied the "*Favia amicorum* complex" in Sabah (Malaysia) and believes that *Bikiniastrea* is distinct but that the status of *Barabattoia* is more doubtful.

DISTRIBUTION AND ECOLOGY (Map #65)

Bikiniastrea is a relatively rare coral that appears to prefer reef slopes. Colonies are usually about 20 cm in diameter but may grow larger. There is a single species, *Bikiniastrea laddi* Wells, 1954, but it may be found after further studies that other species exist that are at present included in *Barabattoia* (see note above).

Favia Oken, 1815
(L: *favus,* honeycomb. Relating to the regular appearance of the corallites.)

DESCRIPTION
Living coral (Col. pl. p. 152)

Most *Favia* colonies are massive and rounded, but there are also encrusting forms. They are usually brown or green, occasionally white or yellow. In some species the peristomal area (around the mouth) is a different color from the rest of the colony. *Favia favus* is generally mottled in shades of brown. Each polyp has a ring of small tentacles, but these are usually retracted during the day.

Corallites have their own walls and are usually

Cycloseris costulata. Sabah, Malaysia, 20 m depth.

Fungia spp. Sabah, Malaysia, 10 m depth.

Heliofungia actiniformis. Sabah, Malaysia, 5 m depth.

Herpolitha limax (top) with *Fungia* spp. Sabah, Malaysia, 10 m depth.

Polyphyllia talpina. Sabah, Malaysia, 6 m depth.

Halomitra pileus. Sabah, Malaysia, 10 m depth.

144

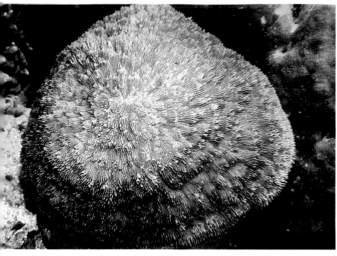

Sandalolitha robusta. Sabah, Malaysia, 12 m depth.

Sandalolitha robusta. Sabah, Malaysia, 7 m depth.

Zoopilus echinatus. Sabah, Malaysia, 4 m depth.

Zoopilus echinatus. Sabah, Malaysia, 15 m depth.

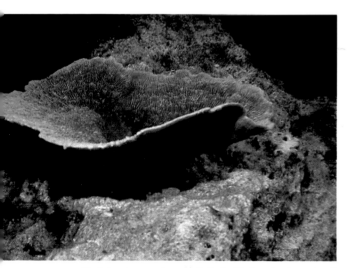

Podabacia crustacea. Sabah, Malaysia, 7 m depth.

Podabacia crustacea (also *Seriatopora* and *Porites*). Sabah, Malaysia, 6 m depth.

145

Favia pallida (X 2.4). Malaysia.

Skeleton

A close examination of perithecal areas reveals that there is usually a fine groove or ridge where costae from adjacent calices meet. Thus costae are not generally continuous between one calice and the next. Margins of both septa and costae are armed with fine or coarse serrations. The columella is well formed, and paliform lobes may be present.

SIMILARITIES

Favia is most likely to be confused with *Montastraea* and *Plesiastrea* (in particular, *Favia stelligera* with *Plesiastrea versipora*). It is possible to distinguish between *Favia* and *Montastraea/Plesiastrea* by looking at the way new corallites are added to the colony. In *Favia* the parent corallite produces a second mouth within the original ring of tentacles and eventually divides to give two separate calices (fission or intratentacular reproduction). Thus it is common to see irregularly shaped corallites in the process of dividing. In *Montastraea* and *Plesiastrea* this method of reproduction is much less common. Instead, new

Intratentacular and extratentacular reproduction.

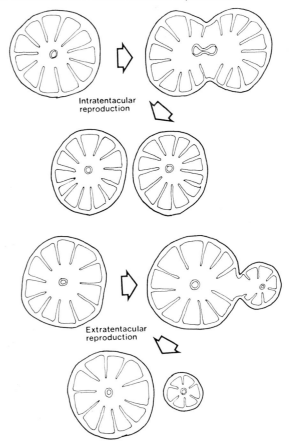

Intratentacular reproduction

Extratentacular reproduction

separated from their neighbors by a groove. In some species the corallites are closely crowded, and in rare cases there may be two or three centers together. Corallites are roundish but may be distorted during asexual reproduction. Such reproduction is intratentacular, *i.e.*, a second mouth appears within the parent corallite and is followed by "fission" to give two separate calices. In most cases corallites are elevated from the surface of the corallum by several millimeters and occasionally by as much as 5 mm. Corallite diameter is variable. Many of the common species have a diameter of approximately 10 mm, but it may reach 20 mm. An exception is *Favia stelligera*, which has small, low corallites about 2 mm in diameter.

Septa are numerous and usually clearly visible, though occasionally obscured by living tissues. They pass over the walls and continue as low costal ridges on exposed perithecal areas. Septa and costae are slightly rough to the touch.

calices are budded off from outside the parent corallite (budding or extratentacular reproduction). This results in the appearance of smaller corallites between the larger ones. The figure explains the difference between these two types of reproduction in diagrammatic form. In addition to these differences, most *Montastraea* and *Plesiastrea* have a distinct crown of paliform lobes on the inner ends of the septa. Paliform lobes may be present in *Favia* but in general are less well developed.

Favia is distinguished from *Bikiniastrea* by its low, unbranched corallites.

Some *Favia* species (*e.g., Favia matthai*) can be mistaken for *Diploastrea,* but *Favia* lacks the widened septa characteristic of this genus.

Favia can be distinguished from *Favites* and *Goniastrea* because in nearly all coralla the majority of calices are clearly separate *(Favia)* rather than united (*Favites, Goniastrea*). Veron and his associates (1977) regard the generic designation of *Favia* and *Favites* species as "somewhat arbitrary," especially as regards the plocoid/cerioid condition. They suggest that, "perhaps the most consistent difference is the nature of the budding, which is usually equal or near-equal in *Favia*, and markedly circumferential in *Favites*."

DISTRIBUTION AND ECOLOGY (Map #66)

Favia is common in nearly all reef localities but does not usually form heads more than a meter or two in diameter. There are possibly 15 species of *Favia* in the Indo-Pacific (Veron *et al.,* record 11 from the Great Barrier Reef).

Favites Link, 1807

(L: *favus,* honeycomb; Gr: *–ites,* like. Describing the typical appearance of *Favites,* with its joined, angular corallites.)

DESCRIPTION

Living coral (Col. pl. pp. 153, 156)

Favites is sometimes encrusting but more often forms massive, irregular hillocks or rounded colonies. At depth these colonies may be flat and plate-like. *Favites* is often brown, green or pinkish in color, occasionally red. Often the peristome contrasts in color with the rest of the colony. For example, the corallite walls may be brown and the peristome green or pink. A ring of tentacles is

Favites abdita (× 1.8). Malaysia.

associated with each polyp but is usually only extended at night.

Corallites are fused, and the common wall is usually acute and often raised more on one side than the other. The width of the wall ranges from about 2 to 5 mm. In *Favites peresi* Faure & Pichon, from the Red Sea, the walls are high and leafy with the fossa 6 to 8 mm deep. Among the many species of *Favites* the calices are rounded, oval, angular or polygonal, and occasionally short series are formed. Calice diameter ranges from over 20 mm to less than 5 mm according to species, and it is common to find a great deal of variation in a single specimen. This is partly a result of unequal fission of corallites and is often particularly noticeable around the margins of the colony.

Septa are prominent and numerous, rising steeply or gently from the fossa. They generally pass over the walls uninterrupted between adjacent calices. The margins of the septa are spiny, and these spines are usually visible and make the coral surface rough to the touch. In some species a layer of fleshy tissue covers the corallum and obscures

Podabacia crustacea. Sabah, Malaysia, 6 m depth.

Goniopora. Sabah, Malaysia, 7 m depth.

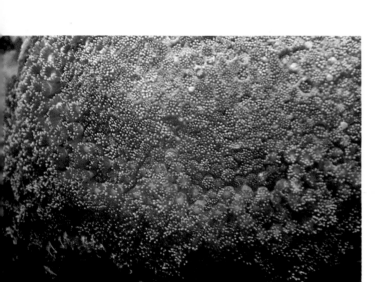

Goniopora. Sabah, Malaysia, 7 m depth.

Goniopora. Sabah, Malaysia, 8 m depth.

Goniopora. Red Sea (Photo: M. Melzac).

Porites. Sabah, Malaysia, 6 m depth.

148

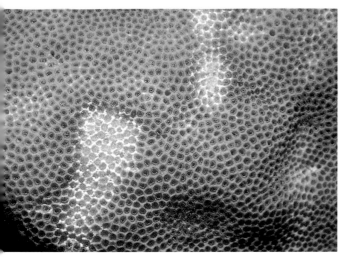

Porites. Sabah, Malaysia, 6 m depth.

Porites. Sabah, Malaysia, 5 m depth.

Porites. Sabah, Malaysia, 5 m depth.

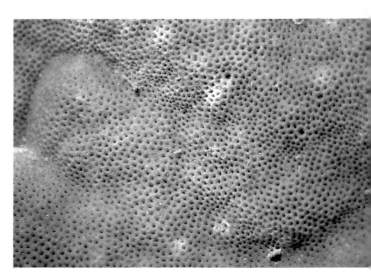

Alveopora. Bali, Indonesia, 20 m depth.

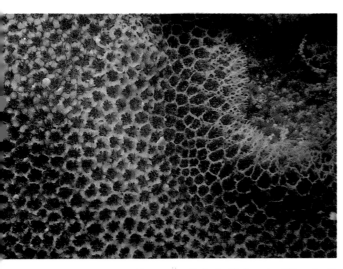

Alveopora. Sabah, Malaysia, 10 m depth.

Caulastrea. Sabah, Malaysia, 15 m depth.

149

the septa, but often the spines show up as small warts.

Skeleton

The spines on the septal margins are usually well developed and may themselves be toothed. Paliform lobes are often absent or poorly developed but may be prominent in some species. The columella is well developed.

SIMILARITIES

The "typical" *Favites* with its high, acute and uneven walls is easily identified, but several species do not show these characters so clearly.

Some *Favites* resemble *Goniastrea* and may be difficult to distinguish underwater. An examination of the skeleton reveals that *Goniastrea* has well developed paliform lobes and fine, even septal teeth. *Favites* can be distinguished either by the lack of paliform lobes or by the presence of ragged septal teeth.

Other *Favites* species can be mistaken for *Favia*, and the main distinction between these two closely related genera is based on the morphology of the corallum. This is plocoid (with separate corallites) in *Favia* and cerioid (with shared corallites) in *Favites*.

Some colonies of the brain coral *Platygyra* have short monocentric valleys and can be confused with certain *Favites* species, (*e.g., P. pini*). In *Favites*, however, the proportion of calices with more than one center is much lower than in *Platygyra*, and the septal spines are stouter and more ragged.

DISTRIBUTION AND ECOLOGY   (Map #67)

This is a common genus found on all parts of the reef. It often occurs as small heads along the reef front, but colonies may grow to a meter or more in diameter. As many as 30 species have been described, but it is likely that a complete revision of the genus would reduce the number to 15 or less. Nine species are described from the Great Barrier Reef (Veron *et al.,* 1977).

Goniastrea Milne-Edwards & Haime, 1848

(Gr: *gonia,* corner; Gr: *aster,* star. Relating to the appearance of the coral, with its joined, polygonal calices.)

DESCRIPTION

Living coral   (Col. pl. p. 156)

The corallum in *Goniastrea* is usually rounded, convex or lobed, occasionally encrusting. Overall color is brown, green or grayish, and the walls and peristome may be different shades. The tentacles are small and are usually retracted during the day.

Corallites are crowded together and are united by their walls. Often the calices are single-centered and polygonal (*e.g., Goniastrea retiformis, G. edwardsi*), with calice diameter ranging from 4 to 10 mm. Other species have a tendency to form short meanders with two or three centers (*G. pectinata*), and one is meandroid with valleys of variable length (*G. australensis,* previously known as *G. benhami*). The width from mid-ridge to mid-ridge in *G. australensis* is usually between 5 and 10 mm.

The fossa or valley in *Goniastrea* species is sometimes constricted, but in general its width is slightly greater than the width of the walls. It may be deep or shallow. Septa are numerous and visible as fine lines radiating from the fossa, up and over the walls. They feel almost smooth to the touch. Sometimes there is a faintly discernible ring around the polyp mouth that corresponds to the notches between the paliform lobes and the main parts of the septa (see below).

Skeleton

Septal margins are finely serrated. Paliform lobes are usually well developed and are clearly visible at the inner ends of the larger septa adjacent to the columella.

Goniastrea aspera (X 1.8). Malaysia.

SIMILARITIES

Goniastrea may be confused with *Favites*, but in general the corallites in *Favites* are larger, the corallite walls much more irregular in height and the septa more spiny. Also, paliform lobes are not developed in *Favites* as they are in *Goniastrea*.

Goniastrea australensis (= *G. benhami*) is similar in appearance to the brain coral *Platygyra lamellina*, but can be identified by the steep, deep valleys, paliform lobes, septa that converge to centers in the valleys and finely serrated septal margins.

Goniastrea species with small corallites bear a superficial resemblance to *Coeloseris*, but there are many differences between the two genera. The septa in *Coeloseris* are leafier, have almost smooth margins and lack paliform lobes. In addition, there is no columella in *Coeloseris*.

DISTRIBUTION AND ECOLOGY   (Map #68)

Goniastrea is common on most reefs and is a hardy coral often found on back reef areas. Many of the colonies are of small or medium size, but others grow to a meter or more in diameter. There are probably eight species.

Platygyra Ehrenberg, 1834

(Gr: *platys,* wide; Gr: *gyros,* round. Probably relating to the wide, sinuous valleys.)

DESCRIPTION

Living coral   (Col. pl. p. 156)

Platygyra commonly forms massive, rounded heads, but some colonies are flattened. A branched species, *Platygyra zelli* Veron, Pichon & Wijsman-Best, is described from the Great Barrier Reef. The corallum is often a combination of green, brown or white, with valleys and walls of contrasting colors. Darker colors generally occur on shaded parts of the colony. A row of small mouths can usually be seen placed at regular intervals along the center of each valley. Sometimes a long, slit-like mouth is present. Tentacles are small and simple but are usually only visible at night.

Platygyra is characterized by its long sinuous valleys, but it is not unusual to see single calices or short series composed of two or three centers. Single calices are polygonal and about 3 to 7 mm in diameter. The width from mid-ridge to mid-ridge

Platygyra lamellina (X 3). Malaysia.

of the meanders is about 3 to 9 mm. In many forms the widths of the wall and the intervening valley are approximately equal. In these types the walls slope down steeply and are either triangular in cross-section or have a rounded outline. Other forms have walls narrower than the valleys, with almost vertical sides.

Septa are closely packed, and most are continuous as they pass between adjacent valleys. Septal margins are rough to the touch although sometimes the spines are obscured by living tissues. There are usually between 13 and 16 septa per cm.

Skeleton

Septa are exsert by several millimeters as they pass over the walls. Septal margins are armed with sharp, ragged teeth. The septa converge to calice centers in single calices and sometimes in short valley systems, but remain parallel in the long valleys. The columella is a well developed spongy structure a millimeter or more in width.

SIMILARITIES

Platygyra species with short series (*e.g., P. pini*) can be mistaken for *Favites*. In *Favites*, however,

Caulastrea. Sabah, Malaysia, 5 m depth.

Bikiniastrea laddi. Sabah, Malaysia, 8 m depth.

Favia pallida. Sabah, Malaysia, 6 m depth.

Favia. Sabah, Malaysia, 5 m depth.

Favia. Sabah, Malaysia, 5 m depth.

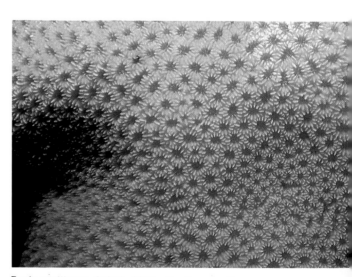

Favia stelligera, Sabah, Malaysia, 5 m depth.

Favites. Sabah, Malaysia, 6 m depth.

Favites acuticollis. Sabah, Malaysia, 5 m depth.

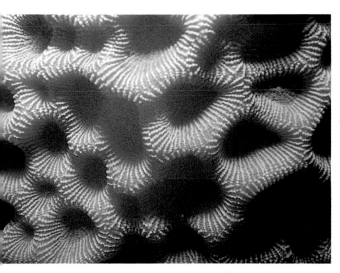

Favites. Sabah, Malaysia, 7 m depth.

Favites. Sabah, Malaysia, 5 m depth.

Favites. Sabah, Malaysia, 5 m depth.

Favites flexuosa. Sabah, Malaysia, 12 m depth.

Platygyra pini (X 2.5). Malaysia.

the proportion of calices with more than one center is much lower than in *Platygyra*, and the septal spines are stouter and more ragged. *P. lamellina* resembles *Goniastrea australensis* underwater, but the skeleton of the latter is readily distinguished by the presence of paliform lobes and by septa that converge to centers in the valleys.

The brain coral *Leptoria phrygia* also has long meanders, but these are narrower and more regular than in *Platygyra*. In addition, the skeletal features in *Leptoria* are finer than in *Platygyra* and the columella is plate-like rather than spongy.

DISTRIBUTION AND ECOLOGY   (Map #69)

Platygyra is common on most reefs and occupies a variety of habitats. It may form colonies a meter or more in diameter. Five species are described from the Great Barrier Reef (Veron *et al.,* 1977), and there may be as many as eight throughout the Indo-Pacific region.

Leptoria **Milne-Edwards & Haime, 1848** (Gr: *leptos,* slender; Gr: *-ia,* ending denoting state of being. Presumably relating to the characteristically narrow valleys.)

DESCRIPTION
Living coral   (Col. pl. pp. 156, 157)

The corallum in *Leptoria* is massive, but the outline of the coral is irregular and gently undulating rather than rounded. It is brown or greenish in color, normally with the valleys the same color as the walls. Tentacles are small and simple and are usually retracted during the day.

Calices are joined in series to form long, sinuous valleys. These are relatively deep (2 to 3 mm) and are a constant width within a single colony, giving a regular appearance. The distance across the valleys from mid-ridge to mid-ridge is seldom less than 3 mm or more than 5 mm.

Septa are closely packed (about 15 to 20 per cm) and clearly visible as they pass up and over the walls. Septal margins are almost smooth to the touch.

Skeleton

Septa are slightly exsert as they pass over the walls. Their margins bear small, fine teeth. The septa are parallel and do not converge to calice centers. In the center of the valley they join to the columella, which is in the form of a single vertical plate. The upper margin of this plate may be lobed, but below this it is normally complete and continuous. There are no paliform lobes.

SIMILARITIES

Leptoria can be confused with the related brain coral *Platygyra* but has a combination of features that enable it to be identified underwater. The undulating outline of *Leptoria* is characteristic, as are the long, sinuous and narrow valleys and the finely serrated septal margins. Conclusive identification

Leptoria phrygia (X 3.4). Malaysia.

of *Leptoria* is made by examining the columella, which is plate-like rather than wide and spongy as in *Platygyra*.

TAXONOMIC NOTE

There has in the past been considerable debate concerning the synonymy of *Leptoria* species. Crossland (1952) suggested that only a single species (*Leptoria phrygia*) was valid, and this view is supported by others, including Veron, Pichon and Wijsman-Best (1977). The alternative is to accept the existence of three species: *L. phrygia, L. gracilis* and *L. tenuis*.

DISTRIBUTION AND ECOLOGY   (Map #70)

Leptoria is usually found along the reef front and upper reef slope and may form colonies several meters in diameter. There is possibly only a single species: *Leptoria phrygia* (Ellis & Solander, 1786).

Oulophyllia Milne-Edwards & Haime, 1848

(Gr: *oulos,* curly or twisted; Gr: *phyllon,* leaf. Presumably relating to the conspicuous valleys and prominent walls.)

DESCRIPTION

Living coral   (Col. pl. p. 157)

Oulophyllia forms massive, convex or rounded colonies. They are usually pale brown in color, sometimes darker or with greenish tinges. The polyps are retracted during the day, but a mass of small tentacles is visible at night.

Corallites are joined in relatively short, discontinuous valleys, but single calices are extremely rare. Calice centers are usually distinct, and a small mouth is visible. The distance from mid-ridge to mid-ridge varies from 1 to 2 cm, with the width of the wall and the valley approximately equal. The depth of the valley may range from 5 mm to over 10 mm, and the intervening walls may be correspondingly low, or high and acute. Septa are prominent, and their edges are slightly rough to the touch. There are about 6 to 12 septa per cm.

Skeleton

Septa are slightly exsert, and their margins are finely serrated. They run from the columellae up and over the walls and also form the connection between adjacent columellae in the valleys. The

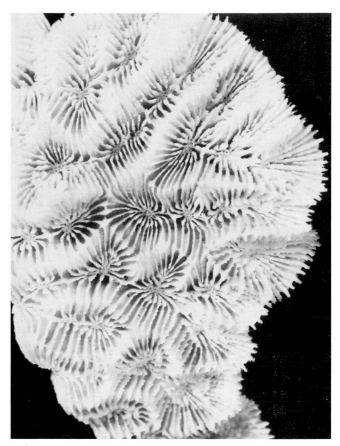

Oulophyllia crispa (X 1.5). Malaysia.

columella centers are well formed and spongy. Paliform lobes may be present at the inner ends of the septa.

SIMILARITIES

Oulophyllia could be mistaken for *Platygyra* but is readily identified by its wide valleys and the smaller number of septa per centimeter.

TAXONOMIC NOTE

Oulophyllia was merged together with *Platygyra* into the genus *Coeloria* by Gardiner (1904). The two genera were subsequently separated (Gravier, 1910), but it is still possible to find *Oulophyllia* referred to as *Coeloria*. Veron and his co-workers (1977) also consider that the genus *Coelogyra*, described by Nemenzo in 1959, should be included in *Oulophyllia*.

DISTRIBUTION AND ECOLOGY   (Map #71)

This is a fairly uncommon coral that appears to prefer reef slopes. Colonies may reach several meters in diameter. There is probably only a single species: *Oulophyllia crispa* (Lamarck, 1816).

155

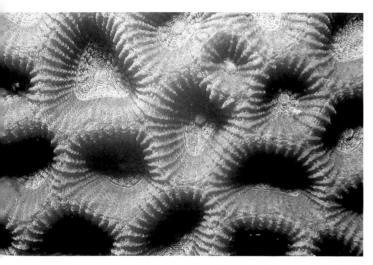

Favites flexuosa. Sabah, Malaysia, 12 m depth.

Goniastrea. Sabah, Malaysia, 4 m depth.

Goniastrea. Sabah, Malaysia, 6 m depth.

Platygyra. Sabah, Malaysia, 9 m depth.

Platygyra. Sabah, Malaysia, 6 m depth.

Leptoria phrygia. Great Barrier Reef, Australia (Photo: W. Deas).

156

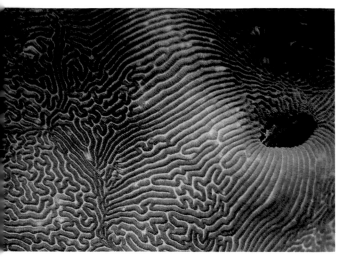

Leptoria phrygia. Sabah, Malaysia, 7 m depth.

Leptoria phrygia. Sabah, Malaysia, 7 m depth.

Oulophyllia crispa. Sabah, Malaysia, 10 m depth.

Oulophyllia crispa. Sabah, Malaysia, 12 m depth.

Hydnophora. Sabah, Malaysia, 5 m depth.

Hydnophora. Sabah, Malaysia, 5 m depth.

Hydnophora Fischer de Waldheim, 1807
(Gr: *hydnon,* tuber; Gr: *phero,* to bear.
Relating to the cone-shaped monticules
typical of the genus.)

DESCRIPTION
Living coral
(Col. pl. pp. 157, 160, 192)

There are both branched and massive *Hydnophora* species, and in this genus growth form is an important diagnostic feature:

H. rigida: corallum branched but with no encrusting or massive base. Branches seldom exceed 4 cm in diameter throughout their length.

H. exesa: massive or encrusting, sometimes producing branches from this base. Branches are stout and usually well over 4 cm in diameter.

H. microconos: massive, usually convex and with no branches. Often there is a free leafy extension around the edge of the colony.

Hydnophora species are usually brown, green or yellowish, with the tips of the monticules paler. Tentacles are often partially extended during the day. They are small (2 to 4 mm long), simple and tightly packed. Sometimes they extend above the level of the monticules and obscure them from view.

Corallites are joined in series, but the walls only rarely form a solid ridge. If they do so, then the ridges are seldom over 20 mm in length. The formation of such ridges occurs in particular toward the tips of branches. In general, however, the walls (collines) are represented by numerous cone-shaped protuberances called monticules or hydnae. Some are flattened on top but others come to a sharp point. Their width and height are variable, but the width at the base seldom exceeds 5 mm. In *H. microconos* the diameter of the monticules is usually only 2 to 3 mm. Often the monticules are packed closely together and do not appear to follow any particular pattern. In other cases, especially on branches, they are arranged in regular longitudinal rows. Septa are usually visible as fine, closely-packed ridges running from the valleys up and over the top of the cones or ridges. They are smooth to the touch.

Skeleton

Septal margins are finely dentate or almost smooth, according to species: *H. rigida,* mostly non-dentate; *H. microconos,* a few teeth at the inner ends of the septa; *H. exesa,* regularly dentate at the inner ends of the septa (adjacent to the columella). The columella usually forms well defined centers in *H. rigida,* but is often continuous around the monticules in the other two species.

SIMILARITIES

Hydnophora is a distinctive genus characterized by the presence of monticules. It could possibly be confused with *Clavarina* and branched forms of

Hydnophora exesa (X 2.5).
Malaysia.

Hydnophora exesa (X 2.5). Malaysia.

Merulina laxa in the cases where the monticules in *Hydnophora* unite to form ridges on the branches. However, a close examination of the corallum will reveal certain areas where monticules are prominent.

DISTRIBUTION AND ECOLOGY (Map #72)

Hydnophora is a fairly common coral that colonizes a variety of reef habitats. *H. rigida* sometimes grows in tracts in shallower areas in much the same way as staghorn, *Acropora*. Massive and encrusting colonies often reach about 2 m in diameter. As many as 20 species have been described, but there is a great deal of intraspecific variation and it is possible that only three species are valid: *Hydnophora exesa* (Pallas, 1766), *Hydnophora microconos* (Lamarck, 1816) and *Hydnophora rigida* (Dana, 1846).

Plesiastrea Milne-Edwards & Haime, 1848
(Gr: *plesios,* recent; Gr: *aster,* star. Relating to the star-like appearance of the calices.)

DESCRIPTION
Living coral (Col. pl. p. 160)
Plesiastrea is usually massive and either rounded or flattened but may be encrusting. It is brown or greenish in color. Tentacles are retracted during the day. Corallites are usually rounded and separate from each other but sometimes are crowded with the walls touching. Calices are about 2 to 3 mm in diameter and are raised slightly above the surface of the corallum. Interspersed among these mature corallites are ones of a smaller size. These have been produced during asexual reproduction by extratentacular budding.

Septa are numerous and their margins are slightly rough to the touch. The main ones pass over the walls and continue on perithecal areas as well defined costae. The costae may be discontinuous or may fuse with those from adjacent calices.

Skeleton
The margins of both septa and costae are finely dentate. The coral surface between the costae is smooth or granulated. The largest septa of the first order reach the columella and have well developed paliform lobes. Septa of the other two orders may not reach the columella, and the paliform lobes may be less well developed or absent.

Plesiastrea versipora (X 2.5). Malaysia.

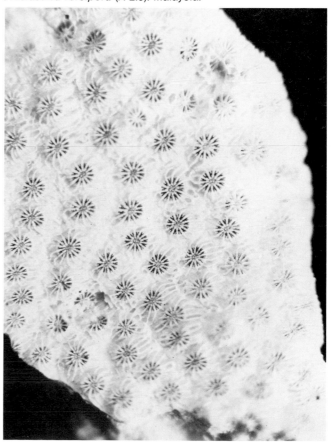

159

Hydnophora. Sabah, Malaysia, 4 m depth.

Hydnophora. Sabah, Malaysia, 6 m depth.

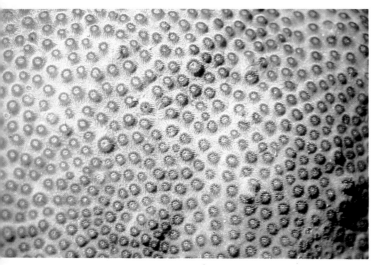

Plesiastrea versipora. Sabah, Malaysia, 20 m depth.

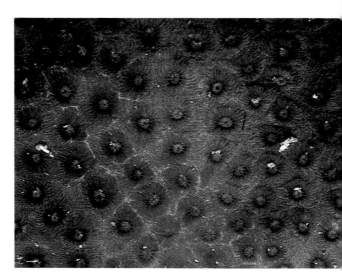

Plesiastrea versipora. Sabah, Malaysia, 10 m depth.

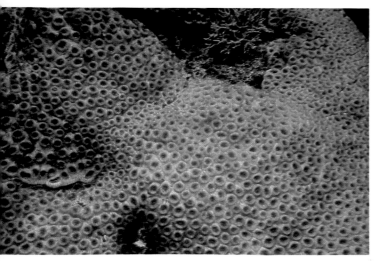

Montastraea. Sabah, Malaysia, 6 m depth.

Montastraea. Sabah, Malaysia, 6 m depth.

160

Diploastrea heliopora. Sabah, Malaysia, 10 m depth.

Diploastrea heliopora. Sabah, Malaysia, 12 m depth.

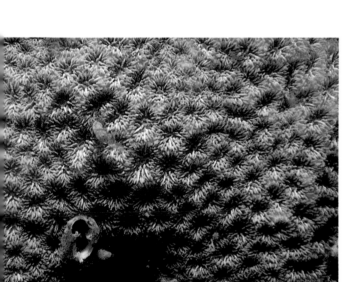

Leptastrea. Sabah, Malaysia, 9 m depth.

Leptastrea. Bali, Indonesia, 15 m depth.

Leptastrea. Sabah, Malaysia, 10 m depth.

Cyphastrea. Sabah, Malaysia, 8 m depth.

SIMILARITIES

Plesiastrea versipora, with its small, slightly protruding corallites, resembles *Cyphastrea,* but an examination of perithecal areas distinguishes between the two genera. In *Plesiastrea* the septa run onto perithecal areas, but in *Cyphastrea* they do not extend beyond the limits of the corallite wall. In this genus the peritheca is more extensive and is covered with tiny spines.

P. versipora can also be confused with *Favia stelligera.* In some cases the hillocky or columnar growth form of *F. stelligera* helps to distinguish this species, but it may be necessary to examine the way in which new calices are added. In *Plesiastrea* asexual reproduction is predominantly extratentacular, whereas in *Favia* it is intratentacular. In addition, the septa are more exsert in *F. stelligera,* and their margins are more coarsely serrated.

DISTRIBUTION AND ECOLOGY   (Map #73)

Plesiastrea may form large colonies several meters in diameter and occurs in a wide variety of reef habitats. It usually forms rounded colonies in exposed shallow areas and plate-like growths on reef slopes where light intensity is low. There is probably only a single species: *Plesiastrea versipora* (Lamarck, 1816). Other *"Plesiastrea"* species have been transferred to *Montastraea* (see taxonomic note under the latter genus).

Montastraea de Blainville, 1830
(L: *montis,* mountain; Gr: *aster,* star. Relating to the protuberant calices and the star-like arrangement of the septa.)

DESCRIPTION
Living coral   (Col. pl. p. 160)

Montastraea usually forms solid, rounded colonies, but encrusting or plate-like growths also occur. Coralla are usually brown, yellow or greenish in color. Each polyp has a ring of small tentacles, but these are usually retracted during the day.

The majority of corallites are circular and separated from each other by a slight gap. They are also elevated several millimeters from the surface of the coral. Mature corallites are usually about 7 to 15 mm in diameter, and interspersed among them are ones of a smaller size. These smaller corallites have been produced during asexual

Montastraea valenciennesi (X 2). Malaysia.

reproduction by extratentacular budding.

Septa are numerous, and their margins are slightly rough to the touch. They radiate from the center of each calice and extend over the walls and onto perithecal areas. These costae may join with others from neighboring calices or may be discontinuous.

Skeleton

The margins of both septa and costae are serrated. The coral surface between the costae is smooth or finely granulated. In some cases the calices are separated by deep grooves. Paliform lobes are usually formed at the inner ends of the septa adjacent to the spongy columella.

SIMILARITIES

Montastraea is confused with *Favia* because growth form and calice size and shape are similar. The two genera are distinguished mainly on the basis of the way in which new calices are added to the colony. In *Montastraea* asexual reproduction is predominantly extratentacular and results·in the appearance of small corallites between the mature ones. In *Favia* it is predominantly intratentacular and mature calices are seen in the process of "fission."

TAXONOMIC NOTE

A comment is made in the monograph *Scleractinia of Eastern Australia* that "*Montastraea* and *Plesiastrea* have always been at the center of a taxonomic debate.'' Until recently, *Montastraea* was thought to be restricted to the Atlantic Ocean, and all Indo-Pacific relations were included in the genus *Plesiastrea* (Vaughan & Wells, 1943; Wells, 1956). Chevalier (1971) stated that true *Plesiastrea* species could be distinguished by the detailed structure of the paliform lobes and by an internal feature of the polyps. Veron *et al.* (1977) agreed with this viewpoint, which is now generally accepted.

DISTRIBUTION AND ECOLOGY (Map #74)

Montastraea is fairly common and is found in most reef localities. It is, however, much less important in the Indo-Pacific than in the Caribbean, where it is one of the major reef-builders. There are probably five or six species in the Indo-Pacific.

Diploastrea Matthai, 1914
(Gr: *diploos,* double; Gr: *aster,* star. Referring to the conspicuous septal arrangement described below.)

DESCRIPTION
Living coral (Col. pl. p. 161)
Diploastrea colonies are usually massive and rounded, occasionally slightly flattened. They are pale brown in color, sometimes with purplish or greenish tints. The polyps have a ring of simple pale-colored tentacles, but these are normally extended only at night.

Corallites are conspicuous and regular in appearance. They are closely packed and take the form of truncated cones. The base of each cone is about 1 cm in diameter, and the center of the cone is raised by 2 to 3 mm. Young corallites are budded off at intervals and can be seen lying between the larger ones.

Septa are conspicuous and thickened where they cross the corallite wall. They drop down to the trough between calices and join with others from adjacent corallites. Thinner septa are just visible lying in the trough and alternating with the stouter ones. Septal margins are rough to the touch.

Skeleton
A distinctive feature of *Diploastrea* is the arrangement of the septa, which can be clearly seen in cleaned skeletons. The main septa are distinctly thickened and stretch from the columella to the

Diploastrea heliopora (X 2.5). Malaysia.

outside of the corallite, where they join with similarly thickened septa from adjacent corallites. Between the thick septa are thinner ones that do not reach the columella. Septal margins have short, coarse teeth. The columella is well developed and usually about 3 to 4 mm in diameter.

SIMILARITIES
Diploastrea is readily identified by its regular, cone-shaped corallites and by the broad columella and septa. It is unlikely to be confused with other corals.

DISTRIBUTION AND ECOLOGY (Map #75)
Occasional on most reefs, especially on upper reef slopes or in areas exposed to swell or currents. Colonies generally grow to a large size, and it is common to find some several meters in diameter. Small gobies are often associated with this coral and can be seen lying on the surface or moving around in search of food. There is a single species: *Diploastrea heliopora* (Lamarck, 1816).

Cyphastrea. Sabah, Malaysia, 5 m depth.

Echinopora. Sabah, Malaysia, 6 m depth.

Echinopora lamellosa. Sabah, Malaysia, 7 m depth.

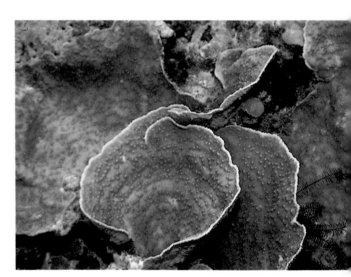

Echinopora lamellosa. Sabah, Malaysia, 7 m depth.

Echinopora horrida. Sabah, Malaysia, 6 m depth.

Echinopora horrida. Sabah, Malaysia, 6 m depth.

Trachyphyllia geoffroyi. Sabah, Malaysia, 12 m depth.

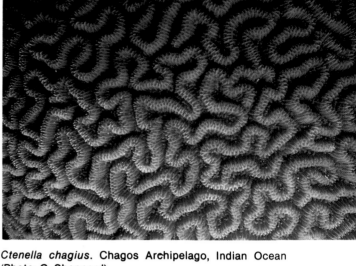

Ctenella chagius. Chagos Archipelago, Indian Ocean (Photo: C. Sheppard).

Galaxea. Sabah, Malaysia, 7 m depth.

Galaxea. Sabah, Malaysia, 20 m depth.

Galaxea. Sabah, Malaysia, 8 m depth.

Acrhelia horrescens. Sabah, Malaysia, 5 m depth.

Oulastrea Milne-Edwards & Haime, 1848
(Gr: *oulos,* curly; Gr: *aster,* star.
Etymology obscure.)

DESCRIPTION
Living coral
Oulastrea usually forms small, rounded colonies, but it may also be encrusting. It has a distinctive coloration: the calices are pale brown while the coenosteum that surrounds them is black and remains so even in cleaned specimens. There is a ring of small tentacles associated with each polyp, but these are usually extended only at night.

Corallites are separate, distinct and between 3 and 5 mm in diameter. A few may be irregular in shape, but most are rounded. The top of the corallite wall is either level with the surrounding coenosteum or raised by less than a millimeter. There is usually a gap of several millimeters between adjacent corallites.

Septa are clearly visible as they run from the center of the calice onto the corallite wall. They then continue over perithecal areas as well defined costae. The surface of the coral is slightly rough to the touch.

Skeleton
Septa are numerous and arranged in cycles. Costae are also prominent, and the margins of both septa and costae are armed with fine spines.

SIMILARITIES
Oulastrea is a distinctive coral and is unlikely to be confused with any other genus.

DISTRIBUTION AND ECOLOGY   (Map #76)
Oulastrea is usually found in muddy areas on the shallow back reef and seldom occurs among dense coral on the fore reef. Colonies are small in size. There is a single species: *Oulastrea crispata* (Lamarck, 1816).

Leptastrea Milne-Edwards & Haime, 1848
(Gr: *leptos,* slender; Gr: *aster,* star. Relating to the shape and appearance of the calices.)

DISTRIBUTION
Living coral   (Col. pl. p. 161)
Leptastrea forms encrusting, flat, convex or rounded colonies. Overall color is normally purple or brown, but often the oral disc and the corallite walls are a different shade. The oral disc may be

Oulastrea crispata (X 5.2). Malaysia.

Leptastrea transversa (X 4.3). Malaysia.

green; in *Leptastrea bottae* the calices are white and the polyps have black centers. There is often a dark or pale line around the calices. Polyps may be partially extended during the day.

Corallites are closely packed, with little or no intervening coenosteum. The walls of adjacent corallites are fused basally, but there is usually a fine furrow above just visible in the living coral. Calices are oval, rounded or polygonal and sometimes laterally compressed or distorted. They range in diameter from 2 to 10 mm, even within a single specimen. Calices are usually fairly shallow, but the fossa may be several millimeters deep. Septa are visible running from the calice center onto the walls; they are smooth or slightly rough to the touch.

Skeleton

Septa are numerous and in cycles. The larger ones of the primary cycle may be slightly exsert and run from the columella onto the walls. They are broken at the top of the corallite wall at the point where adjacent corallites fuse. Septal margins are finely serrated, and paliform lobes may be present at the inner ends of the septa.

SIMILARITIES

Leptastrea could be mistaken for faviids such as *Favites* and *Goniastrea*. The fine line running between adjacent calices is a reliable means of identifying *Leptastrea*. In addition, the calices in this genus tend to be rather irregular in size and shape within a single colony.

DISTRIBUTION AND ECOLOGY   (Map #77)

Leptastrea is a fairly common coral found in most reef habitats. It may be overlooked because

of its low growth profile and the relatively small colony size (seldom exceeding 25 cm in diameter). There are probably seven species.

Cyphastrea Milne-Edwards & Haime, 1848
(Gr: *kyphos,* humped; Gr: *aster,* star. Relating to the protuberant corallites.)

DESCRIPTION

Living coral   (Col. pl. pp. 161, 164)

This coral commonly forms rounded or knobby colonies, but encrusting, plate-like or even branching growths also occur, especially on sheltered reef slopes. Colonies are usually brown or pinkish; some have shades of green or blue. Each polyp has a ring of pale-colored tentacles that may be partially extended during the day.

Corallites are always round and small, and each is distinct, with its own separate wall. Corallite diameter is usually about 1 mm, occasionally as much as 2.5 mm. There is generally a gap of several millimeters between corallites, but in places they may be crowded together so that the walls touch. The majority of corallites are slightly elevated, the walls rising vertically by 3 mm or less.

Septa are visible within the calice and on the corallite walls but do not extend onto perithecal areas.

Cyphastrea chalcidicum (X 6). Malaysia.

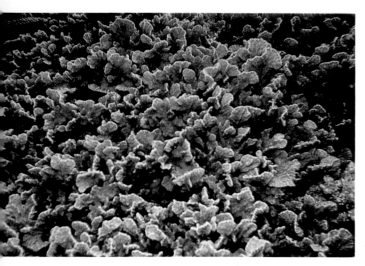

Merulina ampliata. Sabah, Malaysia, 5 m depth.

Merulina ampliata. Sabah, Malaysia, 10 m depth.

Merulina ampliata. Sabah, Malaysia, 10 m depth.

Merulina ampliata. Sabah, Malaysia, 10 m depth.

Merulina ampliata. Sabah, Malaysia, 5 m depth.

Scapophyllia cylindrica. Sabah, Malaysia, 6 m depth.

Cynarina lacrymalis. Sabah, Malaysia, 4 m depth.

Scolymia vitiensis. Sabah, Malaysia, 20 m depth.

Acanthastrea echinata. Sabah, Malaysia, 10 m depth.

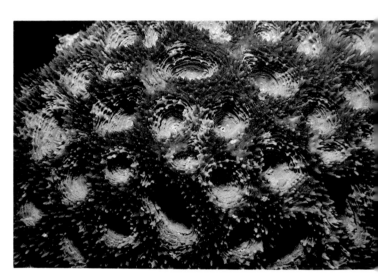

Acanthastrea. Great Barrier Reef, Australia (Photo: W. Deas).

Lobophyllia. Sabah, Malaysia, 5 m depth.

Lobophyllia. Sabah, Malaysia, 8 m depth.

These areas appear smooth, and the septa are only very slightly rough to the touch.

Skeleton
Septa are in cycles, and the larger ones reach the columella. Paliform lobes are usually present, and septal margins are finely serrated. Perithecal areas are ornamented with fine spines or may be blistered and uneven.

SIMILARITIES
Cyphastrea can sometimes be confused underwater with *Astreopora* because both genera have small protruding corallites and form colonies of a similar shape. *Cyphastrea* is readily identified by the vertical narrow corallite walls and the well developed septa. *Astreopora* has cone-shaped corallites with thick walls and poorly developed septa.

Cyphastrea also resembles *Plesiastrea versipora,* but the two corals can be distinguished by examining the perithecal areas. In *Plesiastrea* the septa run onto perithecal areas, but in *Cyphastrea* they do not extend beyond the limits of the corallite wall. The coenosteum is more extensive in *Cyphastrea* and is covered with tiny spines.

DISTRIBUTION AND ECOLOGY (Map #78)
Cyphastrea occurs on most reefs, particularly on the reef slope, but colonies are widely spaced and seldom exceed 50 cm in diameter. Boring organisms such as *Lithophaga* and polychaetes often penetrate the skeleton and sometimes induce abnormalities in the size and shape of the corallites. There are probably five species of *Cyphastrea.*

Echinopora Lamarck, 1816
(Gr: *echinos,* hedgehog, *i.e.,* prickly; L: *porus,* pore. Relating to the raised corallites with their spiny septa.)

DESCRIPTION
Living coral (Col. pl. p. 164)
Echinopora commonly forms foliaceous colonies. In some cases the leaves grow horizontally or in a wide cup and in others they form scrolls that may be open or closed at the top. Several species are branched, often with the branches knobby and irregular. Finally there are semi-encrusting types that form thin, contorted plates over the substrate. These usually have free leafy extensions around the margin of the colony and sometimes short protuberances from the central part. Colony color is usually brown or green, sometimes with yellow or pinkish tinges. Often the margins of the colony are paler than the rest. Tentacles are normally retracted during the day.

Corallites are distinct and are usually separated by several millimeters. They appear as small, rounded, slightly spiky hillocks. Corallite diameter is between 2 and 7 mm but is often about 3 mm. Corallites are raised above the surface of the coral, sometimes by as little as 1 mm, in other cases by as much as 5 mm. Often they are inclined, with one side higher than the other. They are usually thick-walled, with the width of the wall as great as the diameter of the fossa. Calices are normally flat-topped or with a shallow fossa.

The radiating pattern of the septa is usually obscured in the living coral, but faint lines are sometimes visible outside the calice. These correspond to the position of costal ridges or rows of small spines.

Skeleton
Septa are numerous and arranged in cycles. They are slightly exsert, and their margins are usually coarsely serrated. They run down the outside of the corallite wall and continue across perithecal areas as rows of spines or occasionally as costal ridges. In *E. mammiformis* septal and costal margins are smooth or finely serrated. The columella consists of twisted trabeculae.

Echinopora gemmacea (X 3). Malaysia.

Echinopora mammiformis (X 3). Malaysia.

further distinguished by the poorly developed septa and porous skeleton. The corallites in *Cyphastrea* are generally smaller (1 to 2.5 mm) than in *Echinopora* (2 to 7 mm), and foliaceous forms are not produced in this genus.

DISTRIBUTION AND ECOLOGY   (Map #79)

Echinopora is occasional to common on most reefs. Leafy forms are often well represented on the reef slope, where they tend to be flattened or fan-like. In sheltered areas tall scrolls may occur. Branched colonies often grow in tracts several meters across, especially along the reef rim. There are probably five species.

SIMILARITIES

It is possible to confuse *Echinopora* with other corals that also have small, protuberant corallites, such as *Astreopora, Turbinaria* and *Cyphastrea*. *Turbinaria* is distinguished by the lack of ornamentation on perithecal areas, and neither *Astreopora* nor *Cyphastrea* have costal ridges. *Astreopora* is

Moseleya **Quelch, 1884**
(Named for H.N. Moseley, in recognition of his work on deep-sea corals.)

DESCRIPTION
Living coral

Moseleya forms massive, flattened or convex colonies. It is brown or greenish in color, and the

Moseleya latistellata (X 2.5).
Great Barrier Reef.

171

Lobophyllia. Sabah, Malaysia, 6 m depth.

Symphyllia (left) and *Lobophyllia*. Sabah, Malaysia, 6 m depth.

Symphyllia. Sabah, Malaysia, 6 m depth.

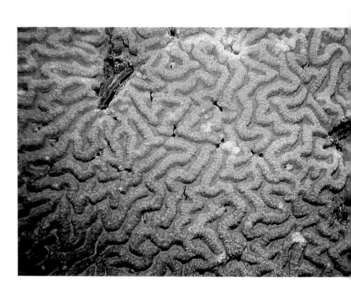

Symphyllia. Sabah, Malaysia, 6 m depth.

Oxypora. Sabah, Malaysia, 15 m depth.

Oxypora. Sabah, Malaysia, 8 m depth.

Echinophyllia. Bali, Indonesia, 20 m depth.

Mycedium. Sabah, Malaysia, 12 m depth.

Mycedium. Sabah, Malaysia, 6 m depth.

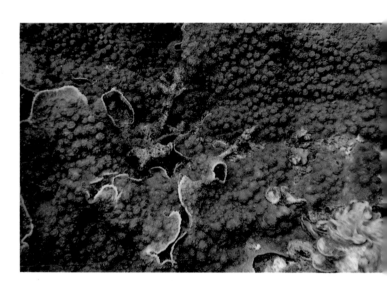

Mycedium. Sabah, Malaysia, 6 m depth.

Pectinia. Sabah, Malaysia, 4 m depth.

Pectinia. Sabah, Malaysia, 5 m depth.

polyps are retracted during the day.

Corallites have shared walls that are high and prominent. There is a large central calice up to 6 cm in diameter and smaller lateral calices up to 3 cm in diameter. Calices are polygonal (usually 4-, 5- or 6-sided), and the fossa is several millimeters deep. Septa are prominent, and their margins are slightly rough to the touch. Septa of adjacent corallites usually fuse on the top of the wall and are thus continuous between neighboring calices.

Skeleton

Septa are in cycles, the largest ones reaching the columella. Septal margins are strongly dentate, and internally there are large dentate paliform lobes. These are not developed to the same degree on every septum, but tend to be particularly prominent on a few larger septa. The columella is small and spongy.

SIMILARITIES

Moseleya could be mistaken for *Favites* or *Acanthastrea*, but a clear distinguishing feature is the presence of the large central calice and well defined paliform lobes.

DISTRIBUTION AND ECOLOGY (Map #80)

Moseleya is apparently often found in turbid water on muddy substrates. Colonies are generally small, consisting of one or several corallites, and are often unattached (Veron *et al.*, 1977). There is a single species: *Moseleya latistellata* Quelch, 1884.

FAMILY TRACHYPHYLLIIDAE

Trachyphyllia Milne-Edwards & Haime, 1848

(Gr: *trachys*, rough; Gr: *phyllon*, leaf. Possibly relating to the indented form of the corallum, which resembles a large and uneven leaf.)

DESCRIPTION

Living coral (Col. pl. p. 165)

Young *Trachyphyllia* are solitary, attached and turbinate. They generally settle on a small stone or mollusc shell but later outgrow this and become

Trachyphyllia geoffroyi (X 1.4). Malaysia.

detached and secondarily free-living (Pichon, 1974). The mature colony is small, low and convex. It is colored some shade or mixture of green, pink, red, blue or brown and often has an iridescent sheen. The polyp is large and fleshy, but tentacles are only extended at night or under conditions of low light intensity. The polyp mouths are 1 to 2 mm in diameter and can be seen lying along the center of the valleys.

Corallites are joined in longitudinal series but are free laterally. The meanders tend to widen and constrict at intervals and the distance from mid-ridge to mid-ridge may vary between 1.5 to 2.5 cm. The valley systems are separated by a gap of several millimeters and the valleys themselves are deep (about 2 cm).

Septa are visible as low ridges, their detail obscured by the covering of fleshy tissue. The surface of the coral is smooth to the touch.

Skeleton

Septa are numerous and slightly exsert. They run from the columella over the walls and then continue several centimeters down the outside as costae. These costae become progressively smaller as they run down the outside of the walls. Margins of both septa and costae are minutely dentate. Paliform lobes are well developed, and the columella is spongy.

174

SIMILARITIES

The living coral resembles *Cataluphyllia* because both corals have a broad oral disc and a fringe of finger-like tentacles. In *Trachyphyllia*, however, the tentacles are generally extended only at night, whereas in *Catalaphyllia* they are extended both day and night. In addition, *Trachyphyllia* is identified by the dentate septal margins and well developed columellae and paliform lobes.

The growth form in *Trachyphyllia* is similar to young *Lobophyllia*, but the latter is readily identified by the large sharp teeth on the septal margins.

DISTRIBUTION AND ECOLOGY (Map #81)

Trachyphyllia is a small coral seldom over 20 cm in diameter. It is rarely found among dense coral but prefers soft sandy or muddy substrates on sheltered reef slopes or in lagoons. There is a single species: *Trachyphyllia geoffroyi* (Audouin, 1826).

Wellsophyllia Pichon, 1980
(Named for Professor J. Wells.)

DESCRIPTION
Living coral

Wellsophyllia forms small colonies that are almost hemispherical in the adult stage but convex or flattened as juveniles. Corallites are joined in short series, and adjacent series are united laterally. Fusion may be incomplete in juveniles, and even in adult colonies the distance between adjacent series is variable. In some cases the walls are only a few millimeters apart, but in others there is a distinct groove almost 10 mm wide. The distance from mid-ridge to mid-ridge across the valley varies both between different specimens and within a single corallum, but usually lies between 15 and 25 mm. The valleys are deep, with the walls sloping steeply downward. Septa are distinct, their margins rough to the touch. There are about 10 to 15 septa per cm.

Skeleton

Septa are slightly exsert, and most have a well developed paliform lobe at their inner end. These lobes have smooth or granular margins, but the rest of the septal margins are armed with small, regular teeth. Septal sides are granular. Costae are present and may be continuous or discontinuous

between adjacent valleys. They also have finely toothed margins and granular sides. Perithecal areas are vesicular. The columella is spongy (trabecular) and well developed.

SIMILARITIES

Wellsophyllia is most closely allied to *Trachyphyllia* but is readily identified by the fused rather than separate meanders. In this respect it resembles large meandrine corals such as *Symphyllia* or *Oulophyllia*. It is distinguished from both of these by the groove along the top of the common wall and by features of the septa and columella.

TAXONOMIC NOTE

In 1902, Verrill described a new coral, *Callogyra*, that he believed probably came from the Indo-Pacific. Subsequently, in his study of corals from Ambon (Moluccas) in 1907, Bedot applied the same name (*Callogyra formosa*) to specimens that appeared to follow Verill's description. It now seems certain, however, that Verrill was describing not an Indo-Pacific form but the well known coral *Colpophyllia* from the Caribbean. Thus Bedot's specimens are new and have been redescribed by Pichon (1980) as *Wellsophyllia*.

DISTRIBUTION AND ECOLOGY (Map #82)

Wellsophyllia is known only from a few isolated

Wellsophyllia radiata (nat. size). Great Barrier Reef. BM(NH) 1894.6.16.34.

Pectinia. Sabah, Malaysia, 5 m depth.

Pectinia. Sabah, Malaysia, 4 m depth.

Pectinia elongata. Sabah, Malaysia, 3 m depth.

Euphyllia (Euphyllia) glabrescens. Sabah, Malaysia, 7 m depth.

Euphyllia (Euphyllia) glabrescens. Sabah, Malaysia, 4 m depth.

Euphyllia (Euphyllia) glabrescens. Sabah, Malaysia, 6 m depth.

Euphyllia (Euphyllia) glabrescens. Sabah, Malaysia, 20 m depth.

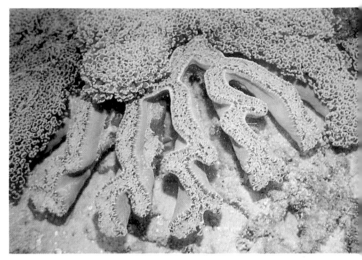

Euphyllia (Fimbriaphyllia) ancora. Sabah, Malaysia, 15 m depth.

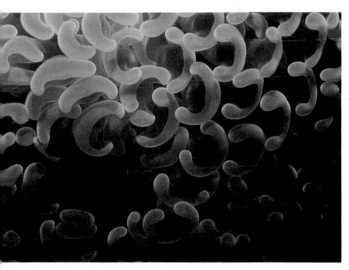

Euphyllia (Fimbriaphyllia) ancora. Sabah, Malaysia, 7 m depth.

Euphyllia (Fimbriaphyllia) divisa. Sabah, Malaysia, 10 m depth.

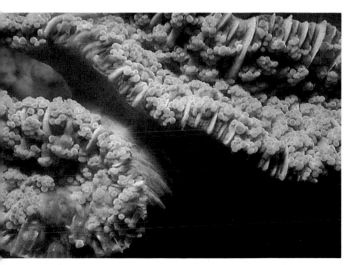

Euphyllia (Fimbriaphyllia) divisa. Sabah, Malaysia, 12 m depth.

Plerogyra. Sabah, Malaysia, 7 m depth.

177

specimens, and virtually nothing is recorded of its distribution on the reef. It is a small coral with a superficial resemblance to *Trachyphyllia* and may thus have been overlooked or misidentified in the past. There is a single species: *Wellsophyllia radiata* Pichon, 1980.

FAMILY MEANDRINIDAE

Ctenella Matthai, 1928
(Gr: *ktenos,* comb; L: *-ella,* suffix denoting diminutive. Possibly relating to the appearance of the septa.)

DESCRIPTION
Living coral   (Col. pl. p. 165)
Ctenella forms massive, encrusting or explanate colonies. These are brownish in color. The tentacles are normally retracted during the day.

Corallites are joined in longitudinal series, and the valleys are usually long and sinuous. The shared walls are prominent and vertical, the distance from mid-ridge to mid-ridge about 1.5 cm. The valleys are about 1 cm deep.

Septa are clearly visible and closely packed (about 20 per cm) as they run over the walls. They feel smooth to the touch, and there is no groove at the top of the shared wall.

Skeleton
The larger septa run from the columella over the walls without interruption. The columella is a solid, almost continuous ridge. Septal margins are smooth.

SIMILARITIES
Ctenella resembles other meandrine corals such as *Platygyra* and *Oulophyllia* but can be distinguished by the lack of spines on the septal margins. In this respect it is similar to *Physogyra*, but the latter can be identified by its distinctive finger-like tentacles and by the leafy, exsert septa. Also, compare this with *Gyrosmilia*, which follows.

DISTRIBUTION AND ECOLOGY   (Map #83)
Occasional along the reef front and slope. There is a single species: *Ctenella chagius* Matthai, 1928.

Ctenella chagius (X 3.5). Chagos Archipelago.

Gyrosmilia Milne-Edwards & Haime, 1851

(Gr: *gyr,* round; Gr: *smilion,* knife. Possibly relating to the growth form and the narrow groove etched along the top of the walls.)

DESCRIPTION
Living coral

Gyrosmilia forms fairly small, rounded heads that may be attached by a narrow peduncle. Little is known of the appearance of the living coral.

Corallites are joined in longitudinal series, and the valleys are long and sinuous. The shared walls are fused laterally, but there is a narrow, shallow groove along the top of the wall. The distance from mid-ridge to mid-ridge is about 6 to 10 mm, and the depth of the valley is about 8 mm. Septa are prominent and leafy, with smooth edges. There are about ten per cm.

Skeleton

The septa alternate in size, and about half are broader than the rest and exsert by 1.0 to 1.5 mm. The septa curve toward the calice centers, but there is no columella. Septal margins are smooth.

SIMILARITIES

Gyrosmilia can be confused with *Physogyra* and

Gyrosmilia interrupta (X 2.7). Red Sea. BM(NH) 1961.5.16.11.

Ctenella. It differs from both in having a narrow groove along the top of the walls. It also lacks the lamellar columella typical of *Ctenella* and is smaller than *Physogyra* (narrower, shallower valley, more septa per cm).

DISTRIBUTION AND ECOLOGY (Map #84)

Gyrosmilia occurs in shallow and deep fore reef areas but does not form large colonies. There is a single species: *Gyrosmilia interrupta* (Ehrenberg, 1834).

FAMILY FLABELLIDAE

DESCRIPTION
Living coral

Flabellids are solitary ahermatypic corals that are cylindrical, turbinate or trochoid in shape. Calices are rounded and seldom exceed 5 mm in diameter in shallow water forms. Polyps may be partially extended during the day and are generally pale or reddish in color. Septa are just visible.

Skeleton

Flabellids such as *Monomyces* and *Gardineria* are characterized by very simple skeletal structures. Septa are few to numerous and are arranged in cycles. They are non-exsert, and the margins are smooth. Septal sides are smooth or granulated. The fossa is several millimeters deep, and the septa drop down steeply. A columella is lacking in *Monomyces* but is well developed in *Gardineria,* consisting of pinnacle-like protrusions. Costae are invariably absent.

SIMILARITIES

Flabellids are distinguished from other solitary corals by a combination of the following features: septa that do not join in the calice and have smooth margins, absence of costae, absence of columella (in *Monomyces*) and non-porous skeleton.

DISTRIBUTION AND ECOLOGY

Flabellids are found in caverns and on the under-surfaces of rocks but are easily overlooked because of their small size. In general they are widely distributed throughout tropical and temperate waters. They have been recovered from depths of 3 to over 3000 meters, with the majority of species coming from deep rather than shallow waters.

Plerogyra. Sabah, Malaysia, 10 m depth.

Plerogyra. Sabah, Malaysia, 8 m depth.

Plerogyra. Sabah, Malaysia, 20 m depth.

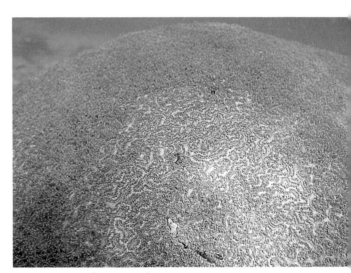

Physogyra lichtensteini. Sabah, Malaysia, 6 m depth.

Physogyra lichtensteini. Sabah, Malaysia, 6 m depth.

Physogyra lichtensteini. Sabah, Malaysia, 6 m depth.

180

Balanophyllia. Hawaii (Photo: Scott Johnson).

Dendrophyllia gracilis. Sabah, Malaysia, 12 m depth.

Dendrophyllia. Sabah, Malaysia, 10 m depth.

Dendrophyllia. Sabah, Malaysia, 10 m depth.

Clumps of *Dendrophyllia* and *Tubastraea* on an underhanging rock face. Sabah, Malaysia, 10 m depth.

Tubastraea micrantha. Sabah, Malaysia, 20 m depth.

181

FAMILY RHIZANGIIDAE

DESCRIPTION
Living coral
The corals belonging to this family are non-reef-building (ahermatypic), but genera such as *Culicia, Phyllangia, Oulangia* and *Cladangia* may be encountered on shallow reefs.

Most rhizangiids are colonial, the colonies formed by stolon-like expansions at the bases of the corallites. These perithecal expansions are usually thin, but in *Cladangia* the corallites are united to their tops. Calices are rounded and up to 5 mm in diameter, occasionally more. Polyps are normally retracted during the day, but the septa are clearly visible. The coral is brown or reddish in color.

Skeleton
Septa are numerous and in cycles, with those of the primary cycle exsert. Their margins are strongly to irregularly dentate, and the septal sides are granular or spiny. Costal ridges are present on the outside of the corallite wall. The columella is usually spongy, rarely solid or absent.

SIMILARITIES
Rhizangiids can be confused with ahermatypic caryophylliids or dendrophylliids, but in general rhizangiids are smaller and have the corallites united basally. Also, they have dentate rather than smooth septal margins and the septa never fuse in the calices.

Culicia sp. (X 4.5). Malaysia.

DISTRIBUTION AND ECOLOGY
Rhizangiids tend to grow on the underside of rocks. This cryptic habit, together with their small size, means that they are readily overlooked. They occur on shallow reefs and have also been dredged from water several hundred meters deep. They are widely distributed throughout tropical and temperate waters.

FAMILY OCULINIDAE
Galaxea Oken, 1815
(Gr: *galaxaios,* milky. Etymology obscure.)

DESCRIPTION
Living coral   (Col. pl. p. 165)
Most *Galaxea* colonies are solid, rounded and relatively small. Massive heads, tall columns and flat plates may also be formed, and a branched form of *Galaxea fascicularis* occurs on sheltered reefs. The overall color is green or brownish, occasionally with purple tinges. Tentacles are nearly always extended during the day and may reach 1 cm in length. They are finger-like and often transparent, green or brown with white tips.

Corallites are separate and distinct and rise at least 2 mm and sometimes over 15 mm above the peritheca . They are round or slightly elliptical in cross section with vertical walls. Diameter varies from 1.5 mm (rare) to about 8 mm, but 5 mm is common. The corallites are generally at least 2 to 3 mm apart, often more. These perithecal areas appear smooth.

Septa protrude above the level of the corallite wall and are clearly visible. They are covered with a mantle of tissue and can sometimes be mistaken for a ring of tentacles.

Skeleton
Septa are numerous and arranged in cycles. They are strongly exsert, protruding several millimeters as thin, sharp blades. Septal margins are smooth, granular or minutely dentate. Costae continue a short way down the outside of the corallite wall but are absent from perithecal areas. The peritheca is slightly rough due to the presence of irregular low vesicles. The columella is weak or absent.

SIMILARITIES
Galaxea is a distinctive coral that is unlikely to

Galaxea fascicularis (branched form) (X 3). Malaysia.

be confused with other genera. The tall, separate corallites and protruding septa are found also in *Acrhelia*, and it is possible that branched *Galaxea* colonies may be mistaken for this genus. The two corals are closely related, but the corallites are smaller in *Acrhelia* and are arranged differently (see the description of *Acrhelia*).

DISTRIBUTION AND ECOLOGY (Map #85)

Galaxea is a common coral that occurs from shallow to deep water and in clear or turbid, calm or exposed conditions. It may form colonies several meters in diameter. There are 24 nominal species of *Galaxea*, but most of these have been synonymized and it is probable that only five or six are valid.

Acrhelia Milne-Edwards & Haime, 1849
(L: *acris*, sharp; Gr: *helios,* sun. Presumably referring to the prominent septa, protruding like rays of the sun.)

DESCRIPTION
Living coral (Col. pl. p. 165)

Acrhelia is a delicate coral with a branching growth form. Colonies are pale brown or pinkish in color and may be small and irregular in shape or larger and hemispherical.

Branches are thin (lateral ones about 5 mm in diameter) and gradually tapering. Corallites are well spaced and arranged in a loose spiral. They project by about 5 mm (excluding the septa) and are usually slanted toward the growing tip. Corallite diameter rarely exceeds 3 mm. The septa are fragile and blade-like and are clearly visible in the living coral. Their position alternates with the tentacles, which are finger-like and usually transparent with white tips. The area between corallites appears smooth.

Skeleton

Septa are in cycles, and the larger ones may protrude by as much as 5 mm. They are fragile and easily broken. Septal margins are smooth or minutely dentate. Costae are restricted to the upper parts of the corallite wall and do not extend onto perithecal areas. The coenosteum is minutely granular or slightly irregular due to the presence of small vesicles.

SIMILARITIES

Acrhelia can be mistaken for a branched form of

183

Tubastraea micrantha. Sabah, Malaysia, 25 m depth.

Tubastraea coccinea. Sabah, Malaysia, 10 m depth.

Tubastraea (at night). Red Sea (Photo: M. Melzac).

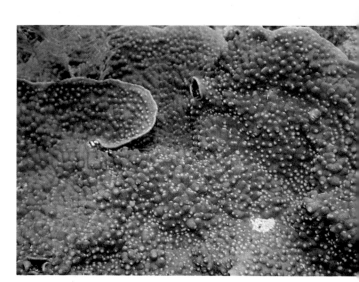

Turbinaria. Sabah, Malaysia, 10 m depth.

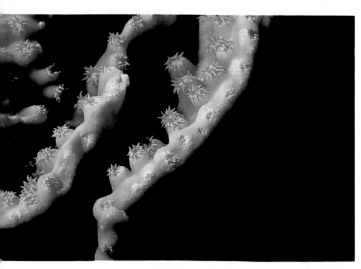

Turbinaria. Red Sea (Photo: M. Melzac).

Turbinaria heronensis. Heron Island, Great Barrier Reef, Australia (Photo: J. Deas).

The bright golden color of these dendrophylliids is brought out by the underwater flash at a depth of about 30 meters. The similarly colored fish is a member of the genus *Anthias*. Photo by Allan Power.

Acrhelia horrescens (X 2).
Malaysia.

Galaxea fascicularis but is distinguished as follows. The corallites in *Acrhelia* are fairly regularly spaced in a loose spiral, whereas in *Galaxea* they are irregularly spaced and tend to grow in clumps. Calices are about 3 mm in diameter in *Acrhelia* (5 mm in *Galaxea*) and branches about 5 mm (8 to 10 mm in *Galaxea*).

DISTRIBUTION AND ECOLOGY (Map #86)

Acrhelia generally forms small colonies less than 20 cm in diameter. It prefers sheltered areas on reef slopes but may also be found along the reef rim. There is a single species: *Acrhelia horrescens* (Dana, 1846).

FAMILY MERULINIDAE

Merulina Ehrenberg, 1834
(L: *merus*, pure; L: *linea*, line. Etymology obscure.)

DESCRIPTION

Living coral (Col. pl. p. 168)

Merulina is often partly encrusting and partly foliaceous, with the leaves arranged in a variety of ways. They may be thin and cabbage-like or flatter and plate-like. Both of these forms often have crests or irregular branched outgrowths arising from the central part. The area of attachment of the colony may be relatively small but in some cases is extensive, so that only the rims are free and foliaceous. Veron and Pichon (1980) suggest that there is a sequential change of growth forms during the life of the colony. Horizontal laminar or encrusting growths occur first and hillocks or vertical plates and branches follow later. Colonies are usually pale brown in color. The tentacles are generally retracted during the day.

Merulina is a meandroid coral with the calices arranged in rows and separated by collines (walls). The valleys and their walls diverge fan-like from the center of the colony to the outside. The calice centers are about 5 mm apart and are usually just visible, but the mouth is scarcely more than 1 mm in diameter. Width across the valley from the middle of one colline to the next is around 3 to 6 mm. The collines are often rounded and slightly wider than the intervening valley, but may be narrower and sharper edged. The valleys are only a few millimeters deep.

Septa are closely packed and are clearly visible as they pass over the walls. They feel fairly smooth to the touch.

Skeleton

Septa protrude by a few millimeters as they pass over the walls. As they enter the valley they converge to the calice centers. Septal margins are

Merulina ampliata (X 2). Malaysia.

armed with small, sometimes ragged teeth. The columella is usually solid, occasionally trabecular.

SIMILARITIES

Merulina is a distinctive coral and is unlikely to be confused with other genera. It resembles *Scapophyllia* and faviid brain corals because of the meandroid arrangement of the calices but is easily distinguished by its foliaceous rather than massive growth form. It is similarly distinguished from *Clavarina*, a closely related genus that is branched rather than foliaceous.

TAXONOMIC NOTE

The genus *Boninastraea* Yabe & Sugiyama, 1935, was created for a merulinid coral with di- to tricentric cerioid calices. A columella is lacking, and the species described (*B. boninensis*) had calices about 10 mm in diameter. This coral was found at Titi-Zima in the western Pacific, and no other specimens have been recorded. The status of this obscure coral is uncertain; it may be an aberrant form of *Merulina*.

DISTRIBUTION AND ECOLOGY   (Map #87)

Merulina is not a particularly common coral, but it occurs in most reef habitats and may form large colonies. At least six species have been described, but Veron and Pichon (1980) consider that all are probably a single species: *Merulina ampliata* (Ellis & Solander, 1786).

Clavarina Verrill, 1864
(L: *clava,* club; L: *-ina,* suffix denoting likeness. Presumably relating to the branching growth form.)

DESCRIPTION
Living coral

Clavarina forms bushy colonies that consist entirely of a network of branches. There is no plate-like structure at the base of the colony. It is usually pale brown in color. The tentacles are retracted during the day.

Branches are fragile and about 1 cm in diameter. The calices are arranged in rows and are separated by collines that run up the length of the branches. Distance across the valleys from mid-ridge to mid-ridge is usually about 4 to 5 mm, but the valley is several millimeters deep. Septa are closely packed and clearly visible as they run from the calice centers up and over the walls.

Skeleton

Septa are stout, and their margins are minutely dentate. They run down the walls and converge to calice centers. The columella is poorly developed.

SIMILARITIES

Clavarina is distinguished from other merulinids by its branched growth form. It is possible to confuse *Clavarina* with *Hydnophora rigida*, which has a similar growth form and in which the monticules

Clavarina triangularis (X 0.5). Great Barrier Reef.

187

Millepora. Sabah, Malaysia, 6 m depth.

Millepora. Sabah, Malaysia, 4 m depth.

Millepora. Sabah, Malaysia, 3 m depth.

Stylaster, growing on *Millepora*. Sabah, Malaysia, 3 m depth.

Distichopora violacea. Enewetak (Photo: Scott Johnson).

Distichopora. Sabah, Malaysia, 3 m depth.

Heliopora coerulea. Sabah, Malaysia, 5 m depth.

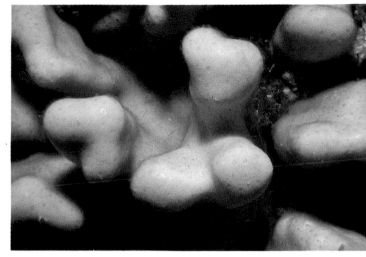

Heliopora coerulea. Sabah, Malaysia, 4 m depth.

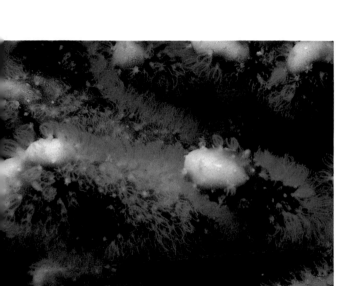

Heliopora coerulea. Sabah, Malaysia, 4 m depth.

Tubipora musica. Sabah, Malaysia, 7 m depth.

Tubipora musica. Sabah, Malaysia, 9 m depth.

Tubipora musica (a broken colony seen from the side). Sabah, Malaysia, 7 m depth.

Clavarina triangularis (X 5.0). Great Barrier Reef.

tend to fuse to form ridges. Such fusion, however, only occurs toward the branch tips, and an examination of the rest of the colony reveals the monticules typical of *Hydnophora*, but not formed in *Clavarina*.

DISTRIBUTION AND ECOLOGY   (Map #88)

A fairly uncommon coral that occurs along the fore reef but seldom forms large colonies. There are probably two species: *Clavarina scrabicula* Verrill, 1864 (with flattened or irregularly shaped branches and deep, well defined calices with paliform lobes) and *Clavarina triangularis* Veron and Pichon, 1980 (with triangular shaped branches and less well defined calices).

Scapophyllia cylindrica (X 2.8). Malaysia.

Scapophyllia Milne-Edwards & Haime, 1848

(L: *scapus*, stalk or shaft; Gr: *phyllon*, leaf. Possibly relating to the columnar growth form.)

DESCRIPTION
Living coral   (Col. pl. p. 168)

Scapophyllia forms massive, often columnar colonies that occasionally have stout, foliaceous edges. They are brown in color. The tentacles are generally retracted during the day.

Calices are united in series to form a pattern of valleys and ridges. Distance from mid-ridge to mid-ridge is about 5 mm, and the width of the wall slightly exceeds that of the valley. The valley is 3 to 4 mm deep, and the walls plunge down steeply. Calice centers are a few millimeters apart, but mouths are tiny and scarcely visible. Septa are closely packed and slightly rough to the touch.

Skeleton

Septa are stout and slightly exsert as they pass over the walls. They converge to distinct calice

centers. The columella is well formed and solid or rod-like. Septal margins are irregular or minutely dentate, and the sides are armed with small spines.

SIMILARITIES

The arrangement of calices is similar in both *Merulina* and *Scapophyllia*, but the latter can be distinguished by its massive corallum. In this respect *Scapophyllia* resembles brain corals of the family Faviidae. It can be identified by the stout exsert septa which have spiny septal sides but irregular or minutely dentate margins. In addition the calices are more distinct than in the faviids, marked by a ring of converging septa and a rod-like columella (not spongy).

DISTRIBUTION AND ECOLOGY   (Map #89)

Scapophyllia may form colonies about 0.5 to 1 meter tall but is not a particularly common coral. It usually occurs along the reef rim and upper fore reef slope. There is a single species: *Scapophyllia cylindrica* Milne-Edwards & Haime, 1848.

Blastomussa merleti (X 2.7). Sudan. BM (NH) 1977.5.5.2.

FAMILY MUSSIDAE

Blastomussa Wells, 1961
(Gr: *blastos,* bud; *mussa,* a coral genus. Relating to the growth form and the way in which new corallites are produced.)

DESCRIPTION
Living coral

Blastomussa is a small colonial mussid that buds off corallites from the edge of the colony. These may form into clumps or tufts or become united laterally to adjacent corallites by their walls. The former (phaceloid) condition is apparently typical of Pacific and eastern Indian Ocean specimens, while the latter (cerioid) form is found in the Red Sea and western Indian Ocean (Veron & Pichon, 1980).

The polyps are fleshy, and a mantle of living tissue usually envelopes the whole corallum. This obscures the skeleton beneath and gives the impression that all the calices are joined. The tentacles are usually retracted during the day, but if expanded are brightly colored and flower-like. The overall color of the coral is brown, greenish or red.

Corallites are rounded and about 5 to 15 mm in diameter depending on the species. In phaceloid specimens they protrude several millimeters from the surface of the coral. Septa are prominent, and their margins are rough or uneven to the touch.

Skeleton

Septa are stout, well spaced and exsert. Their margins have relatively few tall, blunt lobes or sharp teeth. The columella is solid.

SIMILARITIES

Blastomussa is most likely to be mistaken for a faviid but can be identified by its fleshy mantle, the large teeth on the septal margins and the solid columella.

DISTRIBUTION AND ECOLOGY   (Map #90)

This small coral is uncommon and is generally restricted to reef slopes. There are probably two species: *Blastomussa merleti* (Wells, 1961), with corallites up to 7 mm in diameter; and *Blastomussa wellsi* Wijsman-Best, 1973, with corallites 9 to 14 mm in diameter.

191

1   2   3
4   5   6
7   8   9

Cynarina Brueggemann, 1877

(Gr: *kinara,* an artichoke; L: *-ina*, suffix denoting likeness. A reference to the growth form.)

DESCRIPTION

Living coral
(Col. pl. p. 169)

Cynarina is a solitary mussid that is attached by a broad base to hard substrates or is free-living on mud. The corallum is turbinate in shape and about 5 to 6 cm tall. It is rounded or slightly irregular in cross section and does not usually exceed 8 cm in diameter. A fleshy mantle covers the skeleton and is formed into bubble-like expansions over the septa. This coenosarc is often translucent, the septa clearly visible beneath. The tentacles are long and tapering but are normally only extended at night. The living coral is often tinged with green and red.

Septa are prominent, and the larger ones protrude by several millimeters as they pass over the walls. They run down the outside of the corallum and are visible as well defined spiny ridges. The septal margins are also spiny.

Skeleton

Septa are prominent and arranged in cycles. Those of the first cycle are strongly exsert and thickened and may protrude by as much as 10 mm. They have paliform lobes at their inner ends and large, lobate dentations along their margins. These themselves may be toothed, and the paliform lobes are also coarsely serrated or lobed. The costae have dentate margins, and the columella is large and spongy. Smaller septa lie between those of the primary cycle and are thinner, less exsert and have finer teeth.

1. Plate-like, leafy and branching corals growing in profusion on the reef flat. 2. A gorgonian (class Alcyonaria). These sea fans have a horny internal skeleton, but unlike antipatharians have polyps with branched tentacles. Philippines, 15 m depth. 3. *Stylophora*. Sabah, Malaysia, 6 m depth. 4. *Montipora*. The polyps are overshadowed by the small tubercles that ornament the surface of the coral. Sabah, Malaysia, 7 m depth. 5. *Hydnophora rigida* (*Acropora* in the background). Sabah, Malaysia, 4 m depth. 6. *Echinophyllia*. Sabah, Malaysia, 12 m depth. 7. *Turbinaria*. Sabah, Malaysia, 5 m depth. 8. *Millepora*. Sabah, Malaysia, 5 m depth. 9. *Stylaster*. Sabah, Malaysia, 20 m depth.

Cynarina lacrymalis (X 1.2). Malaysia.

SIMILARITIES

Cynarina is a distinctive coral that is readily recognized underwater. It has a differently shaped corallum from the other solitary mussid, *Scolymia*, the fossa is deeper and paliform lobes are present (absent in *Scolymia*). The prominent, strongly exsert ring of primary septa is also characteristic of *Cynarina*.

Cynarina is sometimes mistaken for the young stage of a colonial mussid such as *Lobophyllia,* but the prominent, lobed septa do not occur in *Lobophyllia*.

TAXONOMIC NOTE

Veron and Pichon (1980) consider that *Acanthophyllia* Wells, 1937, which is a poorly known genus, may be synonymous with *Cynarina*. The skeleton appears identical, but as the authors point out, further studies, especially of the polyp, are needed before this opinion can be confirmed.

DISTRIBUTION AND ECOLOGY
(Map #91)

Cynarina is a relatively uncommon coral that is found in protected areas and in deeper water on reef slopes. There is a single species: *Cynarina lacrymalis* (Milne-Edwards & Haime, 1848).

Scolymia Haime, 1852

(Gr: *skolymos,* an artichoke. Presumably relating to the growth form of this coral.)

DESCRIPTION

Living coral   (Col. pl. p. 169)

Indo-Pacific *Scolymia* apparently include a wide range of forms from small solitary coralla to large colonial types (Veron & Pichon, 1980). The solitary coralla are more typical of the genus, but colonial ones are not uncommon. Solitary coralla are flattened and disc-like and may be anything between 3 and 14 cm in diameter. They are rounded or slightly irregular in shape. Colonial coralla are also flat but tend to have a slightly lobed outline. They may reach 20 cm in diameter but seldom have more than ten mouths. Both solitary and colonial types have a fleshy mantle of tissue covering the corallum. This is brown or greenish in color. Tentacles are generally only extended at night.

Septa may be hidden by the fleshy coenosarc, but their position is usually indicated by rows of small warts. These correspond to the sharp spines along the septal margins. Costae are also present and have spiny margins.

Skeleton

Septa are arranged in cycles with the larger one radiating from the columella to the perimeter. Smaller, shorter ones lie between. Septal margins are armed with strong lobed or pointed teeth, the size and shape of which vary according to the size of the septa and corallum. The septa pass over the top of the wall and run a short distance down the outside as costae. They gradually become reduced and represented only as rows of spines. The link between adjacent calice centers may be lamellar (resembling a septum) or trabecular (resembling the columella).

SIMILARITIES

Scolymia can be confused with immature colonial mussids such as *Lobophyllia* but can generally be distinguished by its flatter shape and the reduction of costae on the outside of the corallum.

TAXONOMIC NOTE

Scolymia is well known in the western Atlantic and was thought to be absent from the Indo-Pacific. The genus *Parascolymia* Wells, 1964, was created for the Indo-Pacific form of *Scolymia*, but

Scolymia vitiensis (X 1.2). Malaysia.

Veron and Pichon (1980) consider that there are no valid reasons for separating the two genera. Wells (1964) had suggested differences in the type of linkage formed between adjacent centers during asexual reproduction, but it seems that this is not a reliable feature. Both *Scolymia* and *Parascolymia* are predominantly monocentric, and those di- and tricentric specimens that have been found show both types of linkage—*i.e.,* both lamellar and trabecular (Veron & Pichon, 1980). The same authors also consider that *Homophyllia* is synonymous with *Scolymia. Homophyllia australis* was described from the temperate waters of southern Australia, but Veron & Pichon have studied intermediate types from Lord Howe Island and conclude that this species is probably a cold-water form of *Scolymia vitiensis.*

DISTRIBUTION AND ECOLOGY   (Map #92)

Scolymia is generally restricted to reef slopes and is particularly common in areas that do not support prolific growths of large reef-building corals. There is probably a single polymorphic species in tropical Indo-Pacific waters: *Scolymia vitiensis* Bruggemann, 1877.

194

Acanthastrea Milne-Edwards & Haime, 1848

(Gr: *akantha,* thorn or prickle; Gr: *aster,* star. Relating to the spiny corallites.)

DESCRIPTION
Living coral
(Col. pl. p. 169)

Acanthastrea forms large encrusting colonies or flattish to rounded heads. The coral has a slightly fleshy mantle and is green, brown or reddish in color. Tentacles are generally retracted during the day.

Corallites are either separate and distinct (plocoid) or are united by their walls (cerioid). They are usually polygonal but may be irregular or semi-meandrine with two or three mouths in a row. Calices vary in size even within a single colony, but some at least are a centimeter in diameter and many exceed 2 cm. The fossa dips down several millimeters, and in the center is a small mouth. Septa are prominent and usually run from one calice to the next without interruption but may be separated by a small groove. The surface of the coral is rough and spiny to the touch.

Acanthastrea echinata (X 2). Arabian Gulf. BM(NH) 1978.2.2.270.

Skeleton

Septa are numerous, stout and exsert by several millimeters. In plocoid forms they dip down between calices to a distinct groove, but in cerioid forms they run over the walls between neighboring calices. Septal margins are armed with sharp teeth 3 to 4 mm in length. The columella is prominent and spongy, but where valleys are formed the centers are joined by laminar (plate-like) linkages.

SIMILARITIES

There are several species of *Favites* that have large corallites and spiny septa and can thus be mistaken for *Acanthastrea*. A careful comparison of the spines on the septa will distinguish between the two genera. In *Favites* the spines are relatively small and blunt; in *Acanthastrea* they are coarse, large and sharp. In addition, the polyp in *Acanthastrea* is fleshier than in *Favites*.

Some forms of *Acanthastrea* could be mistaken for *Moseleya,* which also has large calices arranged in a similar way. *Acanthastrea* is distinguished by its fleshier polyp, the distinctive mussid septa and the lack of paliform lobes.

DISTRIBUTION AND ECOLOGY (Map #93)

Acanthastrea is found in a wide range of biotopes but is not a common coral. Colonies may be a meter or more in diameter. There are probably five species.

Lobophyllia de Blainville, 1830

(Gr: *lobos,* lobe; Gr: *phyllon,* leaf. Referring to the meanders, which form separate lobes.)

DESCRIPTION
Living coral
(Col. pl. pp. 169, 172)

Lobophyllia forms massive, convex or rounded colonies. The corallites are either single or joined to form irregular lobes or sinuous meanders. The lobes or meanders are joined at their base, and the stalks vary in length from a few centimeters to 20 cm or more. Corallite width or diameter is usually between 1 and 4 cm but may be larger. The corallites are separated from their neighbors by a gap of 0.5 to 2 cm, but this may be almost obscured in the living coral by a fleshy mantle that passes over the corallite wall.

195

Lobophyllia pachysepta
(X 1.3). Malaysia.

The living tissue is usually green or brown, sometimes pinkish or red. Small mouths are visible in the calices and valleys, but tentacles are normally retracted during the day. When extended, they may be a centimeter or more in length with a rather bulbous base. The corallite walls are covered with numerous fleshy protuberances or warts that correspond to the position of the septal spines. The septa themselves are usually obscured and difficult to see in the living coral.

Skeleton

Small and large septa alternate; most are exsert, the larger ones by as much as 1 cm. Their margins are armed with strong spines several millimeters long. These are either lobed or pointed and may themselves be finely serrated. The septa continue down the outside of the corallites as low costal ridges with spiny edges.

SIMILARITIES

Lobophyllia is a distinctive coral that is unlikely to be confused with other corals. It bears a superficial resemblance to its close relative *Symphyllia* but can be readily identified by the gap between adjacent lobes or meanders. In *Symphyllia* neighboring walls are fused.

DISTRIBUTION AND ECOLOGY (Map #94)

Lobophyllia is a fairly common coral that occurs along the reef rim and fore reef slope. Colonies may reach 2 cm or more in diameter. There are probably four species.

Symphyllia Milne-Edwards & Haime, 1848

(Gr: *syn* = *sym,* together; Gr: *phyllon,* leaf. Referring to the joined meanders.)

DESCRIPTION

Living coral (Col. pl. p 172)

Symphyllia forms massive heads that are rounded, convex or flattened. Corallites are joined in longitudinal series to form a system of valleys and ridges. Occasionally valleys are short or even monocentric. Adjacent lateral walls are fused together, and the walls are stout and high, sometimes dropping more than a centimeter to the valley below. The width from mid-ridge to mid-ridge is usually between 1.5 and 2 cm, but may be wider. The width of the wall is usually the same or slightly less than that of the valley.

The corallum is covered by slightly fleshy tissue that is usually brown, green or white. Sometimes the valleys and walls are contrasting colors; for example, the ridge may be brown and the valleys either white or green. Small mouths are visible in the valleys, but tentacles are generally retracted during the day. The corallite walls are covered with numerous fleshy warts that correspond to the position of the septal spines. The septa themselves are obscured in the living coral.

Skeleton

Septa are numerous, and the larger ones are exsert by several millimeters. Septal margins are

196

Symphyllia cf. *recta* (X 1.3). Malaysia.

armed with strong lobed or pointed spines that themselves may be finely serrated.

SIMILARITIES

Symphyllia is a distinctive coral that is readily separated from meandrine corals belonging to the family Faviidae by the relatively wide, deep valleys and the extremely spiny septa. It shares these features with *Lobophyllia* but can be identified by the lateral fusion between adjacent walls.

DISTRIBUTION AND ECOLOGY   (Map #95)

Symphyllia occurs in most reef biotopes but is not a particularly common coral. Colonies may exceed 1 m in diameter. There are probably four species.

FAMILY PECTINIIDAE

Echinophyllia **Klunzinger, 1879**
(Gr: *echinos,* hedgehog (*i.e.,* spiny); Gr: *phyllon,* leaf. Relating to the spiny surface of this often leafy coral.)

DESCRIPTION

Living coral   (Col. pl. pp. 173, 192)

Echinophyllia is a low-growing coral with an irregular, foliaceous or encrusting growth form. Often the central part of the corallum is attached and solid, the margins free and thinner. Most colonies are brown overall, sometimes with the calice centers green or pink. The polyp tentacles are small and generally remain retracted during the day.

Corallites are prominent and are often separated by a gap of several millimeters. In other cases, especially toward the center of the colony, they may be crowded and joined together. Corallite diameter is usually about 10 mm but may be less or may exceed 20 mm. Corallites are generally elevated several millimeters above the surface of the corallum. The wall is usually vertical but may be slightly inclined. At the edge of the colony, where new growth takes place, the walls are less well developed and the corallites may be superficial. The development of corallite walls also varies according to the degree of calcification, and this is affected by the environment in which the colony is established (Veron & Pichon, 1980). In *Echinophyllia orpheensis* Veron & Pichon, 1980, branched corallites are formed.

Calices are roundish in cross section, but their outline is interrupted by the rough nature of the walls and septa. Septa and costae are visible within the calices and between corallites and have spiny, uneven edges. The living tissue that covers the surface of the corallum is usually slightly fleshy, and the spines may appear as small warts.

Skeleton

Septa are numerous and exsert by several millimeters as they pass over the corallite wall. They continue on to perithecal areas as spiny costal ridges or occasionally as rows of spines. Spines also

Echinophyllia aspera (note alveoli) (X 1.9). Malaysia.

adorn the septal and costal margins and are sharp and irregular, often 2 to 3 mm in length. Paliform lobes are usually present, and the columella is well developed and formed from twisted trabeculae. On the underside of the coral are well developed costae that run parallel and radiate from the center of the corallum. The costal margins are dentate, and the teeth may themselves be spinulose.

SIMILARITIES

Echinophyllia may bear a superficial resemblance to *Echinopora,* but this genus has the perithecal areas densely covered with small spines or occasionally crossed by non-spiny costae. In *Echinophyllia* the costae have prominent spines on their margins or occasionally are reduced to rows of irregularly spaced spines.

Echinophyllia is distinguished from other members of the family Pectiniidae by the prominent, usually protruding corallites with their vertical walls. The corallites around the perimeter of the corallum may be inclined (as in *Mycedium*), but mature ones in the center of the colony show the typical *Echinophyllia* arrangement. Another method of distinguishing between the two genera is to examine the surface of the corallum for alveoli. These small pits formed at the insertion of new septocostae are present in *Echinophyllia* but absent in *Mycedium.*

Colonies in deep, poorly lit waters are usually thin and fragile, and the corallites are superficial. In such cases they resemble *Oxypora* and can only be reliably identified by examining the corallum for slits or pores. These are present in *Oxypora,* absent in *Echinophyllia.*

DISTRIBUTION AND ECOLOGY (Map #96)

Echinophyllia is found in most fore reef areas but has a preference for slightly shaded spots on the reef slope. Colonies may reach a meter or more in diameter. There are probably five species. Ditlev (1980) recognizes only a single species, *Echinophyllia aspera* (Ellis & Solander, 1786).

Oxypora Saville-Kent, 1871
(Gr: *ox,* sharp; *porus,* pore. Probably relating to the spiky appearance of the corallites.)

DESCRIPTION
Living coral (Col. pl. p. 172)

Oxypora may be semi-encrusting but always has free foliaceous margins. Some colonies are loosely attached. The corallum is often only a few millimeters thick and is characteristically brittle and fragile. Colonies are usually brown in color with pink, green or gray calice centers. Tentacles remain retracted during the day. The coral surface is generally covered with a rather fleshy mantle and tends to have a warty appearance due to the underlying spines.

Many of the corallites are separate and distinct, but others are crowded and partially joined together. Calices are rounded to elliptical in shape. They vary in size even on a single corallum, but the diameter is generally between 3 and 8 mm. Calices are superficial or appear slightly raised. Septa are just visible and continue as septocostae outside the calices. These ridges run from the center of the corallum to the perimeter and are almost parallel. They continue on the underside of the coral and have spiny margins. The septocostae have smooth (*O. glabra*) or spiny (*O. lacera*) margins.

Skeleton

There are about eight to 12 septa associated with each calice. These are thickened and exsert at the outer edge of the calice, thus giving the impression of a slightly elevated corallite wall. The margins of

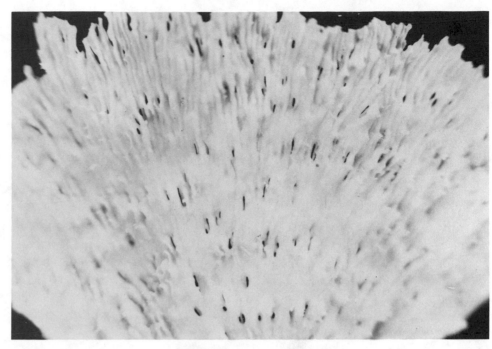

Oxypora lacera (X 1.9).
Malaysia.

septa and costae bear sharp spines that may them-selves have secondary spinules at the tips. A col-umella is present in *O. lacera,* but in *O. glabra* the inner ends of the septa are fused in the center of the calice and the columella is absent. The corallum in *Oxypora* is pierced by numerous small slits or pores.

SIMILARITIES

The thin, fragile corallum and superficial calices are usually sufficient to distinguish *Oxypora* from other pectiniids. It is the only member of the family in which the corallum is pierced by pores or slits.

DISTRIBUTION AND ECOLOGY   (Map #97)

Oxypora may be found in shallow fore reef areas but prefers reef slopes. In general it is not a com-mon coral. Colonies seldom exceed 1 meter in diameter. There are two species: *Oxypora lacera* (Verrill, 1864) and *Oxypora glabra* Nemenzo, 1959.

Mycedium Oken, 1815
·(Gr: *mykes,* knobbed like a fungus; Gr: *-idion,* suffix denoting diminutive. Presumably relating to the knob-like shape of the corallites.)

DESCRIPTION
Living coral   (Col. pl. p. 173)
Mycedium forms foliaceous or semi-encrusting colonies that may exceed 2 m in diameter. Often the folia are contorted or folded, giving the colony an uneven appearance. The edge tends to be deli-cate and easily broken. Most colonies are brown with pink or greenish tinges and often with brightly colored green or red oral discs. Tentacles are not extended during the day.

The majority of corallites are separate, but they may be crowded in places with the walls touching. Corallite diameter varies even within a single specimen but is usually between 5 and 15 mm. Typically the corallites protrude 3 or 4 mm from the corallum. They are inclined at an angle to the coral surface, with the calice facing toward the out-side of the colony. New calices are added around the edge of the corallum, and these are smaller and less protuberant than mature ones.

The septa are slightly obscured by a mantle of living tissue and have a rather uneven appearance. They run from the corallite walls across perithecal areas as well defined ridges; these ridges also con-tinue on the underside of the coral. The surface of the coral is rough to the touch despite the covering layer of living tissue.

Skeleton

Septa are numerous, and their margins are armed with sharp spines. They continue as costae on perithecal areas; these run almost parallel toward the outer margin of the corallum. Costal margins are spiny.

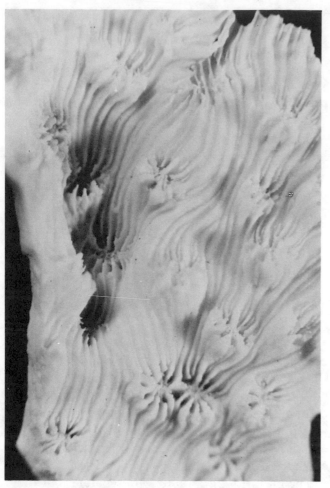

Mycedium sp. (X 1.9). Malaysia.

SIMILARITIES

Mycedium can generally be identified by its protuberant, inclined corallites. Occasionally it may be confused with *Echinophyllia,* and in these cases a reliable method of distinguishing between the two genera is to examine the surface of the corallum for alveoli. These small pits formed at the insertion of new septocostae are present in *Mycedium* but absent in *Echinophyllia.*

DISTRIBUTION AND ECOLOGY (Map #98)

Colonies occur in shallow fore reef areas but are more common on slopes and overhangs. They tend to become fragile and leaf-like at depth. About six species have been described, but recent authors (Chevalier, 1975; Veron & Pichon, 1980) suggest that only a single species is valid: *Mycedium elephantotus* (Pallas, 1766).

Physophyllia Duncan, 1884
(Gr: *physis,* growth; Gr: *phyllon,* leaf. Relating to the leafy growth form.)

DESCRIPTION
Living coral

Physophyllia forms encrusting colonies with free

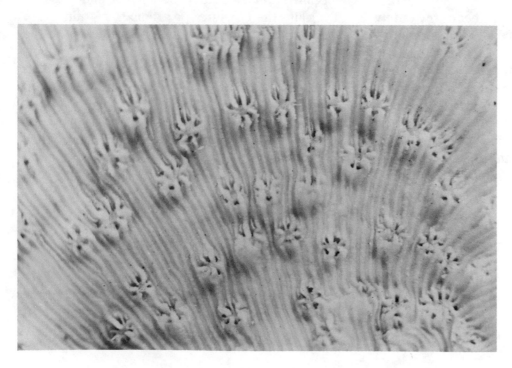

Mycedium elephantotus (X 1.9). Malaysia.

foliaceous margins. There are few records of this coral, and little is known about its color and general appearance.

Corallites are separate but lack distinct boundaries. Their position is marked by a ring of radiating septa which continue as parallel septocostae on perithecal areas. Adjacent septocostae are well spaced, separated by a gap of 2 to 5 mm. Their margins are smooth to the touch. Perithecal areas may be flat or raised into collines.

The majority of calices are superficial, but those toward the margins of the colony may be slightly elevated and inclined. There is usually a large central calice about 15 mm in diameter and subsidiary ones about 5 mm in diameter.

Skeleton

Septal and costal margins are either smooth or armed with fine spines. The corallum is solid, not pierced by pores or slits.

SIMILARITIES

Physophyllia can be recognized by its leafy form, superficial calices and well spaced septa and septocostae. It can be confused with *Oxypora* but lacks the pores and slits characteristic of that genus.

DISTRIBUTION AND ECOLOGY (Map #99)

Little is known of the distribution of *Physophyllia*, but along with other pectiniids, it probably prefers reef slopes. There may only be one species: *Physophyllia ayleni* Wells, 1933. It is possible that this is a form of *Pectinia*. The status of *Physophyllia* will be resolved when more specimens have been found.

Pectinia Oken, 1815
Lettuce coral
(Gr: *pectinis,* comb. Probably relating to the comb-like appearance of the walls, which are often tall, thin and striated.)

DESCRIPTION
Living coral

Pectinia forms encrusting, foliaceous or branched colonies. In many cases there is a distinctive semi-meandrine arrangement of collines which form thin convoluted leaves over the surface of the corallum. These may be up to 5 cm high but are only a few millimeters wide. In some cases the top of the colline is indented by as much as half its height. The walls occasionally enclose only a single calice, but more often they are united longitudinally to enclose a system of deep valleys. The width of the valleys is variable, but in many cases it lies between 1 and 2 cm. Collines are absent in *Pectinia elongata*, which is entirely branching with thin tapering branches.

Calices are superficial and lack true walls (the collines are formed from modified septocostae). The position of calice centers is indicated by the pattern of septa as they converge to the calice centers. Calices are circular or oval in appearance and usually between 2 and 6 mm in diameter. In *P. elongata* they may reach 10 mm in diameter.

Calices are widely spaced and scattered over the coral surface. In the semi-meandrine forms they lie along the floor of the valleys and also occur on the side of the collines. Perithecal areas are crossed by septocostae and give the coral a striated appearance. Some run along the length of the valleys and others pass up and over the walls. Their margins have a slightly warty appearance due to the presence of spines beneath the slightly fleshy mantle. This living tissue is brown or grayish in color, often with green tints and with the top of the walls pale. Tentacles are long and thin but are only extended at night.

Pectinia sp. (X 1.1). Malaysia.

Skeleton

Margins of septa and septocostae are finely and irregularly serrated. Costae are also present on the undersurface of the corallum.

SIMILARITIES

The growth form and other characters of *Pectinia* make it a distinctive genus. *Oxypora* also has superficial calices, but is readily identified by its fragile skeleton penetrated by slits or pores.

DISTRIBUTION AND ECOLOGY (Map #100)

Pectinia occurs in most reef habitats, both in shallow and deep areas. Colonies occasionally reach 1 m or more in diameter. The taxonomic history of *Pectinia* is complicated because of the great variations within species and disagreements about names and synonymies. For many years *Pectinia* was known as *Tridacophyllia*, and as many as 12 species were described. Subsequent studies (Chevalier, 1975; Veron and Pichon, 1980) suggest that only about half this number are valid.

Paracyathus sp. (X 6). Malaysia.

FAMILY CARYOPHYLLIIDAE

DESCRIPTION (Solitary and other small ahermatypic forms.)

Living coral

Most non-reef-building caryophylliids are solitary, but a few form low colonies in which the individual corallites are joined together (*e.g., Polycyathus*). Corallites are trochoid to cylindrical in shape. Shallow-water forms are often less than 5 mm in diameter and seldom exceed 15 mm. They are usually pale in color with transparent polyps. Septa are visible, and the larger ones are slightly or distinctly exsert. They have smooth margins.

Skeleton

Septa are in cycles, and the inner ends of higher cycles (*i.e.,* the smaller septa) may unite to lower cycles. Costae usually run a short way down the outside of the corallite wall. Septal and costal margins are smooth, and the sides are smooth or finely granular. Paliform lobes may be present; the columella is well developed and spongy in appearance. The corallite wall and septa are solid, rarely porous.

SIMILARITIES

Caryophylliids are most likely to be confused with dendrophylliids, and it may be difficult to distinguish between the two underwater. An examination of the skeleton reveals that dendrophylliids have fused septa (Pourtales plan), while in caryophylliids the septa may unite, but not in this particular arrangement. In addition, the skeleton in caryophylliids is solid, rarely porous as it is in dendrophylliids.

DISTRIBUTION AND ECOLOGY

Many caryophylliids are found at depths of thousands of meters, but there are several species that occur in shallow water and can be seen among the reef-building corals of fringing and offshore reefs. They are generally attached to dead coral surfaces or grow in caverns and underhangs, but are easily overlooked because of their small size and cryptic habits. Attached types include *Paracyathus*, *Polycyathus* and *Caryophyllia*. In contrast, *Heterocyathus* settles on small pebbles or shells in soft substrates and becomes free-living as an adult. Caryophylliids are widely distributed throughout tropical and temperate waters.

Euphyllia **Dana, 1846**
Subgenus *Euphyllia* **Dana, 1846.**
(Gr: *Eu-*, true; Gr: *phyllon,* leaf. Possibly relating to the prominent, leafy septa.)

DESCRIPTION
Living coral   (Col. pl. pp. 176, 177)
Euphyllia (Euphyllia) has a phaceloid growth form in which the corallites rise separately from an encrusting base. They are several centimeters tall and usually between 1 and 4 cm in diameter. The majority of calices are rounded, but those that are in the process of dividing are irregular or elongate.

The polyp tentacles are always extended during the day and are unable to completely retract. They are shaped like narrow fingers, have slightly inflated tips and may be several centimeters long when fully extended. They are green, gray, bluish or pale brown in color, usually with the tips white or green.

Septa become visible if the polyp is made to retract. The larger septa are exsert and there are smaller ones between them. Their upper edges feel smooth to the touch.

Skeleton
Septa are numerous and in cycles, the larger ones exsert by as much as 10 mm as they pass over the corallite wall. They continue as costae for a short way down the outside of the wall. Septal margins are smooth, finely granulated or minutely dentate. There is no columella.

SIMILARITIES
Euphyllia (Euphyllia) is readily distinguished underwater by its characteristic growth form and the long, finger-like tentacles. *Heliofungia* has tentacles of a similar shape and size, but the corallum is detached and completely different in form.

The general growth form and arrangement of corallites in *Euphyllia (Euphyllia)* are similar to *Plerogyra*, but the polyps are distinctly different. They are finger-like in *Euphyllia,* inflated and balloon-like in *Plerogyra*. In addition, the septa in *Plerogyra* are more leafy and widely spaced.

DISTRIBUTION AND ECOLOGY   (Map #101)
Euphyllia (Euphyllia) is a common coral that is found in a wide variety of reef habitats. Many colonies are 10 cm or less in diameter, but a few may reach 50 cm. There are possibly only two species: *Euphyllia (Euphyllia) glabrescens* (Chamisso & Eysenhardt, 1821) and *Euphyllia (Euphyllia) cristata* Chevalier, 1971. *E. cristata* is identified by its more exsert septa and by the development of a fifth septal cycle.

*Euphyllia (Euphyllia)
glabrescens* (X 1.1).
Malaysia.

Euphyllia **Dana, 1846**
Subgenus *Fimbriaphyllia* **Veron & Pichon, 1980**
(L: *fimbria,* fringe; Gr: *phyllon,* leaf. Relating to the arrangement of the calices.)

DESCRIPTION
Living coral   (Col. pl. p. 177)

Euphyllia (Fimbriaphyllia) has a flabelloid to flabello-meandroid growth form. The corallites rise from an encrusting base and, when they divide, they do not become separated but remain united in series. Thus meanders of various lengths are formed. They are well spaced and each is separated from its neighbor by a deep trough. The width of the meanders is usually around 1 cm.

The polyp tentacles are always extended during the day and tend to hide the skeleton beneath. They are of two distinct types, which has led to the erection of two species (Veron & Pichon, 1980). *Euphyllia (Fimbriaphyllia) ancora* has long thin tentacles that do not branch except at the base. The tip of each tentacle is expanded into a crescent- or kidney-shaped cap that is usually paler in color than the rest of the tentacle. *Euphyllia (Fimbriaphyllia) divisa* has fairly stout finger-like tentacles that are usually over 5 cm long. They are generally divided into sub-branches, and all the branches give off small side branches. These side branches are finger-like and have slightly expanded tips that are normally rounded or occasionally crescentic. The tentacles in both species are usually greenish or bluish with paler tips.

Septa are visible if the polyps are made to retract. The larger septa are exsert and particularly prominent. Their upper edges feel smooth to the touch.

Skeleton

Septa are numerous and in cycles, the larger ones exsert by as much as 1 cm as they pass over the corallite wall. They continue as costae for a short way down the outside of the wall. Septal margins are smooth, finely granulated or minutely dentate. There is no columella.

SIMILARITIES

Euphyllia (Fimbriaphyllia) is easily recognized underwater by its distinctive tentacles. The skeleton is similar to that in *Plerogyra sinuosa,* but the septa in *Euphyllia* are closer together and less leafy.

The skeleton is also similar to *Cataclyphyllia,* except that the septa in this genus have straight margins and drop gently to the fossa. The living corals are easily distinguished by their polyps.

DISTRIBUTION AND ECOLOGY   (Map #101)

Euphyllia (Fimbriaphyllia) occurs in a wide

Euphyllia (Fimbriaphyllia) divisa (X 2). Malaysia.

variety of reef habitats but appears to be particularly common on reef slopes. Colonies often exceed 50 cm in diameter and may even reach 1 m or more. There are probably two species: *Euphyllia (Fimbriaphyllia) ancora* Veron & Pichon, 1980 (with unbranched tentacles) and *Euphyllia (Fimbriaphyllia) divisa* Veron & Pichon, 1980 (with compound tentacles). These species have been described on the basis of their distinctive polyps, and there appear to be no skeletal differences between the two.

Catalaphyllia Wells, 1971
(Named for Rene Catala, in recognition of his studies on tropical marine fauna.)

DESCRIPTION
Living coral
The corallum in *Catalaphyllia* is monocentric and attached by a small base. As growth continues the corallum breaks free from the substrate, first becoming crescentic (flabelloid), then elongate and sinuous (flabello-meandroid). Polyps are brightly colored, and tentacles are usually extended both

Catalaphyllia jardinei (X 0.5). Great Barrier Reef.

Catalaphyllia jardinei (X 2). Great Barrier Reef.

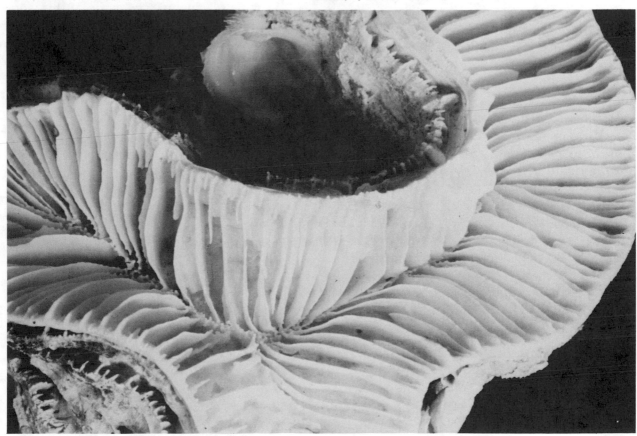

during the day and at night (Veron & Pichon, 1980). These are narrow and finger-like with slightly bulbous tips and form a fringe along the top of the wall. They are gray-brown to purple, often with the tips pink. Oral discs are broad and bright green or purplish in color.

Valleys are 2 to 3 cm wide and appear shallow in the living coral because of the expanded polyps. The polyp mouths are several millimeters in diameter and lie in a row along the center of the valley. Septa are obscured unless the polyps are made to retract.

Skeleton

There are nine to 12 septa per cm that slope evenly from the top of the wall to the bottom of the valley. Depth here is 1.5 to 2 cm. The septa are thin and only slightly exsert, with their margins granular, finely serrated or toothed. Low costae extend down the outside of the corallite wall. The columella is spongy or lamellar but weakly developed.

SIMILARITIES

The living coral can be identified by the broad oral disc and fringe of finger-like tentacles. In these respects it resembles *Trachyphyllia,* except that the tentacles of that genus are normally only extended at night. In addition, *Trachyphyllia* has prominent teeth on the septal margins, paliform lobes and a well developed columella.

Euphyllia (Fimbriaphyllia) has a similar flabello-meandroid skeleton, but the oral disc is narrow and the tentacles are either compound or have distinctive kidney-shaped tips. In addition, the septa in *Cataphyllia* are less exsert and drop evenly to form a relatively shallow, V-shaped valley.

DISTRIBUTION AND ECOLOGY   (Map #102)

Cataphyllia occurs in a variety of reef biotopes but is especially common on soft substrates rather than in areas of dense coral growth. Mature colonies may reach 50 cm in diameter. There is a single species: *Cataphyllia jardinei* (Saville-Kent, 1893).

Plerogyra Milne-Edwards & Haime, 1848

(Gr: *pleres,* full; Gr: *gyros,* circle. Etymology obscure, possibly a reference to the rounded growth form.)

DESCRIPTION

Living coral   (Col. pl. pp. 177, 180)

Plerogyra forms rounded colonies that are built up from large, stalked corallites. The corallites are usually over 5 cm tall and are well spaced from their neighbors. Calices in *Plerogyra simplex* are rounded, but in *Plerogyra sinuosa* some at least are elongate and form meanders of varying lengths. It is also common to find solitary coralla that represent the juvenile phase of *Plerogyra* species. These single corallites are several centimeters tall and range from 2 cm to about 10 cm in diameter.

The skeleton in *Plerogyra* is always obscured by prominent vesicles. These apparently retract at night, when the tentacles themselves are extended (Veron & Pichon, 1980). The vesicles are usually rounded, balloon-like and about 1.5 cm in diameter. In *Plerogyra sinuosa* they are often bulbous only at the base and then taper upward to a blunt point. The vesicles are transparent, white, pale brown or green and are sometimes streaked or mottled with darker markings. Minute flattened comb jellies may creep over the vesicles, appearing as dark brown blotches. The vesicles do not always have a regular outline but may be distinctly lobed in some specimens. The cause of this is unknown.

The vesicles can be made to partially retract so that some of the underlying skeleton is revealed. The septa are leafy and widely spaced, their upper margins smooth to the touch.

Plerogyra simplex (X 2.7). Malaysia.

Plerogyra sinuosa (two specimens) (X 1.1). Malaysia.

Skeleton

Septa are prominent, and the larger ones are exsert by as much as 10 mm as they pass over the corallite wall. They may be separated by a gap of 5 mm or more and drop steeply to the fossa. Septal margins are smooth or occasionally minutely dentate. The degree to which costae are developed is variable, but in general they do not extend for more than a few millimeters down the outside of the corallite wall.

SIMILARITIES

The shape of colonies and arrangement of corallites are similar in *Plerogyra* and *Euphyllia,* but the two genera are easily distinguished by the distinctive tentacles and vesicles. In addition, the septa in *Plerogyra* are more leafy and widely spaced.

Plerogyra can also be mistaken for *Physogyra* because in both genera the corallum is covered with inflated vesicles. The vesicles in *Physogyra* are smaller and less rounded, but the main difference between the two genera is in the arrangement of the meanders. These are free laterally in *Plerogyra*, but in *Physogyra* neighboring meanders are fused into a common wall.

DISTRIBUTION AND ECOLOGY (Map #103)

Plerogyra is especially common on reef slopes and in the shelter of boulders and coral heads. Solitary coralla do not generally exceed 15 cm in diameter with the vesicles fully inflated. Colonial forms are usually less than 50 cm in diameter. There are probably two species: *Plerogyra sinuosa* (Dana, 1846), in which the calices are united to form meanders (juveniles are monocentric, cylindrical or trochoid); and *Plerogyra simplex* Rehberg, 1892, in which the calices are monocentric (irregular when dividing).

Physogyra Quelch, 1884
(Gr: *physa,* air bubble; Gr: *gyros,* circle. Relating to the conspicuous vesicles that cover the corallum.)

DESCRIPTION
Living coral (Col. pl. p. 180)

Physogyra forms massive, rounded colonies that are pale brown in color. Calices are united in series that may be short or long and sinuous. The series are united laterally, and the distance from mid-ridge to mid-ridge is about 10 to 15 mm.

207

Physogyra lichtensteini (X 2).
Malaysia.

The corallum is covered by a mat of vesicles and tentacles. The vesicles are usually extended during the day and the tentacles are extended at night, but there appear to be differences according to geographical location. Veron (1980) reports that specimens from the Great Barrier Reef are covered with small, gray, grape-like vesicles during the day and that elongate, tapering tentacles appear at night. In Malaysia the vesicles are finger-like with bulbous bases and pointed tips, and a few elongate tentacles are usually extended during the day.

The tentacles do not completely retract, but they withdraw sufficiently for the septa to be seen. These are widely spaced, the larger ones often 2 to 3 mm apart, their margins smooth to the touch.

Skeleton

Septa are exsert by several millimeters as they pass over the walls. Septa of adjacent valleys are usually separated by a gap of several mm. They have a leafy appearance and their upper margins are smooth. A narrow ridge runs along the top of the walls, marking the union between adjacent valley systems. The fossa is deep, and the septa drop down steeply. There is no columella.

SIMILARITIES

Physogyra is easily distinguished from other meandrine corals by its distinctive tentacles and by the smooth-edged leafy septa. The vesicles are similar to those in *Plerogyra*, but the arrangement of the corallites is different in the two genera. In *Physogyra* the meanders are joined laterally to their summits; in *Plerogyra sinuosa* they are free laterally.

DISTRIBUTION AND ECOLOGY (Map #104)

Physogyra is not a particularly common coral, but where colonies occur they may exceed 1 m in diameter. They are found in a variety of reef habitats but appear to prefer relatively shallow, protected waters. There are probably three species.

FAMILY DENDROPHYLLIIDAE

(Col. pl. pp. 65, 181, 184, 185)

This family includes several species that are restricted to water many hundreds of meters deep and can only be recovered by dredging. Other species occur over a wider depth range and are found in shallow waters. They may occur on coral reefs, but in most cases they lack symbiotic algae (zooxanthellae) and do not contribute to reef-building. *Tubastraea* and *Dendrophyllia* fall into this category but may colonize reefs in large numbers and are of significant ecological interest. Thus these two genera are described separately. A brief description is given here of a range of small dendrophylliids that may occur in shallow-water habitats.

208

DESCRIPTION
Living coral

In its simplest form (*e.g., Endopsammia, Balanophyllia*) the corallum is solitary and attached to hard substrates. It is cylindrical to trochoid in shape and seldom exceeds 10 mm in diameter. *Heteropsammia* is solitary or consists of several joined corallites. It is free-living on soft substrates, and the base of the coral always encloses the tube of a commensal sipunculid (peanut-worm). Other dendrophylliids (*e.g., Rhizopsammia, Duncanopsammia*) usually form small creeping colonies or low clumps in which the corallites are united at their bases by coenosteum.

These small dendrophylliids are usually brown, green or reddish in color. Polyps are normally retracted during the day but are expanded in a colorful ring at night. Septa are visible and often protrude slightly above the level of the corallite wall. Ridges corresponding to the underlying costae are sometimes visible on the outside of the corallites.

Skeleton

Septa are numerous and drop steeply to a well developed spongy columella. They are arranged in cycles, and the inner ends of some of the cycles are curved and fused to their neighbors (Pourtales plan). Septal margins are smooth, granular or slightly to highly dentate. Septal sides are strongly granulated. Costae may be thick and well developed or reduced to rows of granules. The corallum is porous, with the walls and septa pierced by small holes.

Balanophyllia cumingi (X 3). Malaysia.

SIMILARITIES

The small dendrophylliids described above can be confused with a number of other genera, and it is often necessary to examine the skeleton to be certain of identification. The characteristic arrangement of the septa, their granulated sides and the porous corallum are all distinctive features.

Dendrophyllia de Blainville, 1830
(Gr: *dendron,* tree; Gr: *phyllon,* leaf. Presumably relating to the branched, tree-like growth form of some species.)

DESCRIPTION
Living coral

Dendrophyllia forms low tufts or taller branched colonies. They are often red or orange in color, occasionally grayish or dark green. The polyps are sometimes partially extended during the day but are most clearly seen at night. They are attractive, flower-like and often bright yellow in color.

Corallites are separate and distinct. They are cylindrical or turbinate in shape and protrude by a centimeter or more from the coral surface. Calice diameter is usually around 5 to 15 mm. Perithecal areas appear smooth or are covered with low fine ridges. The larger septa are clearly visible and drop steeply to the calice center. They are usually covered with slightly fleshy tissue and are smooth to the touch.

Skeleton

Septa are numerous and arranged in cycles. They follow the Pourtales plan in which some of the septa curve and unite with their neighbors in a characteristic pattern. Septal margins are smooth or irregularly and finely dentate. The columella is spongy and well developed. Costal ridges are low, fine and crowded closely together. The corallum is porous, with the walls and septa pierced by small holes.

SIMILARITIES

Dendrophyllia is often confused with *Tubastraea* because the two genera have similar growth forms and several other features in common. The only reliable way to distinguish between the two is to examine the septal arrangement. In *Tubastraea* the septa are fewer in number and only occasionally unite at their inner ends. In *Dendrophyllia* they are more numerous and many are united at their inner ends.

Dendrophyllia gracilis (X 1.8). Malaysia.

DISTRIBUTION AND ECOLOGY

Dendrophyllia has a restricted distribution, preferring underhangs and vertical cliff faces. It may be rare or absent at some sites but occur in abundance at others. It is a non-reef-building (ahermatypic) coral with many species found in deep water. There are probably three or four species that occur on coral reefs in relatively shallow water.

Dendrophyllia occurs widely in the Indo-Pacific and is also found in more temperate waters.

Tubastraea Lesson, 1834
(L: *tubus,* tube; Gr: *astron,* star. Relating to the appearance of the calices.)

DESCRIPTION
Living coral   (Col. pl. pp. 181, 184)
Some *Tubastraea* colonies are low and tufted, while others are taller and tree-like. They are red, orange or dark green in color. Polyps are sometimes partially extended during the day, and at night the corallum is hidden by a ring of bright yellow tentacles.

Corallites are separate and distinct. They are cylindrical or turbinate in shape and protrude by a centimeter or more from the coral surface. Calice diameter is usually around 5 to 15 mm. Perithecal areas appear smooth or are covered with fine, low ridges. Larger septa are clearly visible and drop steeply to the calice center. They are usually covered with slightly fleshy tissue and are smooth to the touch.

Skeleton
Septa are arranged in cycles, and some are reduced to ridges on the inner wall of the corallite. In young calices the inner ends of smaller septa curve and unite with their neighbors, but in mature calices most are free and normal. Septal margins are smooth or finely and irregularly dentate. Costal ridges are low, fine and crowded closely together. The corallite wall and the smaller septa are porous.

SIMILARITIES
See *Dendrophyllia.*

DISTRIBUTION AND ECOLOGY
Tubastraea species tend not to grow in areas of dense coral growth but prefer vertical cliff faces and reef slopes. They often thrive where currents are strong. This is particularly true for the black, tree-like *Tubastraea micrantha* (often referred to as *Dendrophyllia micrantha*), which grows with its branches spread out across the direction of water flow. This is presumably an adaptation to ensure that the maximum volume of water flows over the polyps, bringing with it an ample supply of food. *Tubastraea* species occur from the surface to

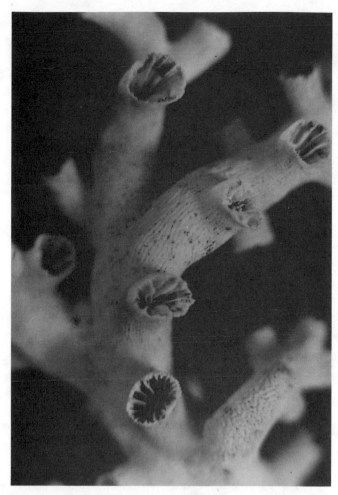

Tubastraea micrantha (X 1.8). Malaysia.

depths of nearly 1,500 meters. There are probably four or five species in shallow Indo-Pacific waters.

Turbinaria Oken, 1815
(L: *turbinatus,* cone-shaped; L: *-aria,* suffix denoting resemblance. Referring to the cone-shaped corallites.)

DESCRIPTION
Living coral   (Col. pl. pp. 184, 192)
Turbinaria often forms vase-shaped convolutions or spreading leaf-like fronds, fans or folds. In other cases layers of lobed plates produce massive, irregular heads. Colonies are usually about 20 to 50 cm in diameter but may be considerably larger. The corallum as a whole is generally brownish, but the polyps, tentacles and peristome may be more

brightly colored. Often the polyps are bright yellow or white and the peristome greenish. Tentacles are usually partially or completely extended during the day and have an attractive flower-like appearance.

Corallites are separate and distinct and may be present on both sides of leaf-like fronds but on the upper surface only of flatter fans. They are rounded, and most protrude by at least 1 mm and up to 15 mm in the form of a truncated cone. In certain places on the corallum they may be inclined, superficial or even slightly sunken into the coenosteum. Corallites are usually about 1.5 to 3.0 mm in diameter at the base, rarely reaching 5 mm. The corallite wall is wide, the top of the wall rounded and the fossa narrow. Corallites may be crowded in places but mostly are separated by smooth coenosteum. Septa are just visible in the living coral but do not extend over the corallite wall.

Skeleton
In young calices the septa follow the Pourtales plan typical of other dendrophylliids, but they

Turbinaria sp. (X 2.5). Malaysia.

revert to the normal condition during subsequent growth. Thus in the adult calice the septa are not curved and their inner ends are not fused together. Septal margins are smooth, granular or irregularly dentate. The columella is usually well developed. The skeleton is spongy and porous.

SIMILARITIES

Turbinaria is a distinctive coral that is unlikely to be confused with other dendrophylliids because of its characteristic growth form. The foliaceous growth form also distinguishes it from *Acropora* and *Astreopora*, both of which have corallites of a similar shape. *Cyphastrea* and *Echinopora* also have small, protruding corallites, but in these two genera the septa are clearly visible within the calice and on the corallite wall. In *Turbinaria* they can just be seen in the calice but do not extend onto the wall.

DISTRIBUTION AND ECOLOGY (Map #105)

Turbinaria is the only reef-building (hermatypic) coral in the family Dendrophylliidae and sometimes contributes significantly toward coral cover. It is especially common on reef slopes, and colonies may be large and come in a variety of forms. Veron and Pichon (1980) note that, "Most *Turbinaria* species from eastern Australia show a range of growth form which is paralleled by few other scleractinian genera." This range of form has led to taxonomic problems and the description of over 50 species. Veron and Pichon recognize nine species from the Great Barrier Reef, and it is possible that as few as 15 occur throughout the Indo-Pacific.

CLASS HYDROZOA

FAMILY MILLEPORIDAE

Millepora Linnaeus, 1758
Fire coral
(L: *mille,* thousand; L: *porus,* pore. A reference to the numerous small pores that cover the surface of the coral.)

DESCRIPTION

Living coral (Col. pl. pp. 188, 192)

Millepora forms branched, plate-like, massive and encrusting colonies. Branches are rounded or flattened; plates are upright and often fuse with each other to form a box-like structure. *Millepora*

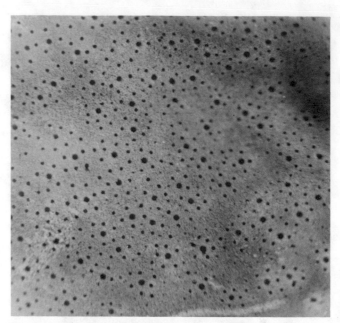

Millepora platyphylla (X 4.5). Malaysia.

is white, yellow or brown in color, and the surface of the coral appears smooth and structureless.

White hair-like tentacles are extended during the day and have a powerful and irritating sting. There are also stinging cells on the coenosteum. Thus *Millepora* has earned itself the name fire coral. A close examination reveals minute pores scattered over the surface of the coral.

Skeleton

The largest pores are about 0.1 mm in diameter and are referred to as gastropores. It is through these that the feeding polyps (gastrozooids) are extended. Around each gastropore are five to seven smaller pores known as dactylopores that contain defensive polyps (dactylozooids). The surface of the coral is finely granulated and may be pitted with shallow cups. These are ampullae, receptacles for the reproductive medusae. The skeleton is pale yellow or yellow-brown.

SIMILARITIES

Millepora is readily distinguished from stony (scleractinian) corals by the presence of minute featureless pores on the coral surface and the lack of corallites and septa. It is larger and more robust than its relatives *Stylaster* and *Distichopora* and is never purple or red in color. In addition, these two genera have minute styles in the gastropores that are lacking in *Millepora*.

Millepora also resembles *Heliopora* in some respects, but this latter genus is distinguished by its blue skeleton and the branched rather than simple tentacles.

DISTRIBUTION AND ECOLOGY (Map #106)

Millepora is an important coral in terms of reef-building and is especially successful in shallow fore reef areas where it may form large tracts or colonies several meters in diameter. *Millepora* occurs in sheltered and exposed sites and thrives in both shallow and deep water. It can make use of other substrates apart from the reef itself; for example, it often forms encrustations over sea fans and sea whips. *Millepora* is the only coral to produce medusae, tiny "jellyfish" that contain the gametes.

There are probably six or seven species in the Indo-Pacific, but the taxonomy of the group is complicated by the wide range of forms in which the coral can occur (see Boschma, 1948).

FAMILY STYLASTERIDAE

Stylaster Gray, 1831

(Gr: *stylos,* style; Gr: *aster,* star. Referring to the pillar-like structure in the center of each gastropore.)

DESCRIPTION

Living coral (Col. pl. pp. 188, 192)

Stylaster forms fragile branched colonies that seldom exceed 20 cm in height. They may be fanlike and oriented in one plane or bushy and more profusely branched. They are usually pink, purple or red, occasionally white. Minute white tentacles are sometimes visible.

Skeleton

There are larger gastropores (0.1 mm diameter) and smaller dactylopores scattered over the surface (see description for *Millepora*). The gastropores have a style in the center that is visible under high magnification. The surface of the coral is pitted or granular and the pores are often slightly exsert.

SIMILARITIES

Stylaster is similar in size and color to *Distichopora* but differs in the position of the gastropores. In *Stylaster* they are scattered over the surface of the branches and are usually slightly exsert. In *Distichopora* they are restricted to the narrow edges of the slightly flattened branches and are never exsert.

DISTRIBUTION AND ECOLOGY (Map #107)

Stylaster occurs in caves and crevices on reef slopes and is occasionally found on the sides of boulders in shallower water. It may be absent or rare in some areas, locally common in others. There are three or four species in the Indo-Pacific.

Distichopora Lamarck, 1816

(Gr: *distoichos,* in two rows; L: *porus,* pore. Relating to the arrangement of the pores in rows along the sides of the branches.)

DESCRIPTION

Living coral (Col. pl. p. 188)

Distichopora forms delicate branched colonies that seldom exceed 10 cm in height. The branches are generally aligned and flattened in one plane. The coral is pink, purple, orange or white in color, sometimes with two colors in the same colony. Minute white tentacles and tiny pores are usually just visible arranged in rows along the narrow edges of the branches. The flat side of the branch has a slightly uneven, knobby appearance.

Skeleton

The pores in *Distichopora* are not scattered at random over the surface of the coral but arranged in continuous rows or series along the narrow edge of the branches. They are superficial or lie slightly below the surface of the coral. The gastropores have a style in the center that is visible under high magnification. The rest of the coral surface is slightly rough with irregular pits and small bumps.

SIMILARITIES

Distichopora could be confused with *Stylaster* or possibly with small colonies of *Millepora*. It is readily distinguished from both by the position of the gastropores, which are restricted to the narrow edge of the slightly flattened branches.

DISTRIBUTION AND ECOLOGY (Map #108)

Distichopora is found in crevices and caves, on ledges and on the sides of boulders. It may be rare or absent in some areas, locally common in others. There are probably three or four species in the Indo-Pacific.

CLASS ALCYONARIA

FAMILY HELIOPORIDAE

Heliopora de Blainville, 1830
Blue coral
(Gr: *helios,* sun; L: *porus,* pore. Possibly relating to the arrangement of the pores, with the small ones grouped around the larger ones.)

DESCRIPTION

Living coral (Col. pl. p. 189)

Heliopora colonies often consist of an encrusting or semi-massive base from which arise a mass of branches or lobes. These are only a few centimeters in height and width, have blunt ends and are usually slightly flattened laterally. In other cases the corallum is laminate or encrusting and lacks branches. Finally, there are tall, wholly branched colonies. Again, the branches are only a few centimeters in diameter and have rounded tips.

Heliopora is known as blue coral, but the blue color of the skeleton is often obscured by brownish living tissues. The polyps (autozooids) are occasionally expanded during the day, when a ring of eight tiny white tentacles can just be seen. These are feather-like with fine side branches. The pores in which the zooids are located are visible as white or black dots less than 0.5 mm in diameter.

Skeleton

The surface of the corallum is smooth and perforated by cylindrical pits of two sizes. The larger ones (about 0.5 mm diameter) are 2 to 5 mm apart and contain the autozooids. The smaller ones (about 0.1 mm diameter) are more numerous and enclose extensions of the internal canal system that contain zooxanthellae. The skeleton itself is imperforate; *Heliopora* is the only alcyonarian coral to produce a skeleton of this type. The blue tint of the skeleton is due to the presence of iron salts.

SIMILARITIES

Heliopora is readily distinguished from scleractinian corals by the tiny pores and the lack of true septa and other corallite structures. In these respects it resembles *Millepora,* but it differs in both color and growth form. In addition, the tentacles in *Millepora* are simple, whereas in *Heliopora* they are branched.

DISTRIBUTION AND ECOLOGY (Map #109)

Heliopora is a fairly common coral that occurs in a variety of reef habitats, especially in shallow areas. Colonies may grow to a meter in diameter and are important reef-builders along with the scleractinian corals. There is a single species, *Heliopora coerulea* (Pallas, 1766).

Heliopora coerulae (X 3.6). Malaysia.

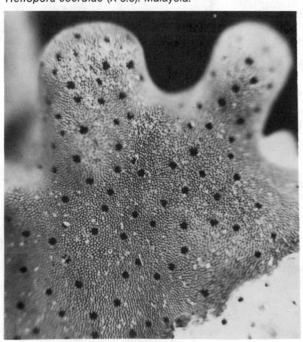

FAMILY TUBIPORIDAE

Tubipora **Linnaeus, 1758**
Organ-pipe coral
(L: tubus, tube; L: *porus,* pore. Relating to the small tubes in which the polyps are situated.)

DESCRIPTION

Living coral (Col. pl. p. 189)

Tubipora forms rounded heads that may reach 1 m or more in diameter. Polyps are expanded during the day and obscure the skeleton beneath. Associated with each polyp is a ring of eight feather-like tentacles several millimeters long. These are green, bluish, gray, white or brown in color. They retract rapidly when touched to reveal the reddish tubes in which they live. The diameter across the top of the tubes is about 1 to 2 mm.

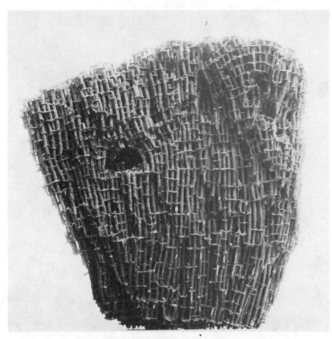

Tubipora musica. Locality unknown.

Skeleton

The skeleton in *Tubipora* is bright red in color and consists of a mass of vertical tubes bound together by horizontal platforms. The general arrangement resembles the pipes of an organ, and it is from this that the name organ-pipe coral is derived. Only the uppermost tubes in the colony are occupied by polyps.

SIMILARITIES

Tubipora is an unmistakable coral, both living and dead.

DISTRIBUTION AND ECOLOGY   (Map #110)

Tubipora prefers shallow, relatively quiet waters and may be locally common. There is much variation in the dimensions of the tubes and color of the polyps, but probably only a single species is valid: *Tubipora musica* Linnaeus, 1758.

ATLAS OF DISTRIBUTIONAL MAPS

The following 110 maps give the ranges of distribution for most of the coral genera presented in this book. The first 28 are covered in the section entitled Atlantic Reef Corals (starting on p. 42), and from # 29 through # 110 are covered in the section entitled Indo-Pacific Reef Corals (starting on p. 67). When a genus has a distribution covering both zoogeographic regions it is repeated in its proper sequence.

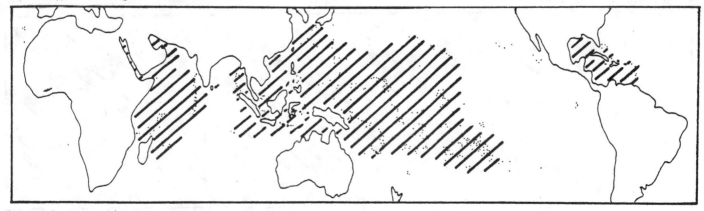

1. Distribution of the genus *Stephanocoenia*.

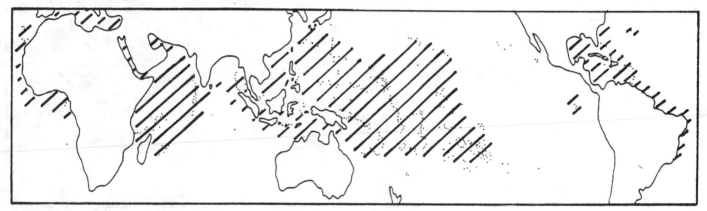

2. Distribution of the genus *Madracis*.

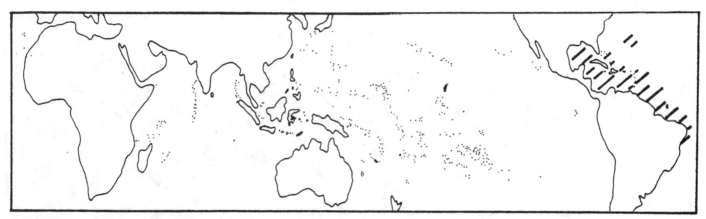

3. Distribution of the genus *Acropora*.

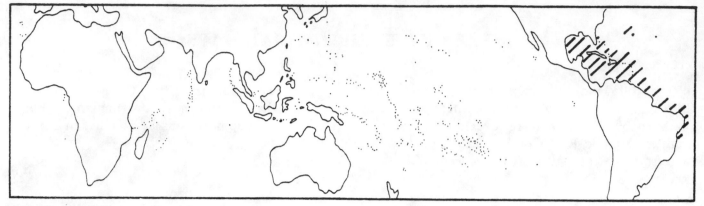

4. Distribution of the genus *Agaricia*.

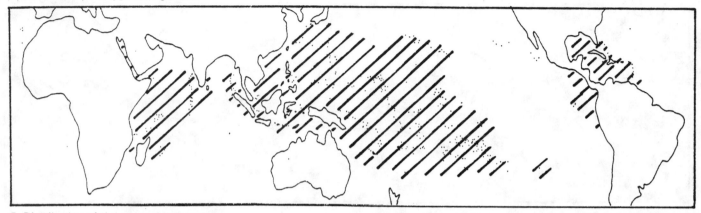

5. Distribution of the genus *Leptoseris*.

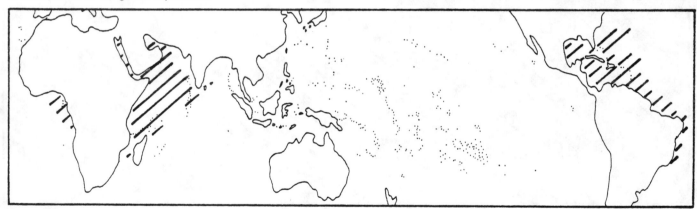

6. Distribution of the genus *Siderastrea*.

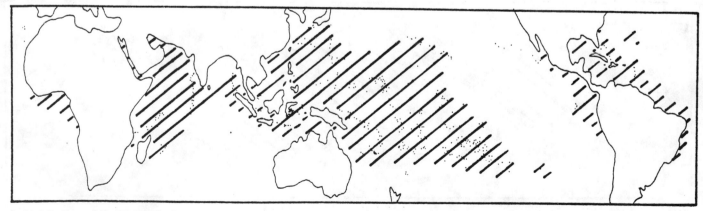

7. Distribution of the genus *Porites*.

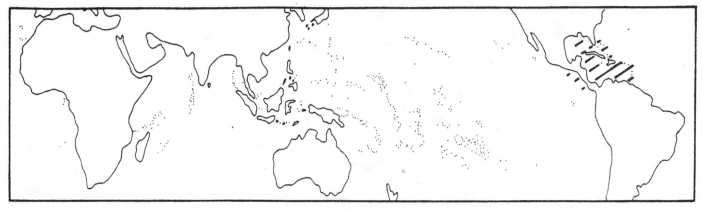

8. Distribution of the genus *Cladocora*.

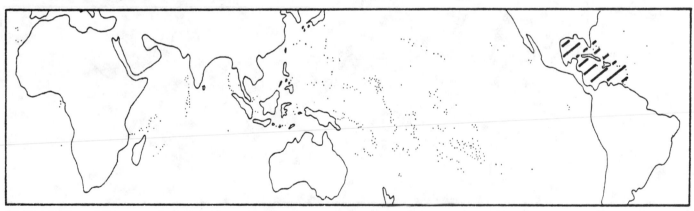

9. Distribution of the genus *Montastraea*.

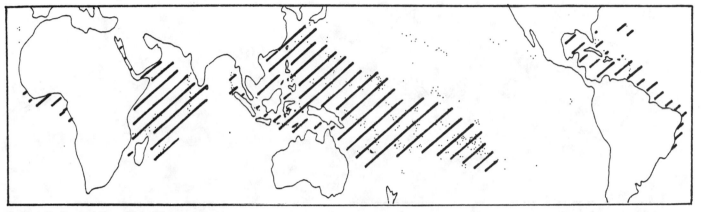

10. Distribution of the genus *Solenastrea*.

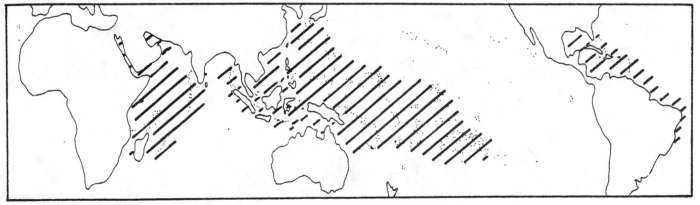

11. Distribution of the genus *Favia*.

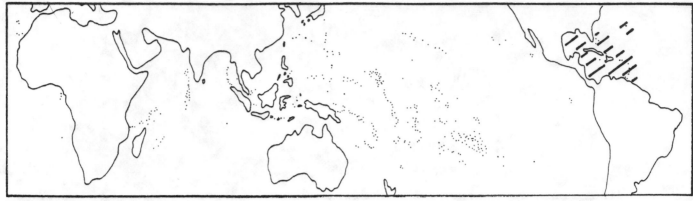

12. Distribution of the genus *Diploria*.

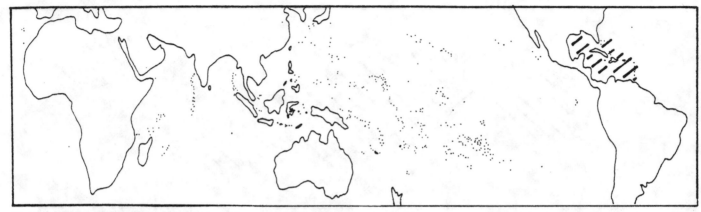

13. Distribution of the genus *Manicina*.

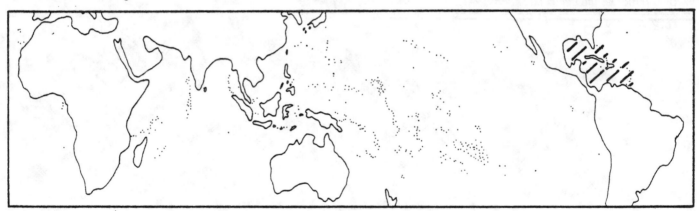

14. Distribution of the genus *Colpophyllia*.

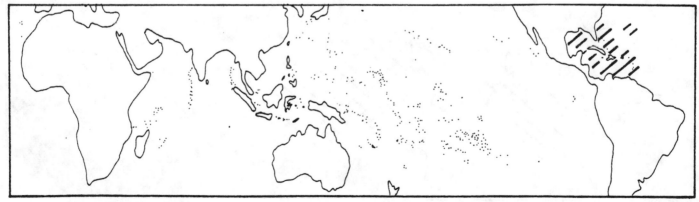

15. Distribution of the genus *Oculina*.

220

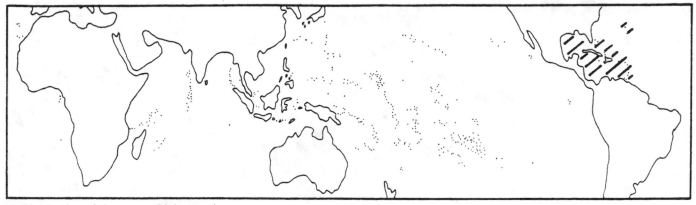

16. Distribution of the genus *Dichocoenia*.

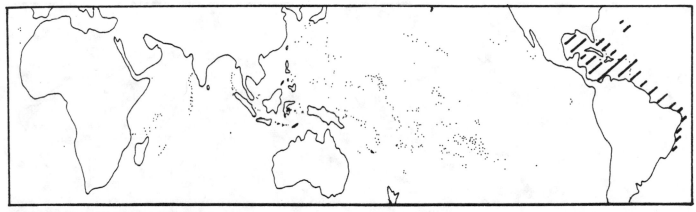

17. Distribution of the genus *Meandrina*.

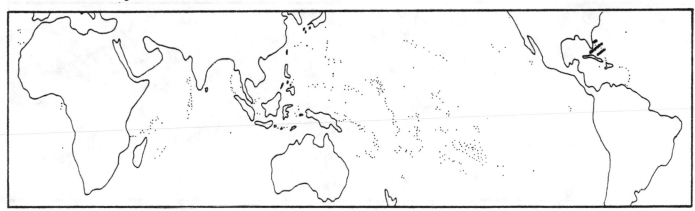

18. Distribution of the genus *Goreaugyra*.

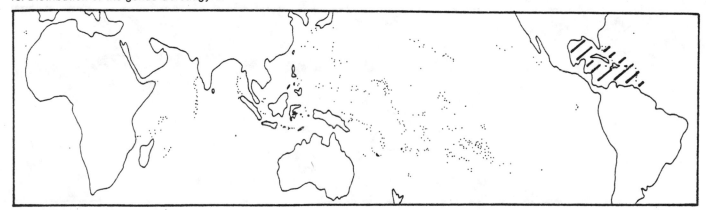

19. Distribution of the genus *Dendrogyra*.

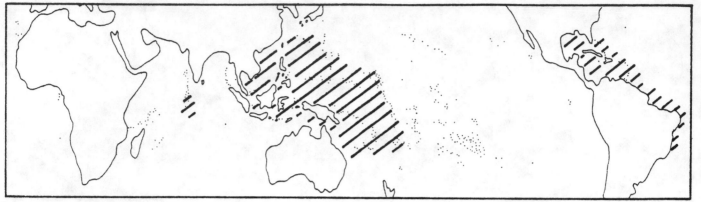

20. Distribution of the genus *Scolymia*.

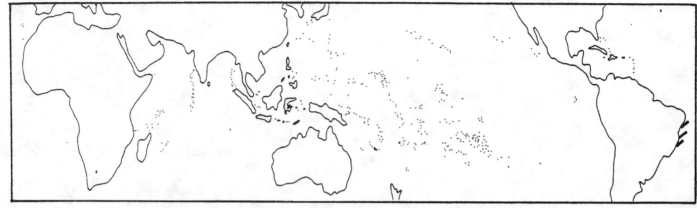

21. Distribution of the genus *Mussismilia*.

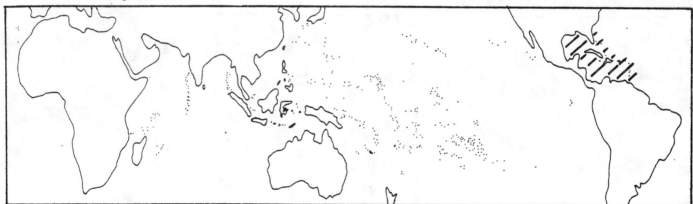

22. Distribution of the genus *Mussa*.

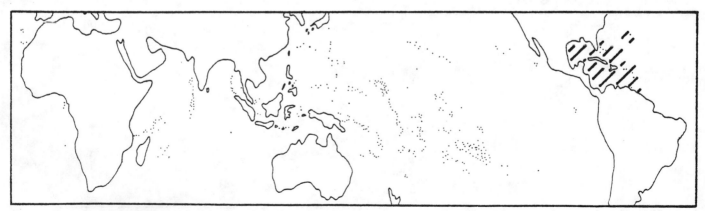

23. Distribution of the genus *Isophyllastrea*.

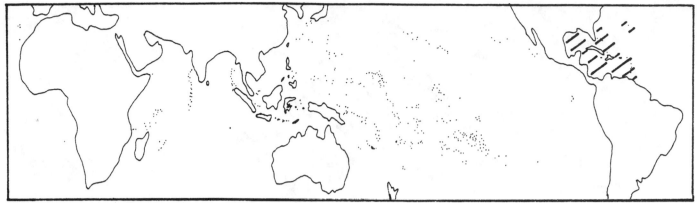

24. Distribution of the genus *Isophyllia*.

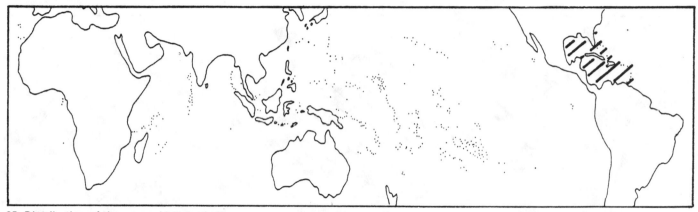

25. Distribution of the genus *Mycetophyllia*.

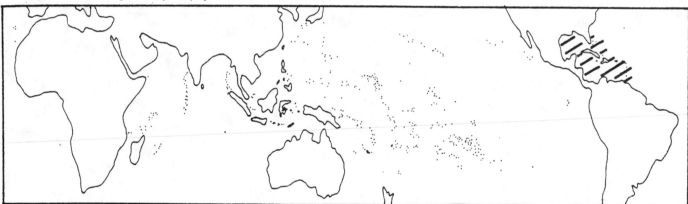

26. Distribution of the genus *Eusmilia*.

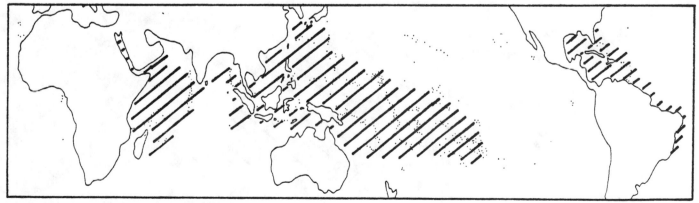

27. Distribution of the genus *Millepora*.

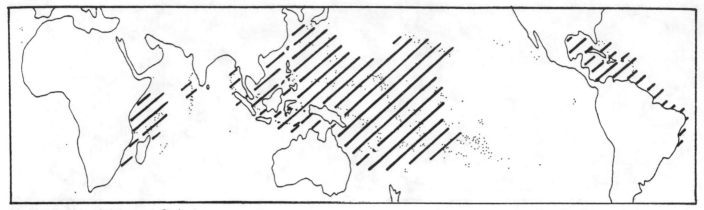

28. Distribution of the genus *Stylaster*.

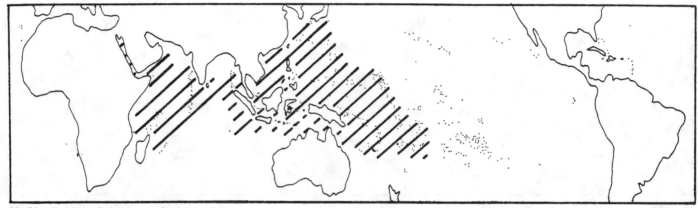

29. Distribution of the genus *Stylocoeniella*.

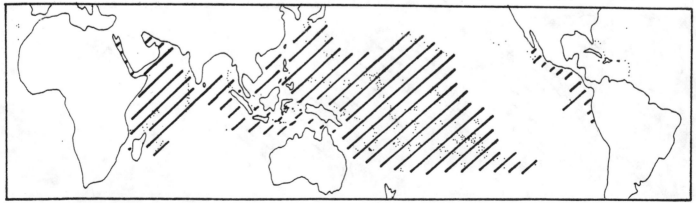

30. Distribution of the genus *Seriatopora*.

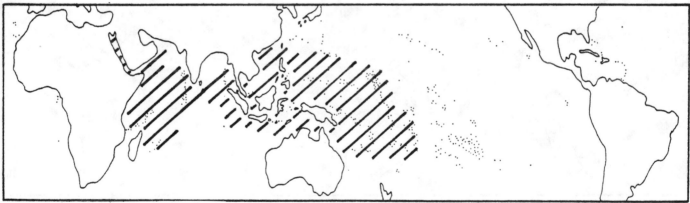

31. Distribution of the genus *Pocillopora*.

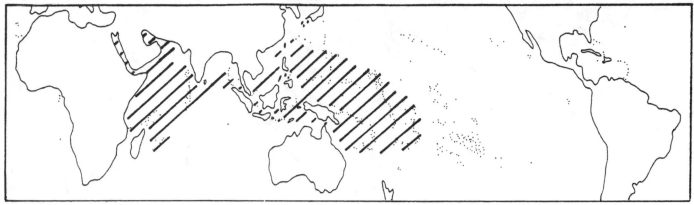

32. Distribution of the genus *Stylophora*.

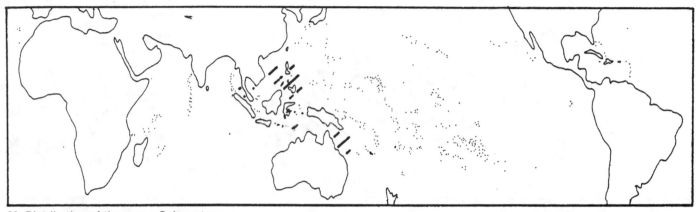

33. Distribution of the genus *Palauastrea*.

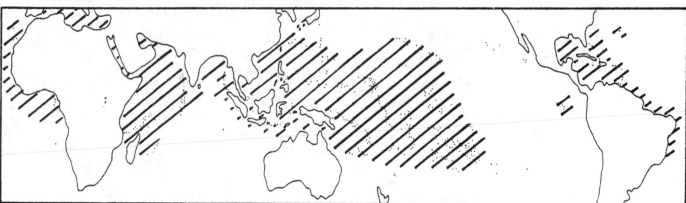

34. Distribution of the genus *Madracis*.

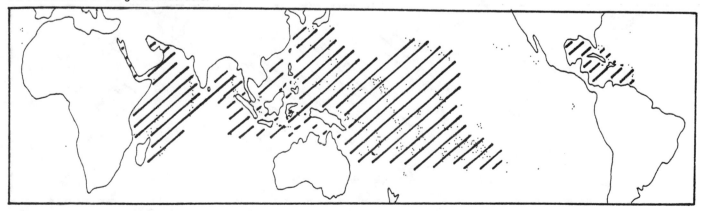

35. Distribution of the genus *Acropora*.

225

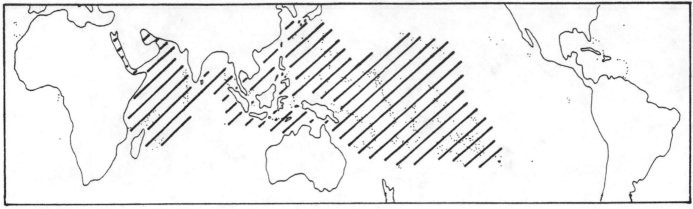

36. Distribution of the genus *Montipora*. .

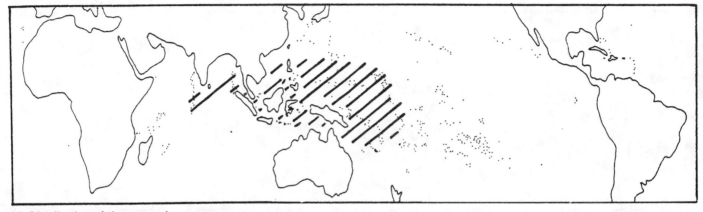

37. Distribution of the genus *Anacropora*.

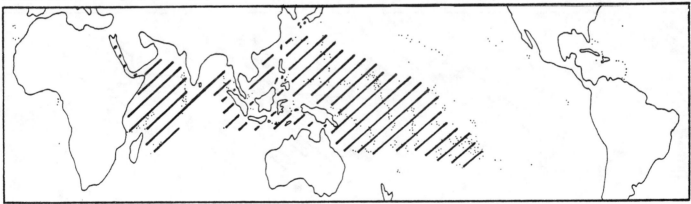

38. Distribution of the genus *Astreopora*.

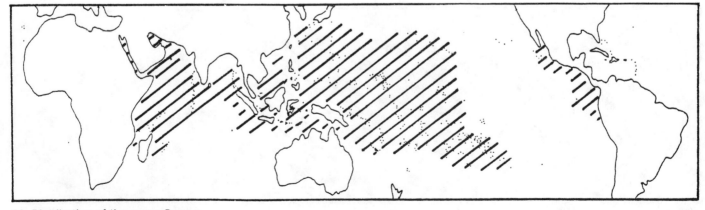

39. Distribution of the genus *Pavona*.

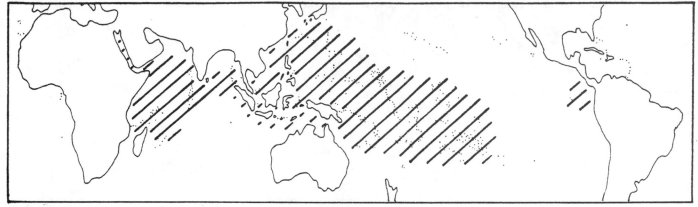

40. Distribution of the genus *Gardineroseris*.

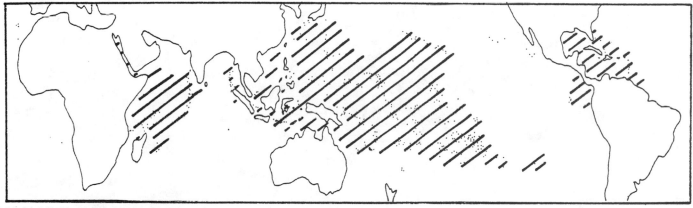

41. Distribution of the genus *Leptoseris*.

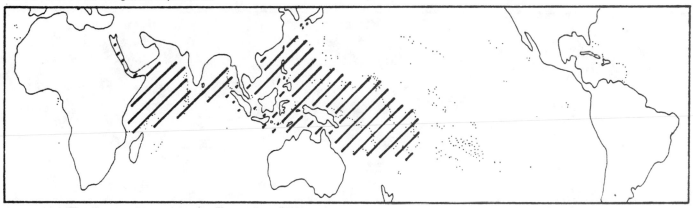

42. Distribution of the genus *Pachyseris*.

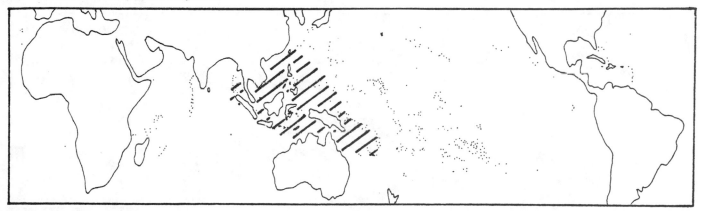

43. Distribution of the genus *Coeloseris*.

227

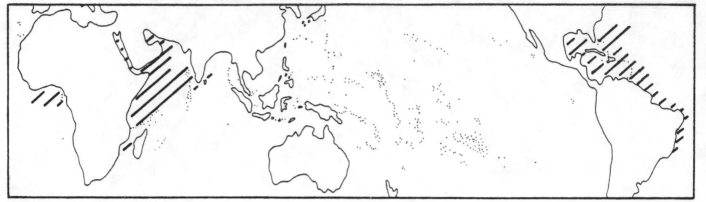

44. Distribution of the genus *Siderastrea*.

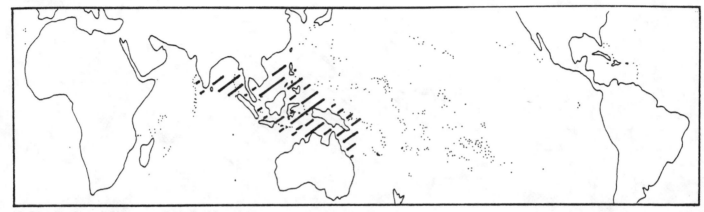

45. Distribution of the genus *Pseudosiderastrea*.

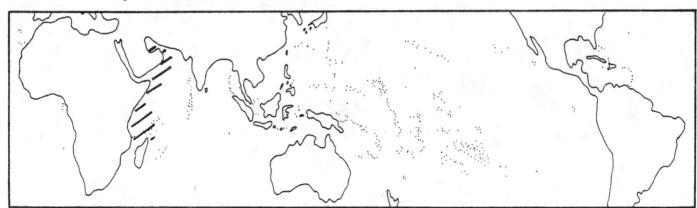

46. Distribution of the genus *Anomastrea*.

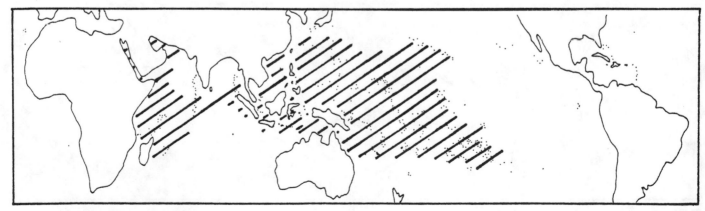

47. Distribution of the genus *Coscinaraea*.

228

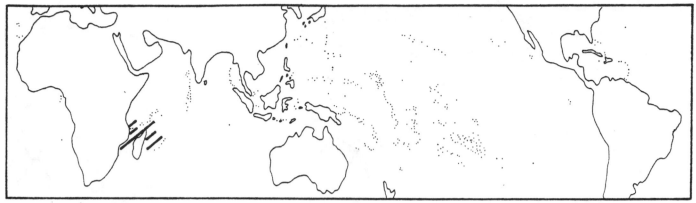

48. Distribution of the genus *Horastrea*.

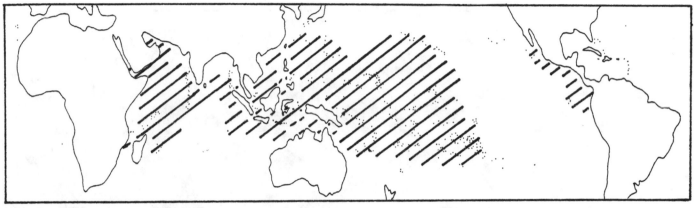

49. Distribution of the genus *Psammocora*.

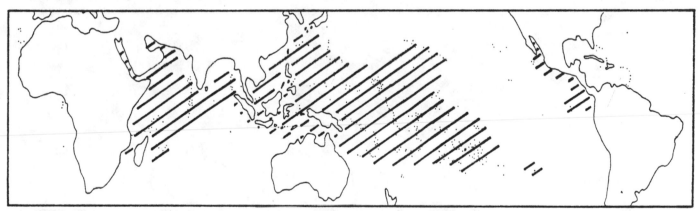

50. Distribution of the genus *Cycloseris*.

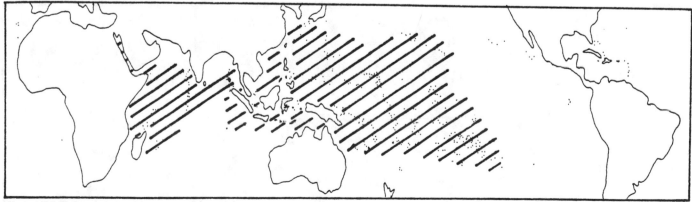

51. Distribution of the genus *Fungia*.

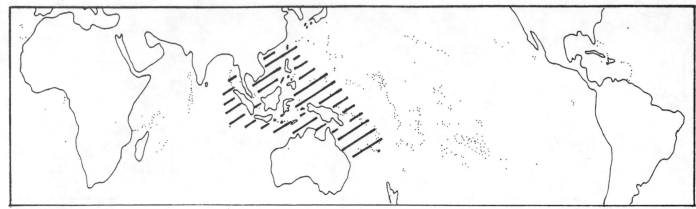

52. Distribution of the genus *Heliofungia*.

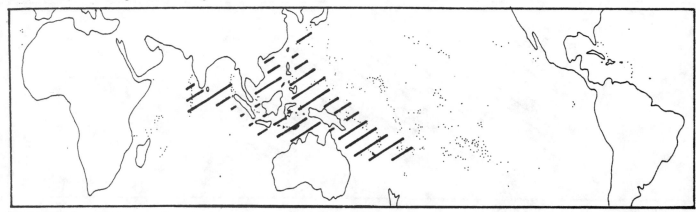

53. Distribution of the genus *Herpetoglossa*.

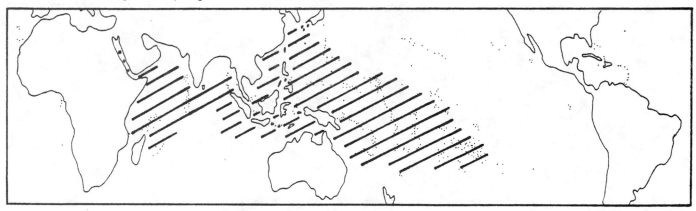

54. Distribution of the genus *Herpolitha*.

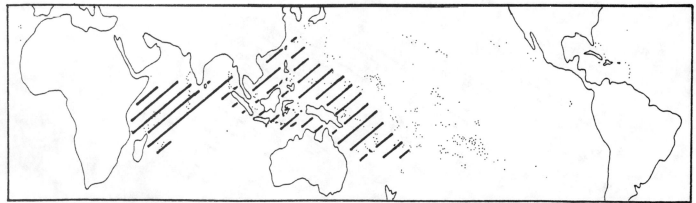

55. Distribution of the genus *Polyphyllia*.

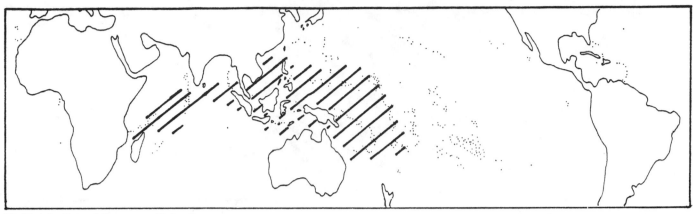

56. Distribution of the genus *Halomitra*.

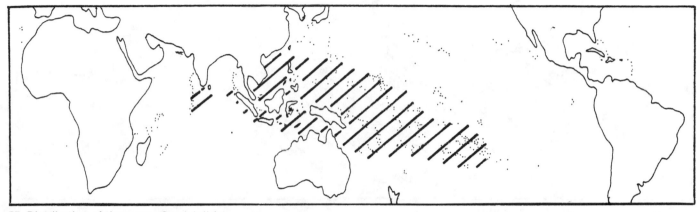

57. Distribution of the genus *Sandalolitha*.

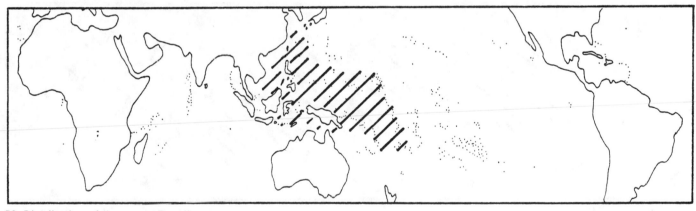

58. Distribution of the genus *Zoopilus*.

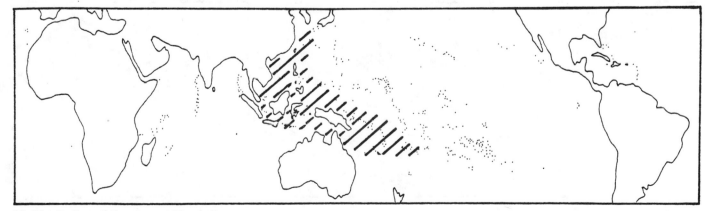

59. Distribution of the genus *Lithophyllon*.

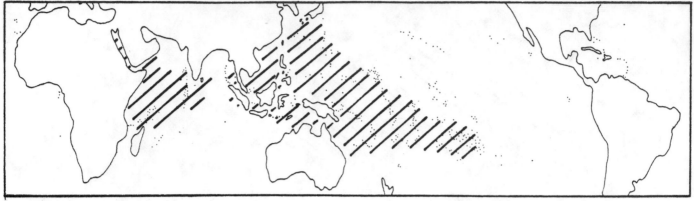

60. Distribution of the genus *Podabacia*.

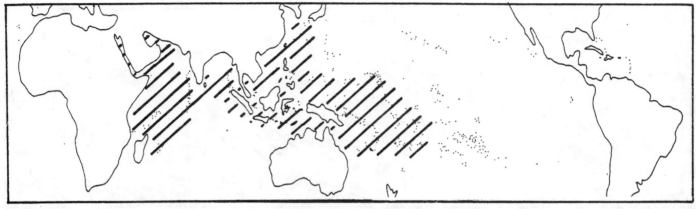

61. Distribution of the genus *Goniopora*.

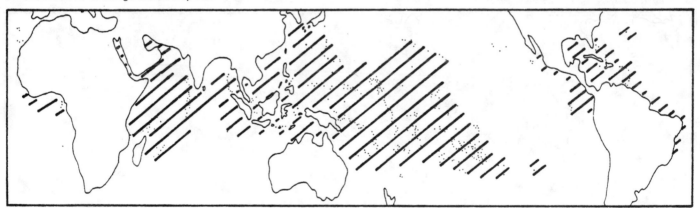

62. Distribution of the genus *Porites*.

63. Distribution of the genus *Alveopora*.

232

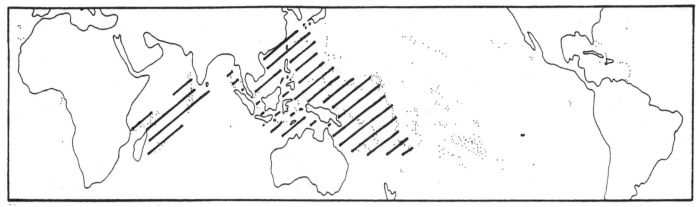

64. Distribution of the genus *Caulastrea*.

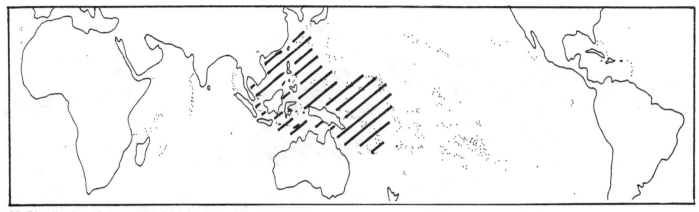

65. Distribution of the genus *Bikiniastrea*.

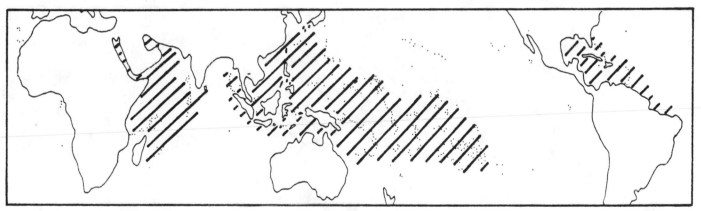

66. Distribution of the genus *Favia*.

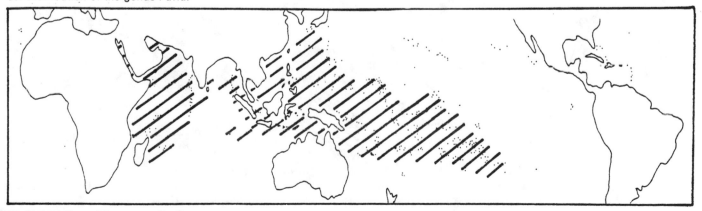

67. Distribution of the genus *Favites*.

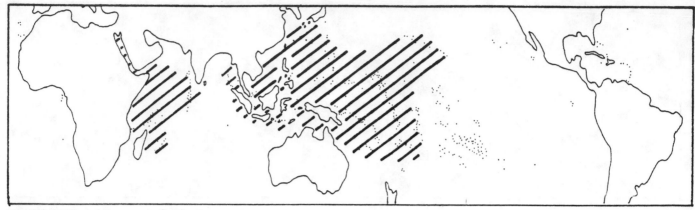

68. Distribution of the genus *Goniastrea*.

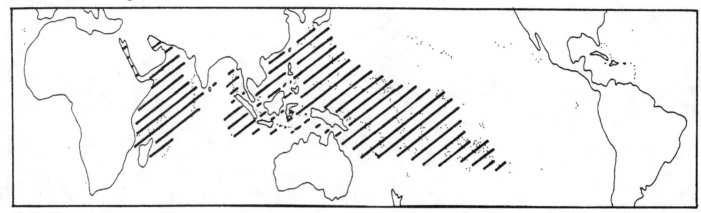

69. Distribution of the genus *Platygyra*.

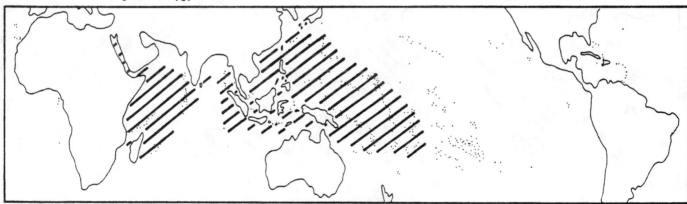

70. Distribution of the genus *Leptoria*.

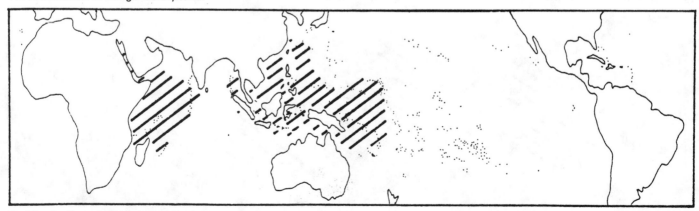

71. Distribution of the genus *Oulophyllia*.

234

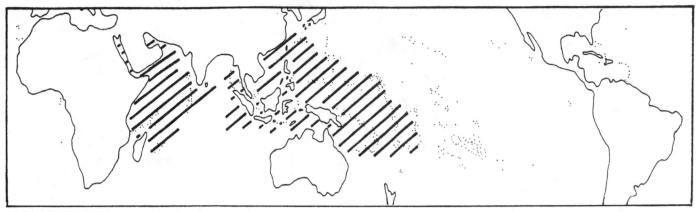

72. Distribution of the genus *Hydnophora*.

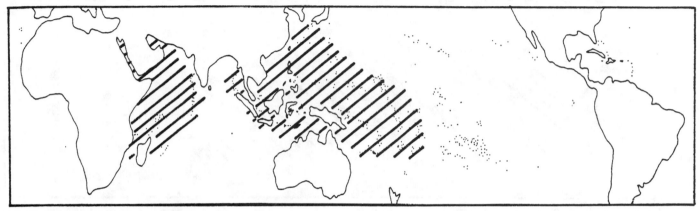

73. Distribution of the genus *Plesiastrea*.

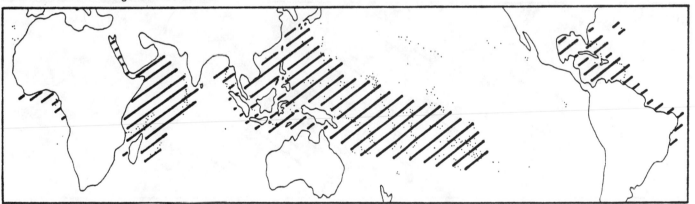

74. Distribution of the genus *Montastraea*.

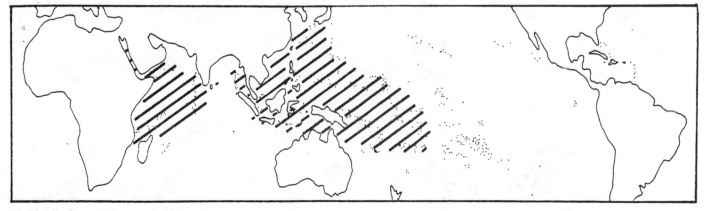

75. Distribution of the genus *Diploastrea*.

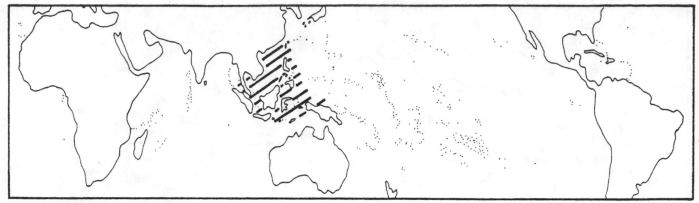

76. Distribution of the genus *Oulastrea*.

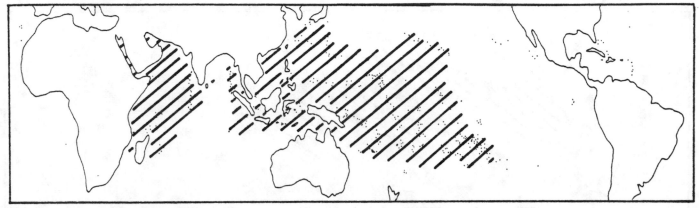

77. Distribution of the genus *Leptastrea*.

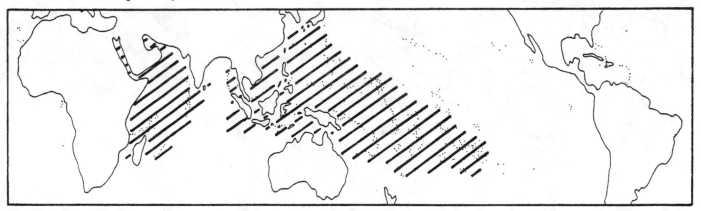

78. Distribution of the genus *Cyphastrea*.

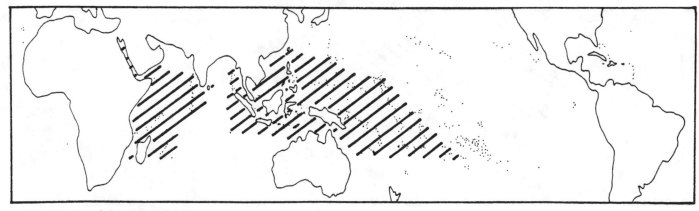

79. Distribution of the genus *Echinopora*.

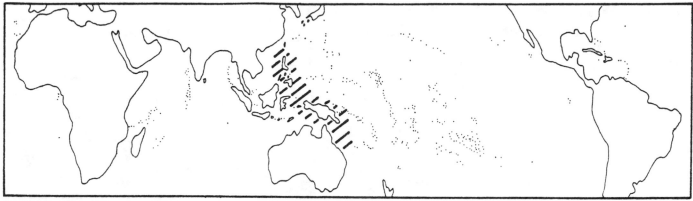

80. Distribution of the genus *Moseleya*.

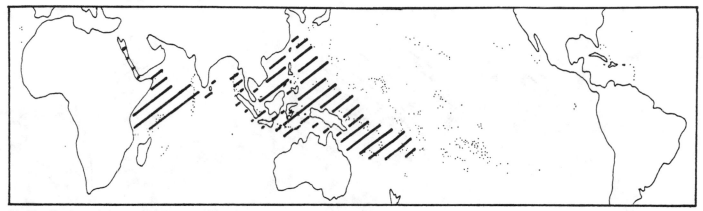

81. Distribution of the genus *Trachyphyllia*.

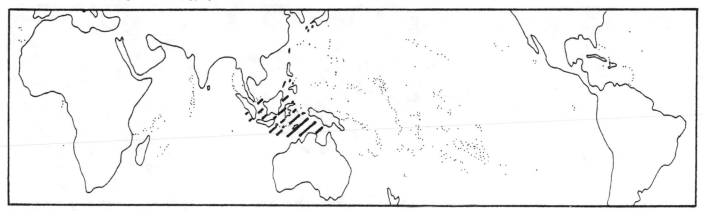

82. Distribution of the genus *Wellsophyllia*.

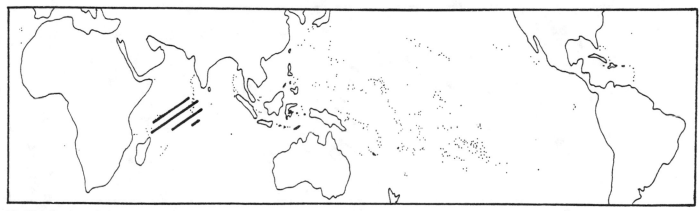

83. Distribution of the genus *Ctenella*.

237

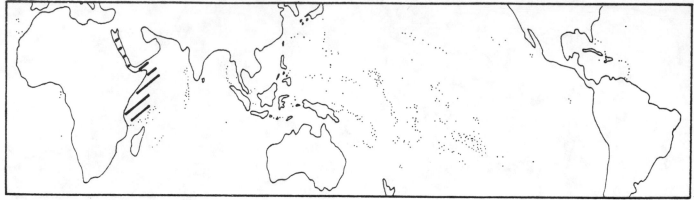

84. Distribution of the genus *Gyrosmilia*.

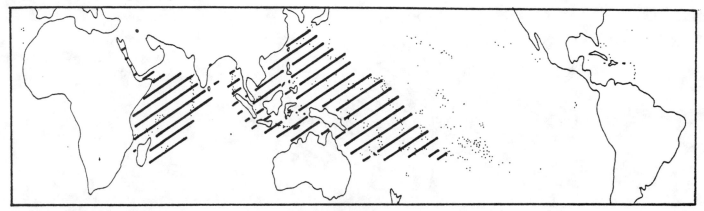

85. Distribution of the genus *Galaxea*.

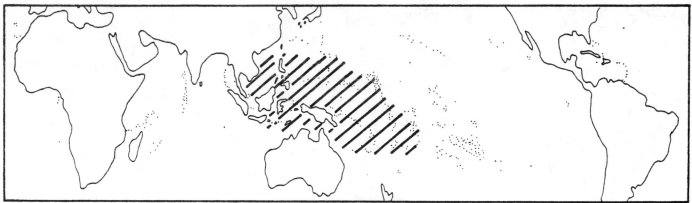

86. Distribution of the genus *Acrhelia*.

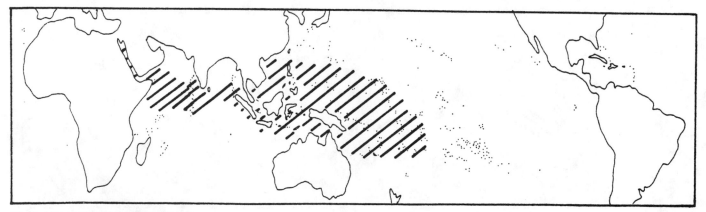

87. Distribution of the genus *Merulina*.

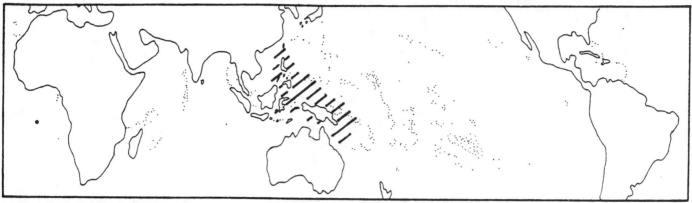

88. Distribution of the genus *Clavarina*.

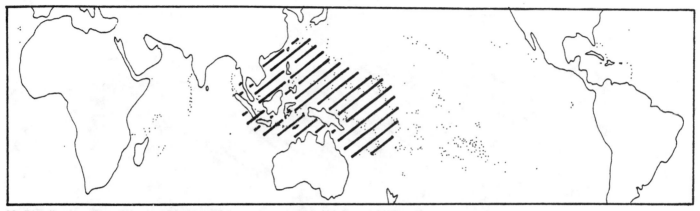

89. Distribution of the genus *Scapophyllia*.

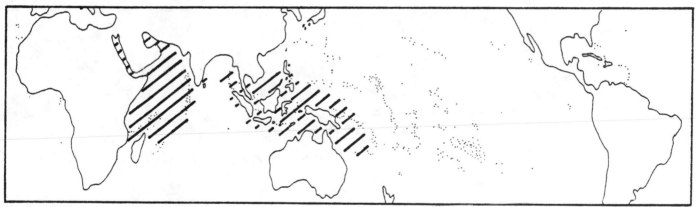

90. Distribution of the genus *Blastomussa*.

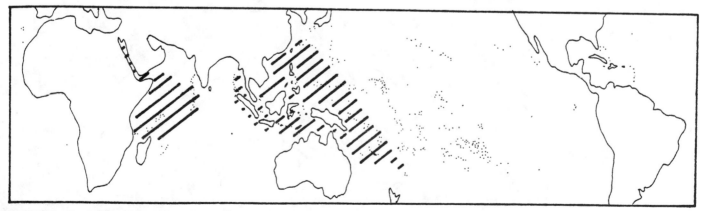

91. Distribution of the genus *Cynarina*.

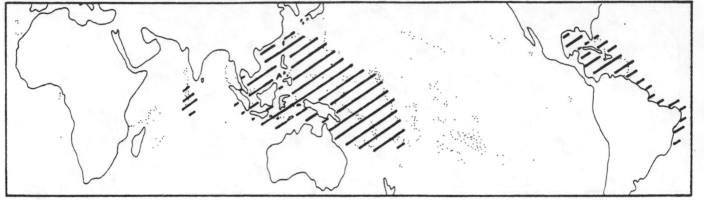

92. Distribution of the genus *Scolymia*.

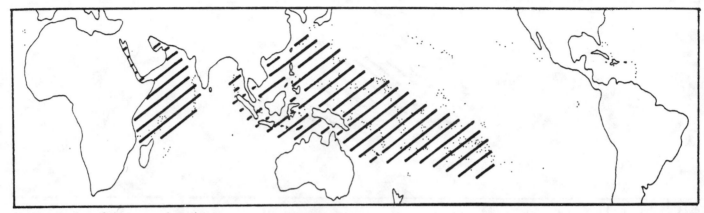

93. Distribution of the genus *Acanthastrea*.

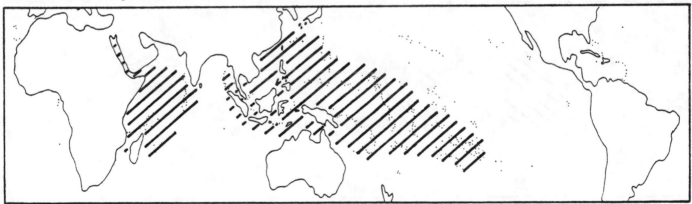

94. Distribution of the genus *Lobophyllia*.

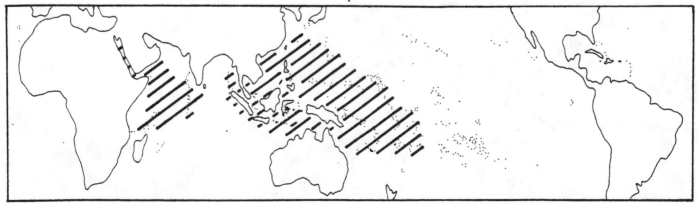

95. Distribution of the genus *Symphyllia*.

240

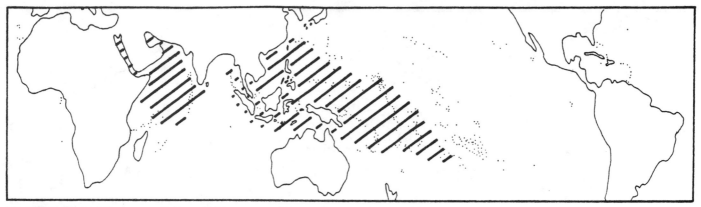

96. Distribution of the genus *Echinophyllia*.

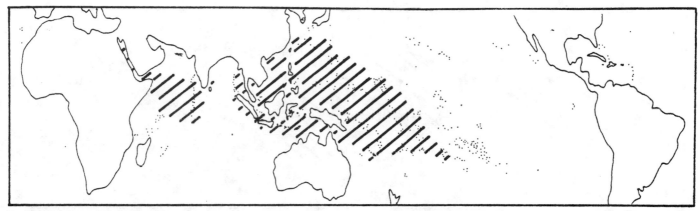

97. Distribution of the genus *Oxypora*.

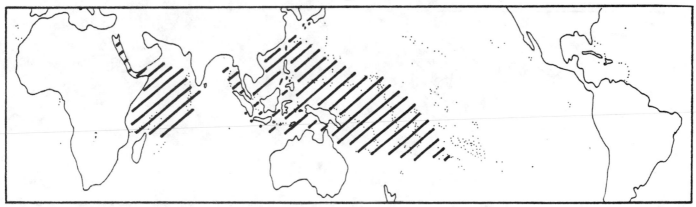

98. Distribution of the genus *Mycedium*.

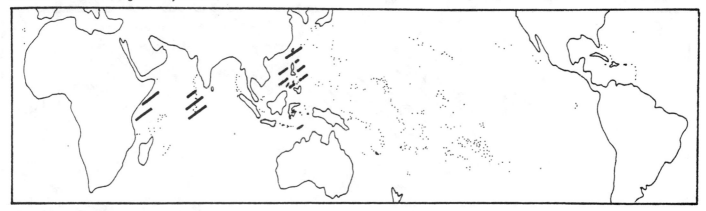

99. Distribution of the genus *Physophyllia*.

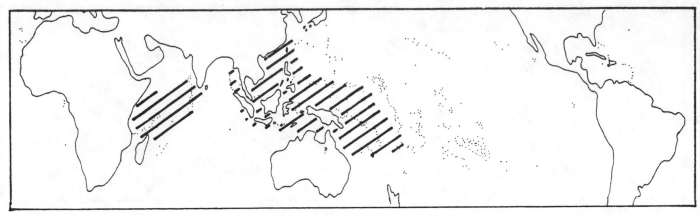

100. Distribution of the genus *Pectinia*.

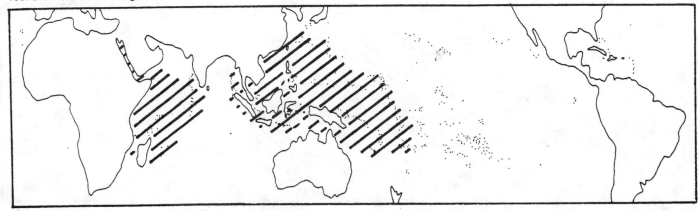

101. Distribution of the genus *Euphyllia*.

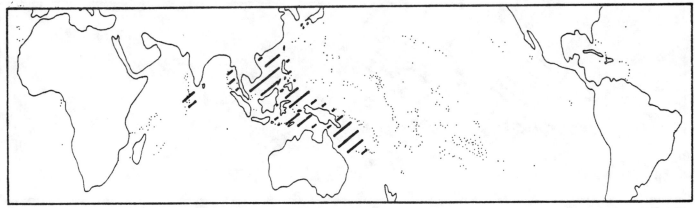

102. Distribution of the genus *Catalaphyllia*.

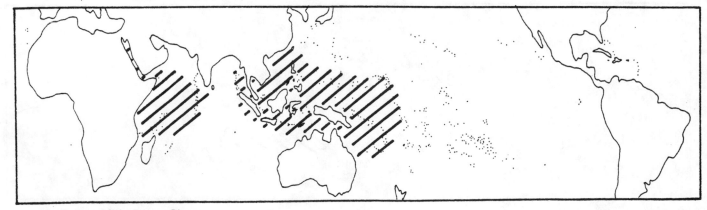

103. Distribution of the genus *Plerogyra*.

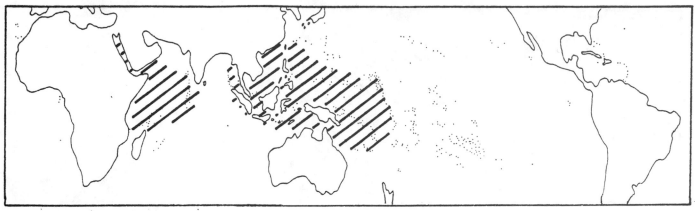

104. Distribution of the genus *Physogyra*.

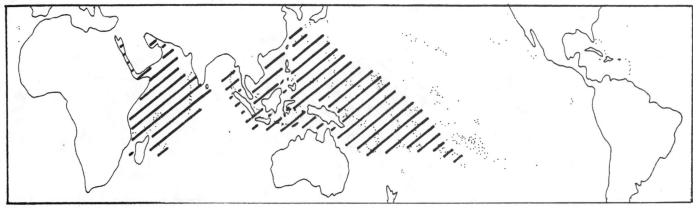

105. Distribution of the genus *Turbinaria*.

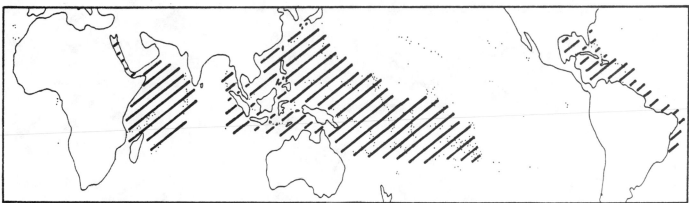

106. Distribution of the genus *Millepora*.

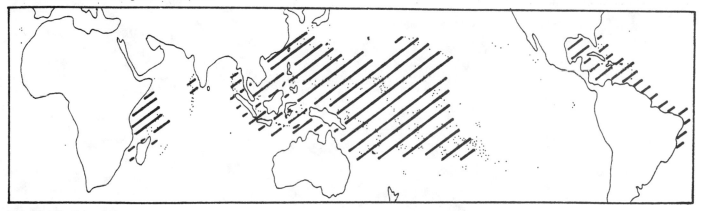

107. Distribution of the genus *Stylaster*.

243

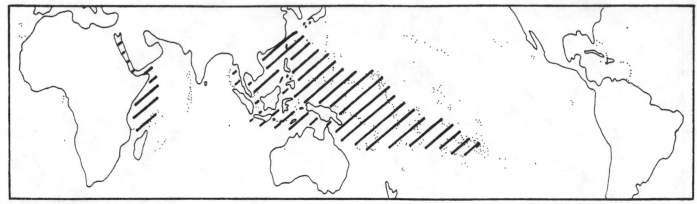

108. Distribution of the genus *Distichopora*.

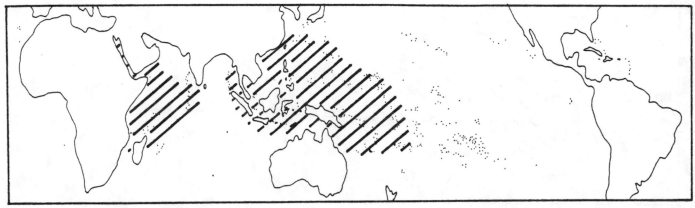

109. Distribution of the genus *Heliopora*.

110. Distribution of the genus *Tubipora*.

244

Glossary

Ahermatypic: corals that lack zooxanthellae and do not contribute to reef-building.

Atoll: a roughly circular reef that encloses a central lagoon.

Axial: referring to the corallite formed at the tip of a branch.

Back reef: a shallow, usually impoverished, part of the reef facing away from the reef front toward land or shallow water.

Bank reef: a reef formed by growth of corals on an underwater hillock. The top of the reef is not exposed.

Barrier reef: a reef formed at the margin between the continental shelf and deep oceanic waters.

Biotope: an area with particular physical and biological features; *e.g.*, reef front, lagoon, back reef, exposed fore reef, etc.

Calice: upper, open end of the corallite.

Cerioid: closely packed corallites with fused walls.

Coenosarc: an extension of the polyp that stretches over the surface of the skeleton.

Coenosteum: skeletal material deposited outside the corallite wall.

Colline: elongate wall or ridge formed between corallites or groups of corallites.

Columella: a skeletal structure that develops in the central axis of the calice. It is usually either styliform (rod-like), papillose, trabecular (both spongy in appearance) or lamellar (formed from a series of interconnecting vertical plates).

Corallite: skeletal parts deposited by a single polyp.

Corallum: the skeleton of solitary and colonial corals.

Costae: extension of the septa outside the corallite wall.

Dendroid: corallum formed from spreading branches of single corallites.

Dissepiments: skeletal structures left by the polyps.

Ecomorph: an intraspecific variant produced in response to environmental factors.

Edge zone: a horizontal fold of the polyp wall that extends over the corallite wall.

Etymology: formation and meaning of words.

Explanate: spread out flat.

Exsert: a term used to describe septa that protrude above the top of the corallite wall.

Extratentacular (= **intercalicular**): describing a form of asexual reproduction in corals in which a new mouth is produced from the edge zone or coenosarc and thus lies outside the parental ring of tentacles.

Flabellate: corallum in which the meanders arise from a common base but are free laterally. They may be relatively short (crescentic) or elongate and sinuous (flabello-meandroid).

Fore reef: the main seaward facing part of the reef, stretching from shallow to deep water.

Fossa: the central depression in a calice, usually partly filled by the columella.

Fringing reef: reef growing adjacent to island or mainland shores.

Hermatypic: corals that contain zooxanthellae and contribute to the building of reefs.

Hydrocorals: hydrozoan coelenterates that produce a calcareous skeleton.

Imperforate: referring to skeletal structures in corals (*e.g.*, walls, septa, coenosteum) that are solid rather than porous.

Insert: a term used to describe septa which do not protrude above the top of the corallite wall.

Intratentacular (= **intracalicular**): describing a form of asexual reproduction in corals in which the oral disc invaginates to produce a new mouth within the parental ring of tentacles.

Isotherm: a line linking points of equal temperature.

Meandroid: corallum in which the corallites are fused in longitudinal series to produce a pattern of valleys and ridges.

Mesenteries/mesenterial filaments: the mesenteries are radial partitions lying within the gastrovascular cavity of the coral polyp; mesenterial filaments may be produced from their free inner margins.

Oceanic reef: a reef that has its base in deep oceanic waters.

Octocorals: alcyonarian coelenterates that produce a calcareous skeleton.

Oral disc: upper surface of the polyp, extending from the mouth to the outer ring of tentacles.

Paliform lobe: a vertical lobe-like protrusion formed at the inner end of a septum, adjacent to the columella.

Perforate: referring to skeletal structures in corals (*e.g.*, walls, septa, coenosteum) that are porous rather than solid.

Peristome: area within the inner ring of tentacles and immediately surrounding the mouth.

Peritheca: surface of the coenosteum between the corallites.

Phaceloid: growth form in which tall, separate corallites arise from the basal part of the corallum.

Planula: the planktonic larval stage of corals.

Platform reef: a reef formed by growth of corals on an underwater hillock.

Plocoid: separate, well defined corallites.

Polymorphic: existing in more than one form.

Polyp: the living part of a coral.

Reef crest: an emergent part of the reef, just behind the reef front.

Scleractinian: true or stony corals belonging to the Class Zoantharia.

Septa: calcareous, plate-like structures that radiate from the wall toward the center of the corallite. They are aligned vertically and alternate with the mesenteries.

Septal cycles: relating to the formation and arrangement of the septa. Septa are laid down in radial series or cycles, the first cycle consisting of six primary septa, the second of six secondary septa, the third of 12 tertiary septa, and so on.

Septal margin: the upper free edge of the septum.

Septal orders: relating to the size of septa. Equal sized septa form a single order; subequal or unequal septa form two or more orders. Orders do not necessarily correspond to cycles (see above).

Septocostae: extensions of the septa that unite adjacent calice centers. They are found in corals where the corallites lack walls and there is no clear distinction between septa and costae.

Shelf reef: a reef that has its base on the relatively shallow floor of the continental shelf.

Solitary: referring to corals that grow as a single polyp with a surrounding skeleton.

Synapticulae: small bars that make lateral links between adjacent septa.

Thamnasterioid: a corallum in which corallite walls are indistinct and the septa run uninterrupted between calice centers.

Trochoid: top shaped.

Turbinate: shaped like an inverted cone.

Zooxanthellae: unicellular algae (dinoflagellates) that live in coral tissues.

Bibliography

Bak, R.P.M. (1975). Ecological aspects of the distribution of reef corals in the Netherlands Antilles. *Bijdr. Dierk.*, 45: 181-190.

Barnes, J., Bellamy, D.J., Jones, D.J., Whitton, B.A., Drew, E.A., Kenyon, L., Lythgoe, J.N. and Rosen, B.R. (1971). Morphology and ecology of the reef front of Aldabra. *In:* Regional variation in Indian Ocean coral reefs. *Symp. Zool. Soc. Lond.*, 28: 87-114. [Eds.: Stoddart, D.R. and Yonge, M.] Academic Press, 584 pp.

Bedot, M. (1907). Madreporaires d'Amboine. *Rev. Suisse. Zool.*, 15(2): 143-292.

Blainville, H.M. de (1830). Zoophytes *In: Dictionnaire des Sciences naturelles.* Paris. 60: 310-358.

Boschma, H. (1948). The species problem in *Millepora. Zool. Verh. Leiden,* 1: 1-111.

Boschma, H. (1957). List of described species of the order Stylasterina. *Zool. Verh. Leiden,* 33: 1-72.

Bruce, A.J. (1976). Coral reef caridea and "commensalism." *Micronesica,* 12(1): 83-98.

Buddemeier, R.W. & Kinzie, R.A. (1976). Coral growth. *Oceanogr. Mar. Biol. Ann. Rev.,* 14: 183-325.

Burchard, J.E. (1980). *Coral Fauna of the Western Arabian Gulf.* ARAMCO. Dhahran, Saudi Arabia. 128 pp.

Chevalier, J.P. (1971). Les scleractiniaires de la Melanesie francaise (Nouvelle Caledonie, Iles Chesterfield, Iles Loyaute, Nouvelles Hebrides). 1ere Partie. *Exped. Francaise recifs coralliens Nouvelle Caledonie,* Edn. Fond. Singer-Polignac, Paris. 5: 5-307.

Chevalier, J.P. (1975). Les scleractiniaires de la Melanesie francaise (Nouvelle Caledonie, Iles Chesterfield, Iles Loyaute, Nouvelles Hebrides). 2eme Partie. *Exped. Francaise recifs coralliens Nouvelle Caledonie,*Edn. Fond. Singer-Polignac, Paris. 7: 5-407.

Colin, P.L. (1978). *Caribbean Reef Invertebrates and Plants.* TFH Publications Inc., Ltd. 512 pp.

Connell, J.H. (1976). Population ecology of reef building corals *In: Biology and Geology of Coral Reefs,* Vol. 3, Biol. 2: 205-245 [Eds., Jones, O.A. and Endean, R.]

Dana, J.D. (1846-1842). Zoophytes. *U.S. Exploring Exped. 1838-1842,* 7: 1-740.

Dana, T.F. (1975). Development of contemporary Eastern Pacific coral reefs. *Mar. Biol.,* 33: 355-374.

Deas, W. & Domm, S. (1976). *Corals of the Great Barrier Reef.* Ure Smith. Sydney. 125 pp.

Dinesen, Z.D. (1980). A revision of the coral genus *Leptoseris* (Scleractinia: Fungiina: Agariciidae). *Mem. Qd. Mus.,* 20(1): 181-235, pls. 1-16.

Ditlev, H. (1976). Stony corals (Coelenterata: Scleractinia) from the west coast of Thailand. *Phuket Marine Biological Center Research Bulletin,* No. 13: 1-14.

Ditlev, H. (1980). *A Field-guide to the Reef-building Corals of the Indo-Pacific.* Scandinavian Science Press Ltd., Klampenborg. Dr. W.. Backhuys, Publisher. Rotterdam. 291 pp.

Durham, J.W. (1962). Corals from the Galapagos and Cocos Islands. *Proc. Calif. Acad. Sciences, 4th series.* 41-56.

Dustan, P. (1975). Growth and form in the reef-building coral *Montastrea annularis. Mar. Biol.* 33: 101-107.

Ehrenberg, G.G. (1834). Beitrage zur physiologischen Kenntniss der Corallenthiere im Allgemeinen und besanders des Rothen Meeres. *Abh. K. Akad. Wiss. Berl., 1832:* 250-380.

Ellis, J. & Solander, D. (1786). *The natural history of many curious and uncommon zoophytes.* London. 1-208, pl. 1-63.

Esper, E.J.C. (1797). *Die Pflanzenthiere.* Fortsetzungen 1, Nurnberg. 1-230.

Fell, H.B. (1967). Cretaceous and tertiary surface currents of the oceans. *Oceanogr. Mar. Biol. Ann. Rev.,* 5: 317-341.

Gardiner, J.S. (1903-1906). In: *Fauna and Geography of the Maldive and Laccadive Archipelagoes.* 1 & 2. Cambridge University Press. 957 pp., 93 pl.

George, J.D. & George, J.J. (1979). *Marine Life.* Harrap, London. 288 pp.

Goreau, T.F. (1959). The physiology of skeleton formation in corals. 1. A method for measuring the rate of calcium deposition by corals under different conditions. *Biol. Bull. mar. biol. lab., Woods Hole,* 116: 59-75.

Goreau, T.F. & Wells, J.W. (1967). The shallow water Scleractinia of Jamaica: revised list of species and their vertical distribution ranges. *Bull. Mar. Sci.,* 17: 442-453.

Harrigan, J.F. (1972). The planula larvae of *Pocillopora damicornis:* lunar periodicity of swarming and substratum selection behaviour. Ph.D. Diss. University of Hawaii, 213 pp.

Hubbard, J.A. (1972). *Diaseris distorta,* an "acrobatic" coral. *Nature, Lond.,* 236: 457-459.

Kohn, A.J. (1961). The biology of atolls. *Bios,* 32: 113-126.

Lamarck, J.B.P. de (1816). *Histoire naturelle des Animaux sans vertebres.* Paris. 2, 1-568.

Laborel, J. (1970). Madreporaires et hydrocoralliaires recifaux des cotes bresiliennes, systematique, ecologie, repartition verticale et geographique. *Annls. Inst. oceanogr., Paris,* 47(1): 171-229.

Lang, J.C. (1971). Interspecific aggression by scleractinian corals. The rediscovery of *Scolymia cubensis* (Milne-Edwards & Haime). *Bull. Mar. Sci.,* 21(4): 952-959.

Lang, J.C. (1973). Interspecific aggression by scleractinian corals: 2. Why the race is not only to the swift. *Bull. Mar. Sci.,* 23(2): 260-279.

Lehman, J.T. & Porter, J.W. (1973). Chemical activation of feeding in the Caribbean reef-building coral *Montastrea cavernosa. Biol. Bull.,* 145: 140-149.

Lewis, J.B. (1974). The settlement behaviour of planulae larvae of the hermatypic coral *Favia fragum* (Esper). *J. exp. mar. Biol. Ecol.,* 15: 165-172.

Linnaeus, (1758). *Systema naturae, I. Regnum animale.* Ed. X.

Loya, Y. & Slobodkin, L.B. (1971). The coral reefs of Eilat, Red Sea. *In:* Regional variation in Indian Ocean coral reefs. *Symp. zool. Soc. Lond.,* 28, 117-139. [Eds.: Stoddart, D.R. & Yonge, M.] Academic Press, 584 pp.

Maragos, J.E. (1973). Order Scleractinia *In:* Devaney, D.M. and L.G. Eldredge (Eds). Reef and Shore Fauna of Hawaii. Bish. Mus. Press, Honolulu. *Bernice P. Bishop Museum Publ.* 64(1).

Mariscal, R.N. & Lenhoff, H.M. (1968). The chemical control of feeding behaviour in *Cyphastrea ocellina* and in some other Hawaiian corals. *J. Exp. Biol.,* 49: 689-699.

Matthai, G. (1928). A monograph of the recent meandroid Astraeidae. *Cat. Madreporarian Corals Br. Mus. (Nat. Hist.),* 7: 1-288.

Mergner, H. & Scheer, G. (1974). The physiographic zonation and the ecological conditions of some South Indian and Ceylon coral reefs. *In: Proc. second Int. Coral Reef Symp.* 2. Great Barrier Reef Comm., Brisbane. 3-30.

Milne-Edwards, H. & Haime, J. (1848). Note sur la classification de la deuxieme tribu de la famille des Astreides. *C.R. Hebd. Seances Acad. Sci.* 27(20): 490-497.

Milne-Edwards, H. & Haime, J. (1849). Memoire sur les polypiers appartenant a la famille des Oculinides, au group intermediaire des Pseudastreides et a la famille des Fongides. *C.R. Hebd. Seances Acad. Sci.* 29: 67-73.

Muscatine, L. (1973). Nutrition in corals. *In: Biology and Geology of Coral Reefs,* Vol. 2, Biol. 1, 77-115. (Eds.: Jones, O.A. & Endean, R.)

Nemenzo, F. (1959). Systematic studies on Philippine shallow water Scleractinians. II Suborder Faviida. *Nat. Appl. Sci. Bull. Philippines,* 16(1-4): 73-135.

Newell, N.D. (1959). Questions of coral reefs. Part 1. *Nat. Hist. Mag.,* 68: 118-131.

Patton, W.K. (1976). Animal associates of living reef corals. *In: Biology and Geology of Coral Reefs,* Vol. 3, Biol. 2: 1-34. [Eds.: Jones, O.A. & Endean, R.]

Pearse, V.B. & Muscatine, L. (1971). Role of symbiotic algae in coral calcification. *Biol. Bull.,* 141: 350-363.

Pichon, M. (1974). Free living scleractinian coral communities in the coral reefs of Madagascar. *In: Proc. second Int. Coral Reef Symp.,* 2. Great Barrier Reef Comm., Brisbane, 173-181.

Pichon, M. (1977). Recent studies on the reef corals of the Philippine Islands and their zoogeography. *In: Proc. third Int. Coral Reef Symp.,* 149-154.

Pichon, M. (1980). *Wellsophyllia radiata* n. gen., n. sp., a new hermatypic coral from the Indonesian region (Cnidaria, Anthozoa, Scleractinia). *Revue suisse Zool.,* 87: 253-259.

Pillai, C.G. (1969). Stony corals of the seas around India. *In: Proc. Symp. Corals and Coral Reefs, Mandapan Camp, Jan. 1969.* 191-216.

Pillai, C.G. (1971). Composition of the coral fauna of the southeastern coast of India and the Laccadives. *In:* Regional variation in Indian Ocean coral reefs. *Symp. zool. Soc. London.,* 28, 301-327. [Eds.: Stoddart, D.R. & Yonge, M.] Academic Press, 584 pp.

Pillai, C.S.G. & Scheer, G. (1976). On a collection of scleractinia from the Strait of Malacca. *In: Proc. second Int. Coral Reef Symp.,* 445-464.

Pomponi, S.A. (1979). Ultrastructure of cells associated with excavation of calcium carbonate substrates by boring sponges. *J. mar. biol.,* 59: 777-784.

Porter, J.W. (1972). Ecology and species diversity of coral reefs on opposite sides of the isthmus of Panama. *Bull. Biol. Soc. Wash.,* 2: 89-116.

Quelch, J.J. (1884). Preliminary notice of new genera and species of 'Challenger' reef-corals. *Ann. Nat. Hist. Zool. Bot. Geol., Ser. 5,* 13: 292.

Quelch, J.J. (1886). Report on the reef corals collected by H.M.S. Challenger during the years 1873-76. *Sci. results voyage Challenger, Lond.,* Zool. 16: 1-203.

Rinkevich, B. & Loya, Y. (1979). The reproduction of the Red Sea coral *Stylophora pistillata* I. Gonads and planulae. *Mar. Ecol. Prog. Ser., 1,* 1 (2): 133-144.

Robertson, R. (1970). Review of the predators and parasites of stony corals, with special reference to symbiotic prosobranch gastropods. *Pac. Sci.,* 24 (1): 43-54.

Rosen, B.R. (1971a). Annotated check list and bibliography of corals of the Chagos Archipelago (including the recent collection from Diego Garcia), with remarks on their distribution. *Atoll Research Bull.,* 149: 67-88.

Rosen, B.R. (1971b). The distribution of reef coral genera in the Indian Ocean. *In:* Regional variation in Indian Ocean coral reefs. *Symp. zool. Soc. Lond.,* 28, 263-299. [Eds.: Stoddart, D.R. & Yonge, M.]

Rosen, B.R. (1975). The distribution of reef corals. *Rep. Underwater Assoc.,* 1: 1-16.

Scheer, G. (1971). Coral reefs and coral genera in the Red Sea and Indian Ocean. *In:* Regional variation in Indian Ocean coral reefs. *Symp. zool. Soc. Lond.,* 28, 329-367. [Eds.: Stoddart, D.R. & Yonge, M.] Academic Press, 584 pp.

Scheer, G. & Pillai, C.S.G. (1974). Report on the scleractinia from the Nicobar Islands. *Zoologica,* 42 (122): 1-75.

Sheppard, C.R.C. (1979). Interspecific aggression between reef corals with reference to their distribution. *Mar. Ecol. Prog. Ser.,* 1: 237-247.

Smith, F.G.W. (1971). *Atlantic Reef Corals.* Univ. of Miami Press, 164 pp.

Stehli, F.G. & Wells, J.W. (1971). Diversity and age-patterns in hermatypic corals. *Systematic Zoology,* 20 (2): 115-126.

Stephenson, T.A. & Stephenson, A. (1933). Growth and asexual reproduction in corals. *Sci. Rep. Gt. Barrier Reef Exped.,* 3(7): 167-217.

Stoddart, D.R. (1973). Coral reefs of the Indian Ocean. *In:* Biology and Geology of Coral Reefs [Eds.: Jones, O.A. & Endean, R.] Vol. 1 Geol. 1: 51-92.

Stoddart, D.R. & Pillai, C.S.G. (1973). Coral reefs and reef corals in the Cook Islands, South Pacific. *Oceanography of the South Pacific, 1972. comp. R. Fraser. New Zealand National Commission for UNESCO,* Wellington. 1973.

Vaughan, T.W. (1907). Recent Madreporaria of the Hawaiian Islands and Laysan. *U.S. natl. Mus. Bull,* 49 (9): 1-427.

Vaughan, T.W. (1918). Some shoal-water corals from Murray Islands, Cocos Keeling Islands and Fanning Islands. *Pap. Dep. mar. Biol. Carnegie Inst. Wash.,* 9 (Publ. 213): 51-234.

Vaughan, T.W. & Wells, J.W. (1943). Revision of the sub-orders, families and genera of the Scleractinia. *Geol. Soc. Am. Spec. Pap.* 44: 1-363.

Veron, J.E.N. & Pichon, M. (1976). Scleractinia of Eastern Australia. Part I. Families Thamnasteriidae, Astrocoeniidae, Pocilloporidae. *Australian Institute of Marine Science Monograph Series,* 1: 1-86.

Veron, J.E.N., Pichon, M. & Wijsman-Best, M. (1977). Scleractinia of Eastern Australia. Part II. Families Faviidae, Trachyphylliidae. *Australian Institute of Marine Science Monograph Series,* 3: 1-233.

Veron, J.E.N. & Pichon, M. (1980). Scleractinia of Eastern Australia. Part III. Families Agariciidae, Siderastreidae, Fungiidae, Oculinidae, Merulinidae, Mussidae, Pectiniidae, Caryophylliidae, Dendrophylliidae. *Australian Institute of Marine Science Monograph Series,* 4: 1-443.

Verrill, A.E. (1901). Variations and nomenclature of Bermudian, West Indian and Brazilian corals, with notes on various Indo-Pacific corals. *Trans. Conn. Acad. Arts Sci.,* 11: 63-168.

Wallace, C.C. (1978). The coral genus *Acropora* (Scleractinia: Astrocoeniina: Acroporidae) in the central and southern Great Barrier Reef province. *Mem. Qd. Mus.,* 18 (2): 273-319.

Wells, J.W. (1950). Reef corals from the Cocos-Keeling Atoll. *Bull. Raffles Mus.,* 22: 29-52.

Wells, J.W. (1954). Bikini and nearby Atolls: (2) Oceanography (biologic). Recent corals of the Marshall Islands. *Prof. Pap. US. geol. Surv.,* 260 (1): i-iv, 385-486.

Wells, J.W. (1956). Scleractinia *In* Moore, R.C., *Treatise on Invertebrate Paleontology.* Coelenterata. Univ. Kansas Press, F., F328-F440.

Wells, J.W. (1961). Notes on Indo-Pacific Scleractinian Corals. III. A new reef coral from New Caledonia. *Pac. Sci.,* 15(2): 189-191.

Wells, J.W. (1966). Evolutionary development in the scleractinian Family Fungiidae. *Symp. Zool. Soc. Lond.,* 16: 223-246.

Wells, J.W. (1971). Notes on Indo-Pacific scleractinian corals. VII. *Catalaphyllia,* a new genus of reef corals. *Pac. Sci.,* 25 (3): 368-371.

Wells, J.W. (1972). Notes on Indo-Pacific scleractinian corals. VIII. Scleractinian corals from Easter Island. *Pac. Sci.* 26 (2): 183-190.

Wells, J.W. (1973). Two new hermatypic scleractinian corals from the West Indies. *Bull. Mar. Sci.,* 23(4): 925-932.

Wells, J.W. & Lang, J.C. (1973). Appendix. Systematic list of Jamaican shallow-water Scleractinia. *Bull. Mar. Sci.,* 23(1): 55-58.

Woodhead, P.M.J. & Weber, J.N. (1969). Coral genera of New Caledonia. *Mar. Biol., 4*(3): 250-254.

Yabe, H. & Sugiyama, T. (1935). Revised lists of the reef corals from the Japanese seas and of the fossil reef corals of the raised reefs and the Ryukyu limestone of Japan. *J. Geol. Soc. Jpn.,* 42: 379-403.

Yabe, H. & Sugiyama, T., (1941). Recent reef building corals from Japan and the south sea islands under the Japanese mandate. I. *Sci. Rep. Tohoku Univ. second ser. (Geol),* Spec. vol. 2: 67-91.

Zou, R. (1975). *Reef building corals of shallow waters of Hainan Island.* Peking Science Press. 66 pp.

Index

Numbers set within parentheses refer to color photos; numbers set in **bold type** refer to main references.